D0849665

Franklin D. Roosevelt's Diplomacy
and American Catholics, Italians, and Jews

Studies in
American History and Culture, No. 37

Robert Berkhofer, Series Editor

Director of American Culture Programs
and Richard Hudson Research Professor of History
The University of Michigan

Other Titles in This Series

Franklin D. Roosevelt's Diplomacy
and American Catholics, Italians, and Jews

by
Leo V. Kanawada, Jr.

UMI RESEARCH PRESS
Ann Arbor, Michigan

Produced and distributed by
UMI Research Press
an imprint of
University Microfilms International
Ann Arbor, Michigan 48106

Library of Congress Cataloging in Publication Data

Kanawada, Leo V.
    Franklin D. Roosevelt's Diplomacy and
American Catholics, Italians, and Jews.

    (Studies in American history and culture ; no. 37)
    Revision of thesis (Ph. D.)—St. John's University,
1980.
    Bibliography: p.
    Includes index.
    1. United States—Foreign relations—1933-1945.
2. Roosevelt, Franklin D. (Franklin Delano), 1882-1945.
3. Catholics—United States—Politics and government.
4. Italian Americans—Politics and government. 5. Jews—
United States—Politics and government. I. Title. II. Series.

E806.K34 1982   327.73   82-16077
ISBN 0-8357-1382-2

Contents

Preface

Ethnicity is not a new term. In twentieth-century America, ethnicity—the character or quality of an ethnic group—has surfaced in a myriad of situations and circumstances, involving both the nation's domestic and foreign policies. Only recently, through mass media coverage of the "black revolution" and other ethnic movements emerging from the 1960s, has the term "ethnicity" become widely known in America. In this brief time, many have begun to challenge society's assumption that ethnic groups should—as quickly and completely as possible—disappear into one enormous "melting pot." Moreover, several authorities on this subject have even asserted that ethnic groups, through expanded immigration, have become vital, highly conscious forces within almost all contemporary societies, exercising a primary role in social change, political decision making, and in expressing and advocating group interests. To the current stream of ethnic self-assertion should be added an area that deserves the attention of the American people: the influence of the ethnic factor on American diplomacy.

In an international crisis or confrontation, the concept that the United States speaks with one voice, that the President represents the views of a unified public opinion, or that the United States acts in its own self-interest, must be tempered by the fact that "ethnicity" can be shown to be a decisive force in the decision-making process. In the brief duration of the Ford administration, Greek-Americans, Jewish-Americans, and Cuban-Americans have had a significant impact on our foreign policy and on foreign policy positions of the candidates during the Presidential election of 1976. Both President Ford and Secretary of State Kissinger, as well as the mass media, were quick to acknowledge the role played by Greek-Americans, by their numbers and presence at congressional hearings, in maintaining the embargo on material to Turkey during the Cyprus crisis of the summer of 1974. Jewish-Americans were also highly critical of Kissinger's "even-handed" policy in regard to Arab-Israeli relations, the influence of which continued in the policies pursued by Presidents Carter and Reagan in the Middle East. Similarly, Cuban-Americans discouraged the renewal of diplomatic and economic relations with

Castro's Cuba. And, within the past year, the hierarchy of the Catholic-American community impressed President Reagan with their outright opposition to supplying military assistance to El Salvador. If, in these several areas prominent in American diplomacy today, ethnic groups occupy such a pivotal role, it should not be surprising that the same held true for the presidency of Franklin D. Roosevelt.

The contention of this book is that, during the years prior to the outbreak of World War II, Catholic-Americans, Italian-Americans, and Jewish-Americans turned the entrance of the Oval Office into a revolving door, making religio-ethnic pressure more of a factor in determining Roosevelt's foreign policy than has thus far been realized.

In the negotiations with the Soviet Union concerning recognition in 1933, for example, it is unlikely that Roosevelt would have accorded recognition in 1933 if Russia did not agree, as it did, to allow religious freedom to American nationals within its borders as demanded by America's Catholics. Also, contrary to the prevailing view that Roosevelt was not motivated by Catholic-Americans to intervene in the anticlerical movement in Mexico in the mid-1930s, but offered merely pious rhetoric in their behalf, this work details the political power and influence of America's Catholics to cause a president to intervene personally—and pursue a course of covert involvement—in this matter. And, during the Spanish Civil War, when it seemed that aid to the Spanish government might become a reality in Congress, with the apparent blessing of the Roosevelt administration, Roosevelt leaked a story to the press specifically calculated to arouse Catholic opposition and defeat such a policy. That political maneuver succeeded in May of 1938.

Italian-American pressure at the outbreak of the Italo-Ethiopian War, orchestrated in part by Generoso Pope, the influential editor of *Il Progresso Italo-Americano* and confidant of Roosevelt, provides perhaps the best example of an ethnic minority succeeding in its quest to alter American foreign policy, particularly the proposed Neutrality Act of 1936. As a consequence of the persistence of the Italian-American community, Roosevelt and the Congress decided to extend the proposal for passage of the Neutrality Act for another year and still sell United States manufactured goods to Italy at normal levels, thereby assuring Mussolini hegemony in Ethiopia.

Finally, in comparison with the assertions of several scholars who minimized the efforts taken by the Roosevelt administration to rescue Jews from Nazi-dominated Europe and to assist in the demands of the Jewish-American community to keep Palestine open to Jewish refugees, this book shows that the efforts were considerable. When the British government proposed to terminate Jewish immigration into Palestine prior to the election of 1936, and during the fall of 1938, Roosevelt privately intervened and succeeded in altering British policy. Immigration into Palestine from 1936 to the announcement of the British White Paper in 1939 can be credited to the pressure exerted by Roosevelt on London in behalf of America's Jews. In addition, Roosevelt continually sought to persuade the British to adhere to the Balfour Declaration and the League Mandate to relocate Palestinian Arabs in adjacent Arab states, and convert Palestine into a Jewish National Home. After *Kristallnacht* in November of 1938, for example, and on the eve of the British White Paper in 1939, he revealed to London his financial plan to assist in the resettlement of Palestinian Arabs.

My findings on the impact of these American minorities are significant enough for the American people and historians, even those who have recently published definitive works on FDR's behavior in foreign affairs, to reconsider and reappraise their conclusions regarding various prominent events during Roosevelt's presidency. In this way the debate will be kept alive, and that has to be pleasing to all who strive to understand this most majestic man.

In writing this book, I have had the help of a host of people. I am especially thankful for the assistance, and encouragement to pursue my topic, of Dr. Frank Freidel of Harvard University, who read the entire manuscript and directed my attention to significant materials in the Joseph C. Green and Jay Pierrepont Moffat Papers; and Dr. Piotr Wandycz of Yale University. At St. John's University, I am indebted to my mentor, Professor Frank Coppa, who provided me with that invaluable guidance, advice, and counsel necessary to complete a project of this nature; and to Professors Thomas Curran and Frederick W. Marks, who read, corrected, and rendered support along the way. Professors William E. Leuchtenburg of Columbia University, James MacGregor Burns of Williams College, Robert Dallek of UCLA, Leonard Dinnerstein of the University of Arizona, and Thomas A. Bailey of Stanford University also offered me encouragement and advice in countless ways, for which I will always be extremely appreciative.

One could not conclude such a book without interviewing those who worked closely and loyally for President Roosevelt, and to those numerous associates I am most grateful for their patience and insights. It must be noted that a very great difficulty in the research was that President Roosevelt did not generally commit to paper his innermost thoughts concerning political or ethnic considerations pertaining to his foreign policies, and therefore much had to be gathered from those who shared his confidence and understood his actions and eventual decisions. Consequently, to Grace Tully, James A. Farley, Thomas Corcoran, Benjamin V. Cohen, John W. McCormack, James Roosevelt, W. Averell Harriman, Emanuel Celler, John W. Pehle, and Isador Lubin, I thank you again and again for making the Roosevelt years come alive for me, and hopefully for all who read this book.

Anyone who studies the New Deal or Franklin D. Roosevelt similarly owes a debt of gratitude to those who labor with you and for you at the various institutions throughout the country, and I wish to extend my special appreciation to these archivists, librarians, assistants, and new friends: Dr. William Emerson and his staff at the Franklin D. Roosevelt Library; Dr. David Wigdor, Carolyn Sung, Ruth Nicolson, Marilyn Parr, Izell Washington, Gary Kohn, and Charles J. Kelly at the Manuscripts Division of the Library of Congress; William Lind at the National Archives; Marte Shaw at Harvard; Nathan M. Kaganoff, Martha Katz-heimer, and Nehemiah Ben-Zev at the American Jewish Historical Society; Judy Schiff and Kathy Straka at Yale; Jean Holliday at Princeton; Edmund Berkeley, Jr., at the University of Virginia; John Reynolds at Georgetown University; Father Robert Trisco and Dr. Anthony Zito at Catholic University of America; and Dr. H. Warren Willis at the United States Catholic Conference. Some of the most significant data was uncovered in the archives of Catholic University of America, and at the United States Catholic Conference in Washington, D.C. The American Jewish Historical Society on the campus of Brandeis University in Waltham, Massachusetts, provided very meaningful material which has yet to be published.

That I have been able to proceed to this point in my life, I owe the deepest gratitude and loving affection to my parents, Leo and Anne Kanawada. To have reached this point in my educational career, I wish to remember my former professor of history at Bucknell University, Dr. J. Orin Oliphant, and the man who gave me the opportunity to succeed at the Maxwell School of Citizenship at Syracuse University, Dr. Warren B. Walsh. Moreover, my research could never have been attempted or concluded without the kind hospitality of Evelyn and Willard Hitch of Woodbridge, Virginia; Diane, Marie, and Ward Lattin of Bethesda, Maryland; and John and Linda McCarthy of Nashua, New Hampshire.

Finally, as all historians know, one cannot possibly accomplish any work without the support of a very special person—one's wife. To Carol, my wife, I will always be grateful not only for the typing of the manuscript, but primarily for her patience, understanding, and love.

I

Catholic-Americans

Your Administrative Committee has earnestly and diligently sought to have the President use his good offices that the Mexican Government would change its Constitution and laws which beget persecution of the Church.... In answer, the President did use his good offices in this respect and personally expressed his mind to the Mexican Ambassador and asked the latter to convey that mind to his Government. The President specifically informed the Mexican Ambassador that he, the President, was speaking informally, but he asked that the present Mexican Government take positive steps to allow full liberty of religious worship to all the citizens of Mexico; that it cease its persecution of the Catholic Church.... Your Administrative Committee was informed, as a consequence of this conversation, indirectly by the Mexican Government that the Mexican Government would.... take steps to have priests minister in states where they were now forbidden.

John J. Burke to the Chairman, Administrative Board of the National Catholic Welfare Conference, October 31, 1935

1

Russia and Recognition

Throughout his first two terms in office, President Franklin D. Roosevelt had more to fear than fear itself in the area of foreign policy; he had to come face to face with the power and influence of America's Catholics. Embroiled in the domestic difficulties created by the Great Depression, Roosevelt hoped to avoid confrontations over foreign affairs. Foreign policy would be best kept on a back burner, and Catholics generally agreed. However, three exceptions aroused the Catholic community and marshalled their forces into action. One concerned the attitude of the United States toward Mexico when a wave of anticlericalism emerged there in 1934. A second dealt with the possibility that the United States might support the communist-backed Loyalist government in Spain with arms and ammunition during the Spanish Civil War. But it was to be the third exception—the question of the United States recognizing the Soviet Union in 1933—that was to educate Roosevelt and provide him with his first lesson as President in ethnic politics. He would never forget the implications.

In the spring of 1933, Roosevelt contemplated recognizing the Soviet Union. No public announcement, however, came from the White House before October of 1933. During this five- to six-month period, the President had to deal with considerable opposition to his plan, particularly from the Catholic-American community. At first, Catholics abhorred any talk of recognizing the Soviet Union. But as time passed they began to demand that, in return for recognition, Roosevelt insist on religious freedom for American nationals in the Soviet Union as well as for the Russians themselves.

Initially, Roosevelt had no intention of yielding to their demands. Pressure from church officials, influential laymen, and the Catholic news media, however, along with fear of losing the most important bloc in the Democratic Party, caused him to adopt their policy demands. And when the negotiations were completed in November 1933, Roosevelt proudly acknowledged his role in achieving these aims. The Catholic community responded with enthusiasm.

As the new administration took office in 1933, Roosevelt had several good reasons for reversing United States policy toward the Soviet Union in the direction of normal diplomatic relations. Henry Morgenthau, Jr., Director of the Farm Credit Administration and later Secretary of the Treasury, favored any new program that would increase agricultural productivity and profits, and "incidentally show the President how useful he could be."[1] The attractiveness of the Russian market was indeed appetizing. Other nations in Europe were assisting their nationals in extending credit to Soviet purchasing agents, and Amtorg—the Soviet purchasing agency in the United States—was also anxious to initiate purchases with American industry if the United States government would underwrite the sales. Shortly after Roosevelt moved into the White House, Morgenthau's Farm Credit Board, the Reconstruction Finance Corporation, and the Treasury began to look into the possibility of trading with the Soviet Union.[2]

While the implementation of Soviet-American trade would help to invigorate economic recovery during the depression, Roosevelt also perceived that, owing to the difficulties prevalent in Europe and in Asia, the announcement of recognition could open the door to a joint coalition between the United States, Britain, and the Soviet Union for the containment of aggression, especially that of the Japanese. Recognition of Russia would be observed by many to indicate that the American government was desirous of checking this danger in the Far East.[3]

Secretary of State Cordell Hull similarly indicated that he wanted a rapprochement with Russia. Since the Soviet Union had shown a desire to cooperate with other nations by attending conferences in the interest of world peace, he believed that the European situation might also be riveted by the cooperativeness of Britain, France, and a reconciled America and Russia.[4] Moreover, with recognition of the Soviet Union, Hull saw that the United States would be able to gather first-hand information inside of Russia comparable to that which the American Communist Party and Amtorg were acquiring in America.[5] With Roosevelt and his close advisors favorably inclined toward the resumption of diplomatic relations, the granting of recognition would nevertheless primarily depend upon American public opinion, and for the Roosevelt administration that meant the Catholic-American community.

Roosevelt did want to increase trade and use recognition as a diplomatic tool, but not at the cost of alienating America's Catholic population.[6] In the spring of 1933, Morgenthau recorded that many people in the administration were concerned about the recognition question, "not only because of their convictions but also because they realized there could be no move toward recognition if it meant leaving this important source of opinion [the Catholic-American community] alienated from the President."[7] Likewise, Herbert Feis, the economic advisor to the State Department, reminisced that Roosevelt—during his first weeks in office—told his associates that he "intended to try to arrange for a resumption of diplomatic relations if a satisfactory agreement could be reached; [that it was] foolish and futile for the United States to remain distant toward so important a power as the Soviet Union." However, Feis continued, Roosevelt would only resume diplomatic relations "when it might be done without arousing strong domestic opposition. He waited and watched."[8] It did not take long for Roosevelt to observe the reactions in the Catholic community.

Throughout his tenure in office, Roosevelt would be especially concerned with the positions expressed by the hierarchy of the Catholic Church, and their collective attitudes as reflected by the National Catholic Welfare Conference (NCWC) and transmitted to the White House by John J. Burke, General Secretary of the NCWC. Roosevelt was aware of Burke's prestige and good work for the Catholic Church in America, and was also aware of the fact that Burke maintained close contact with the State Department during the previous administration. In 1933, Burke continued his ties with the State Department and the White House because he was convinced that the Roosevelt administration was preparing to recognize Russia.[9]

Burke believed that the NCWC would have to either support, or oppose, or say that the recognition of Russia was "a matter that is civic, dealing with the civic stability of the particular government, and that it does not mean any endorsement of moral, religious, or social teachings."[10] Later in the year, Burke would be the conduit to the President for the final, collective view of the Church hierarchy on recognition. That view opposed "unqualified recognition"—recognition without conditions. It also concluded that the church would not make a public protest if, prior to recognition, the Soviet government made certain "concrete concessions" on religious freedom.[11] However, even before Roosevelt received this definitive position from the Administrative Committee of the NCWC, he became fully cognizant of the views emanating from the Catholic community.

On March 25, 1933, *The Brooklyn Tablet* publicly condemned the "sinister campaign to have our government formally grant recognition to Soviet Russia—the avowed enemy of all religion.... We here and now give notice to all concerned in the government of our great republic that twenty million Catholics will look upon this step as treason...."[12] From the predominantly Catholic state of Massachusetts came a petition against recognition signed by 673,586 voters.[13]

The foremost critic in the Catholic community, however, was Dr. Edmund A. Walsh, S.J., Vice-President of Georgetown University and head of the Georgetown School of Foreign Service. During the early months of the new administration, Father Walsh was engaged in a series of ten public lectures dealing with communism, and countering arguments urging the recognition of Russia. He was highly regarded and the most vocal of the leading spokesmen among Catholic-Americans on the issue of recognition. At a mass meeting of the American Legion held on April 18th in Washington, Walsh shared the platform with several prominent Americans who disapproved equally of granting recognition.[14] Also in April, Walsh criticized former New York governor and presidential candidate, Alfred E. Smith, who, as a prominent Catholic, had recently advocated recognition for trade reasons. In the last of ten lectures opposing recognition of Russia, Walsh criticized not only Smith's statements but also his role as spokesman for Catholic-Americans. Walsh observed that Smith had a wide constituency concerning his domestic policies, but that his "Russian views are not shared by that great majority of Americans of his own faith who see eye to eye with him in most other respects."[15]

Perhaps the most influential, particularly with Roosevelt, of all the members of the hierarchy was Patrick Cardinal Hayes of New York. His association with Roosevelt was well known among those who understood the functioning of the White House. Hayes understood that recognition of Russia was "being discussed as an economic question in the hope that it is a way open to revive trade."[16] In a letter to Hayes, Father Walsh wrote that he had "learned from authoritative sources here in Washington that Your Eminence's opinion is highly valued by President Roosevelt. In fact, it was said that he would do nothing affecting Catholic interests until he had learned the attitude of Cardinal Hayes...." Walsh wanted Hayes to write to Roosevelt to the effect that "nothing be done in this matter until the President could hear the point of view of Catholic representatives," and Walsh continued, "I am confident that nothing will be done [until such representation is made]."[17] Throughout this period before recognition, Hayes admitted that he was "in touch with President Roosevelt" and was "letting him know how concerned the Church is with regard to recognition."[18]

During the spring and summer of 1933, Roosevelt publicly remained uncommitted on recognition and, on several occasions, refrained from concluding any sort of agreement with Russia. At a May 16 press conference he said that he "had in mind no formal recognition of the Russian Government."[19] Roosevelt did want to have someone act as a trade commissioner between the United States and Moscow and begin the process of doing business with the Russians. However, when he was informed in June of 1933 that the Reconstruction Finance Corporation "had nearly completed arrangements for financing the sale of about seventy thousand bales of cotton to Russia (payment to be made 30 percent in cash and 70 percent in one-year credit), Roosevelt took his time about giving his clearance to the bargain; and while it was still being considered, Amtorg backed away."[20] Again, in August, when Amtorg desired to buy seventy-five million dollars worth of raw materials and fifty million dollars worth of machinery, Roosevelt thought that the United States should limit its sales to Russia and require a down payment. Consequently, these conditions helped to negate any agreement.[21] Finally, when Morgenthau, in late September, "asked the President whether... he wanted him to go ahead and make loans to Russia, the President fended him off."[22]

Throughout this period, Roosevelt was torn between his desire to consummate some association with the Russians and his need to maintain the support of the Catholic community. He did maintain close contacts with the Church at this time, speaking at graduation ceremonies at the Catholic University of America in June and at the Catholic Charities Conference Dinner in New York City in early October. On both occasions, Cardinal Hayes was "overwhelmed with an abiding gratitude for [this] presence," and congratulated Roosevelt for his "strong, uncompromising utterance on Religion [which] will live in history. It will do incalculable good."[23] Likewise, the Church kept in close contact with Roosevelt, particularly through the State Department.

In July of 1933, Father Burke had several significant meetings on the issue of recognition with key officials in the State Department, particularly Undersecretary of State William Phillips. Prior to his meeting with Phillips on July 24, Burke was told by Jefferson Caffrey, the Assistant Secretary of State, that he did not know if any plan to recognize Russia was presently contemplated, but was certain that only Roosevelt would initiate such a pronouncement.[24] Nevertheless, Burke wished to convey to the State Department the consensus view of the hierarchy of the Catholic Church on recognition as represented by the Administrative Committee of the National Catholic Welfare Conference.

At his meeting with Phillips, he stressed that the bishops of the Administrative Committee of the NCWC were all strongly opposed to recognition, but "they would not make any public protest." Moreover, Burke concluded by questioning whether or not the United States could afford to grant recognition to a government that upheld communistic theories and "not only denied God but sought to destroy God. Would not such a grant," Burke said, "give the impression to many that the United States Government did not care especially what principles underlying government were taught or held, so long as a government was outwardly stable; that the material and not the spiritual was the ultimate test?"[25] Here was the key concept from the Catholic hierarchy that Roosevelt needed, and which afforded him the opportunity to avoid a massive defection by the Catholic community over recognition. The United States had to show that it did care what principles the Soviet government taught and that the Russians did not seek to deny or destroy God. From this point onward the hierarchy—Father Burke, William Bullitt and Father Walsh—consolidated the attitude of the Catholic community for Roosevelt, upon which the decision of recognizing Russia would depend.

The position of the Roosevelt administration toward recognition was best explained by Phillips at his meeting with Father Burke in July of 1933. Phillips told Burke that recognition had nothing to do with the religious attitudes of a government. The United States recognized Mexico even though Mexico was persecuting the Catholic Church. As far as Russia was concerned, Phillips said that the United States was in a dilemma. The reasons to oppose recognition no longer prevailed. Russia disavowed any connection with the Third International; she was devoid of funds to push communist propaganda; and "the question of Russia's debts to the United States was practically a dying or dead question." In fact, no debtor nation to the United States was paying its debt.[26]

Phillips maintained that the recognition of Russia was not being considered in order to obtain trade advantages for the United States. Burke was surprised and asked "if such recognition would be given because the United States was finding it more and more necessary to have as many nations meet together and try to agree on policies that would benefit the world economic situation." Phillips nodded some evidences of agreement, even though Burke thought that Phillips was not at liberty to make known the reasons which might lead the United States to recognize Russia. Although Phillips spoke in strict confidence, Burke came away from the meeting fully convinced that the recognition of Russia by the United States was being seriously considered.[27]

When the interview ended, Phillips said that he would convey Burke's views to Roosevelt.[28] Similarly, during this period the bishops of the NCWC, representing the Church hierarchy, instructed Burke to submit a memorandum of their position and request the Secretary of State to bring it to the attention of the President. It was this final position that summarized "the mind of the Administrative Committee of Bishops of the National Catholic Welfare Conference with regard to the question of recognition by our Government of the present Russian Government."[29]

Before receiving this memorandum and request from the leadership of the Catholic-American community in late September, no memorandum from the State Department to the President regarding recognition contained any reference to religious rights or freedom. Even Hull's letter to Roosevelt in September, outlining the advantages of recognizing the Soviet Union, contained no plea to secure a promise from the Russians that freedom of religion be granted.[30] With this memorandum the opinion of the hierarchy (without doubt representing for Roosevelt the conviction of millions of Catholic-Americans) coupled with the work of Father Burke, caused the

Roosevelt administration, when dealing with the Russians, to insist on religious guarantees prior to recognition.

What the memorandum requested had a profound impact on the administration's policy toward recognition. Specifically, it warned the administration that recognition would be "interpreted by millions of our citizens" as toleration of "irreligion and immorality."[31] Although the bishops believed that recognition of Russia was risking great injury to their own institutions and would hinder the religious, moral, social, and political welfare of the country, the administrative committee did not desire to make a public protest on this question because it was "ever willing, even seemingly, to interfere in what might be termed purely political affairs, and it recognizes that it does not know all the considerations that enter into the solution of such a problem." The statement was encouraging to Roosevelt and the State Department, for a public protest now could essentially be avoided. Furthermore, Father Burke concluded the letter with the way in which avoidance of such a confrontation could be accomplished. He said that the Administrative Committee requested that, if recognition was given, the United States should "inform and assure the public that the ground for such recognition is only the political stability of the Government recognized"; that recognition would in no way mean that America sympathized with "the religious and moral institutions and teaching of the Government in question."[32]

Roosevelt and the State Department understood the importance of this statement of Catholic attitudes, and immediately adopted it as part of their overall policy regarding the recognition of the Soviet Union. This policy was to be espoused by Roosevelt up to and during the negotiations with the Russians, and was reinforced with other proposals added to the President's thinking by those in and out of government (Catholics and non-Catholics alike) throughout the fall of 1933.

With the position of the Catholic community now well known in the State Department, William Bullitt—slated to become our first Soviet Ambassador—urged Hull to negotiate for "protection of the civil and religious rights of Americans in Russia which are inadequately protected under current Russian practice."[33] It should be noted that Bullitt, as a member of the inner circle at the State Department, had been working for Roosevelt without the knowledge of the department on the matter of recognition since August.[34] Roosevelt frequently employed this tactic during his tenure in office. Moreover, in another undated memorandum to Roosevelt, Bullitt, aware of the attitude expressed by the hierarchy, stressed that recognition "will inevitably bring sincere charges that the United States Government is making friends with a government avowedly an enemy of God and a persecutor of religion," and therefore a "promise from the Soviet Government, in writing, would be the surest guarantee that the above mentioned points would be allowed and observed. It would be highly desirable to obtain such a promise prior to negotiations for recognition."[35] Specifically, it warned the administration that recognition would be "interpreted by millions of our citizens" as toleration of "irreligion and immorality." Curiously, Bullitt's memorandum bore a stark resemblance to the memo forwarded to the State Department by the Catholic hierarchy.

In view of his concern about the influence and importance of the Catholic community, Roosevelt asked Bullitt to "Please speak to me about this."[36] Later, Roosevelt remarked that he was very proud of the fact that he had insisted on the inclusion of religious rights as a prerequisite to recognition.[37]

R. Walton Moore, counselor in the State Department and advisor to the President, also expressed his concern about Americans in Russia having the right to worship in their homes and churches. Moore did not know how far Roosevelt could push the Russians on this point, but he suggested that "in view of the agitation among religious bodies in this country, we should obviously go as far as we can."[38]

Although Moore had emphasized "religious bodies" in his memorandum, the President was primarily worried about Roman Catholics.[39] In discussing the impending recognition of Russia with Henry Morgenthau, Jr., Roosevelt related a conversation he had with Henry Wallace, his future vice-president. He said that Wallace came over to the White House "very much worried about our recognizing Russia on account of the religious effect it will have in this country."[40] Later, Wallace recalled this conversation with Roosevelt and how important it was for the President to get religious freedom in the agreement. At that time, Wallace noted, Roosevelt told him about the effort over freedom of religion and the attempt to prevent the Russians from engaging in covert activities in the United States. Both points received great emphasis. "I had made some of those points with Roosevelt prior to that," Wallace observed, "and I've no doubt the Catholics had made some of those points with Roosevelt.... He felt he'd put some things over very much against Litvinov's will."[41]

Before Roosevelt sent his invitation on October 20, 1933, to the Soviet government requesting them to send a negotiator to Washington to hold discussions that might lead to recognition, he had a very significant meeting with Father Walsh, the leading Catholic spokesman opposing recognition. Although Roosevelt had ascertained the policy objectives of the Catholic hierarchy from Father Burke, he was informed by a friend of long standing that Father Walsh could place "the A.F. of Labor, the American Legion, The Bishop Freeman Committee and the Catholics squarely behind the Administration's program for Russia, solely on economic grounds, and with reasonable protection of our own interests." With Walsh anxious to relay certain information to Roosevelt, a conference was quickly arranged.[42]

Father Walsh met Roosevelt at the White House on October 20, the very day that Roosevelt announced to the press that he had invited the Soviets to send a representative to Washington to initiate discussions. From all indications the meeting between Roosevelt and Walsh established, first of all, official government policy on religious liberty to be followed by Roosevelt up to and including the negotiations with Maxim Litvinov, the Russian arbiter. Walsh impressed upon Roosevelt that the Catholic Church in America desired "his powerful support in defense of fundamental human liberties," and Walsh recommended several objectives. He demanded "complete liberty of conscience for all, whether citizens of Russia or nationals of a foreign jurisdiction residing in Soviet territory." Secondly, the meeting established that private and public exercises of religious beliefs be guaranteed to all. And finally, that all "Bishops, priests, other ministers of religion, and laymen,—now in confinement under charges connected with religion"—be released.[43] The Jesuit priest emphasized that if religious liberty for the citizens of Russia, or nationals of a foreign country, and private and public exercise of religious beliefs were not guaranteed "and published *before recognition or at least simultaneously* . . . the liberties now being assailed in Russia will never be restored." Recognition without these conditions, Walsh concluded, would be "wholly alien to American ideals and abhorrent to Christian instincts."[44]

Walsh recalled that at the meeting with Roosevelt, in reply "to certain observations I had made respecting the difficulty of negotiating with the Soviets, he (Roosevelt) answered with that disarming assurance so characteristic of his technique in dealing with visitors: "'Leave it to me, Father; I am a good horse dealer.'"[45] During the meeting, Roosevelt must have been at his persuasive best, for Walsh agreed to discontinue his attack on the President's policy of recognition. "Father Walsh's cooperation on the matter emerged as one of the major coups of the President in preparing public opinion for recognition."[46] As a result of this meeting, Roosevelt consented to incorporate the religious liberty proposal and Walsh attempted, through numerous telephone calls, to "contribute something to the tranquility of mind needed for the forthcoming negotiations." Walsh's final act was also of utmost importance. He cancelled a lecture in Providence, Rhode Island, and substituted one on "Capitalism at the Crossroads." Roosevelt told McIntyre (secretary to the President) to "thank him and tell him I appreciate it." The subject of the lecture was to have been "Recognition of Soviet Russia."[47]

After the meeting with Roosevelt and the President's announced invitation to the Russians, Walsh told the press that "continued public controversy and debate at this time appear to me to be superfluous and may prove dangerous. The President should not be hampered, or annoyed, or embarrassed as he undertakes to fulfill his constitutional duty and exercise his constitutional prerogative in the conduct of our international relations." He pointed out that Roosevelt had guaranteed nothing to the Russians except to hear their point of view. Moreover, if the United States and the Soviet Union solved the various difficulties that existed between them, Walsh said that he would be "the first to support renewed diplomatic relations." To Walsh, Roosevelt did not commit the United States to any course of action; he only provided an invitation to hold a conference.[48]

Walsh's view was correct. When Roosevelt released the correspondence inviting the representatives of Russia to the United States, he advised the press that his action did not mean recognition. "The press, however, not only announced recognition, but in many cases fixed what they considered the precise day on which it was to take place." Actually, the press tended to listen to Litvinov, "who announced before he sailed that everything would be settled in a half hour."[49] Litvinov was not aware of the fact that Roosevelt would not extend recognition unless the demands for religious freedom were initially granted.

A similar statement was issued by the Most Reverend Joseph Schrembs, Bishop of Cleveland and Episcopal Chairman of the Department of Lay Organizations of the National Catholic Welfare Conference. Schrembs hoped "that the United States Government, in its forthcoming discussions bearing on recognition of Soviet Russia, will ask guarantees with regard to freedom of religious worship...[and] that no one will question the good faith of the Administration in its new move with regard to Russia." In order to acquire diplomatic recognition from the United States, Schrembs felt that it was not too much to ask Russia to promise religious freedom to its citizens.[50] Roosevelt agreed.

By late October, the American people were well aware that Roosevelt had invited Litvinov to the United States to discuss an agreement leading toward recognition between the two countries.[51] In the front-page editorial, *The Brooklyn Tablet*—representing millions of America's Catholics—emphasized that it was "not interested in the so-called Japanese issue, or the advantages or disadvantages of a trade agreement, or the arbitration of international debts, or in the grand hurrah of the Soviet propagandists here and abroad." *The Brooklyn Tablet* wanted the persecution of the Catholic religion in Russia to stop. It had "opposed recognition of Soviet Russia because of the discrimination, destruction and organized campaign against religion," and because of the propaganda directed against "democratic government and constitutional freedom." But now, this leading Catholic newspaper moved to the position of supporting recognition if various guarantees were agreed upon. It concluded the editorial by appealing to Roosevelt "to ask and insist upon guarantees with regard to religious freedom and subversive propaganda, at the coming discussions in Washington. Otherwise recognition should be barred."[52] The Church hierarchy and the Catholic press were resolved to trust in the "good faith of President Roosevelt . . . [and] believed that considerable good might be brought out of an otherwise regrettable situation; that freedom of religious worship for Americans in Russia might eventually lead to freedom of worship for the Russian people themselves."[53]

Roosevelt knew that the religious plank had to be accepted by the Russians as quickly as possible. He was well aware of the fact that the press and the educational institutions of the Catholic Church solidly supported his domestic programs; that negotiations with Russia threatened the support of Catholic leaders; and that a week after Litvinov would arrive the American hierarchy of the Catholic Church would meet and these bishops might pass resolutions that could seriously hamper negotiations. It should be noted that Roosevelt was "so concerned about the views of Catholic-Americans that he invited many bishops from around the country to the White House" to consult with them about this issue.[54] Roosevelt, it seems, was determined to announce publicly during their meeting that the Russians had accepted the proposals for religious freedom.[55]

In November of 1933, the religious issue became paramount. Even though Roosevelt had previously decided to accept the major points stipulated in the memorandum by Walsh and Bullitt, he was urged to accept a similar memorandum from the Pope. This note from the Pope was passed through Cardinal Hayes's representative, Monsignor Robert F. Keegan, stressing the hope of Catholics for religious freedom of worship. Cardinal Hayes in a note marked "confidential" wrote on November 2: "The President conferred with the Monsignor for more than one hour in his private study, receiving him most cordially and substantially accepting the points of the memorandum."[56]

On the day prior to Litvinov's arrival, Roosevelt and the State Department began their final preparations and strategy. The religious issue had top priority. That afternoon Hull, Bullitt, Morgenthau, and Phillips all met with Roosevelt to set down the principal points to be considered. The discussion centered mainly on the demand for freedom of religion for Americans in Russia as well as how to curtail Soviet propaganda in the United States. According to Phillips, these subjects were well "buttoned up" and had "to be accepted by Litvinov."[57]

The Administration also possessed additional items of information from Father Walsh, supplementing his recent memorandum on religion in Soviet Russia. Walsh informed Roosevelt that Boris Skvirsky, the unofficial Soviet representative in the United States, had cabled Moscow concerning the matters of religion that would be discussed with Litvinov. Moscow reacted favorably and promised to consider the propositions which Walsh had outlined in his memorandum to Roosevelt; the same propositions which America's Catholics, Walsh said, hoped that Roosevelt could "persuade Mr. Litvinov to accept."[58] The scene was now set for the negotiations with Litvinov.

Initially, the talks had begun under the supervision of Secretary Hull. However, upon his departure for South America, Acting Secretary Phillips assumed leadership, with the "vastly more important and pivotal conversations between Litvinov and President Roosevelt at the White House."[59] How important were the religious demands of the Catholic community as the conference began? At the first meeting with Litvinov on November 9, at the State Department, Hull reflected Roosevelt's desire to settle the religious issue prior to the granting of recognition, and the overall significance of this issue. "Hull gave the impression," Morgenthau said, "that the religious issue is the most important one, and that it was very much uppermost in his mind." At first Hull cautioned that, if diplomatic relations between Russia and the United States could not commence "without first coming to an agreement on the religious issue, the Roosevelt Administration would be overthrown at the next election."[60]

According to Morgenthau, the American position was that "we wanted a formal statement in writing on the religious question," but "Litvinov kept answering that he could not give any statement informal, or otherwise, as it would be binding on his country and, therefore, he did not wish to make any statement." Later, after a discussion with the President, Litvinov and the Soviet government agreed to such a public statement. However, some confusion of intention did exist, for Hull had to emphasize that the United States was "only talking about protecting American nationals in Russia, and not about the religious issue as it affected Russian citizens, and that the U.S.A. was desirous of securing permission for nationals for freedom of religious worship while in Russia."[61]

Litvinov argued that Americans were already permitted to practice their religion and therefore a statement was unnecessary. Whether American nationals were permitted to worship in Russia or not (or whether all Russians were to be granted religious freedom), the administration knew that a statement, any statement, on religious liberty was essential in order to maintain Catholic-American support. Morgenthau recorded that Hull said that "we have to face criticism if we do not handle the question of debts and religion simultaneously with recognition."[62] Confusion still existed in Litvinov's mind, for at a conference later in the day, "a carefully prepared document in regard to religious freedom of our nationals in Russia" was given to Litvinov, and he responded that "*we* are not interested in the religion of our national[s]."[63]

Meanwhile, at the White House, the President saw the need for some personal diplomacy. He had previously promised Catholic Church spokesmen to fight for religious freedom for Russians as well as American nationals in the Soviet Union. Meeting with Hull, Bullitt, Moore, and Phillips upstairs in his study for tea, Roosevelt was pleased that something was advanced on the religious issue. However, Roosevelt wanted Litvinov all to himself in order to resolve the religious question and called for a meeting with Litvinov for the following day which, Phillips surmised, would "be the crisis."[64] Thus began three days of conversations between the President and Litvinov, wherein Bullitt reported that Litvinov said that "I can't understand the President; he hasn't talked about anything but religious freedom to me, and I want to discuss important things like trade relations, etc. What is the idea?"[65] Years later, Bullitt revealed that when Litvinov's "persistent refusal to agree to the guarantees [particularly the one on religious freedom] prompted the negotiators to hand him a schedule of steamship sailings with the choice of sign or go home...the State Department was most certainly resorting to drastic action."[66]

On November 10, Roosevelt spoke to Litvinov a second time, urging him to agree to the demand that religious freedom be granted to Americans in Russia. Roosevelt was adamant and reiterated that such an agreement was essential, and that Litvinov could return to Moscow if his government "refused to give in."[67]

The Brooklyn Tablet similarly learned that "an agreement with Russia is not ready as yet." The Soviet Union, according to the *Tablet*, wanted the American government to agree to recognition first and then specific terms would be discussed.[68] Of course, Roosevelt insisted on just the opposite procedure. After considerable debate Litvinov sought instructions from Moscow, and, on November 11, "he was authorized to try to draw up a statement which would satisfy the wishes which the President had expressed.[69]

Roosevelt had succeeded. However, he apparently paid a price and, as he would do so often throughout his political life, he compromised—not only with Litvinov, but also with those church spokesmen and leaders to whom he promised, in the memorandum he endorsed, to insure religious freedom for American nationals *and* Russians. Consequently, religious liberty for the Russian people was not advanced one iota. What transpired between the President and Litvinov during these last hours of negotiation on the religious question shows how concerned Roosevelt was to ease, according to Rexford Tugwell, "the annoyance of the Roman Catholics, who had been so much opposed to recognition."[70]

In November of 1933, James A. Farley, Postmaster General and chairman of the National Democratic Committee, had dinner with Roosevelt and asked about the problem of religious freedom at the negotiations. "Oh, I was very definite on that," Roosevelt told Farley, "I told Litvinov the situation must be cleared up, because the people of this country give everyone the right to freedom of religious belief, and there is no reason why Russia should impose her ideas on Americans who might be in that country. I said guarantee of religious freedom must be given Americans before anything could be done."[71]

A few days later at a Cabinet meeting, Farley said that Roosevelt "felt the agreement would be very pleasing to the people of this country, and that those who had opposed recognition on religious grounds would no longer do so. He acknowledged that the safeguards to religion involved Americans alone, but expressed himself confident he had opened the door to similar bargaining by other countries."[72] Farley wanted Roosevelt to press Litvinov, as did many clergymen of all faiths, to accept the proposition that *all Russians* would acquire religious freedom. But, as much as Roosevelt would have desired that end result, he was primarily concerned with the fact that the agreement "would greatly facilitate the acceptance of recognition in the United States, particularly on the part of Roman Catholic leaders, if the Russian government would publicly concede the right of American nationals residing there to worship as they saw fit."[73]

Possibly, the best picture of what occurred between Roosevelt and Litvinov, and of Roosevelt's sensitivity to Catholic-American opposition and opinion, was drawn by Frances Perkins, Roosevelt's Secretary of Labor. Perkins said that Roosevelt wanted Russia to agree to permit the free practice of religion, and he knew how irritated Americans were on this issue. He was sensitive to public opinion and did press Litvinov constantly. According to Perkins, Litvinov gave stock answers that religion "wasn't totally prohibited," anyone who wanted to pray to God could, and so forth. However, Roosevelt never gave up on the issue, stating at one point that in America people could not "understand this idea that people shouldn't have access to religion—any kind they want. That's all I ask, Max—to have Russia recognize freedom of religion." In addition, Roosevelt did tell Perkins that he had been in contact with leading religious leaders in the United States, "probably Chicago Cardinal, Samuel Stritch—he is such an intelligent man," but "this was done very quietly."[74]

As a result of the authorization by Moscow to draw up a statement on religioius freedom, the President met again with Litvinov on November 12. Their conference lasted two hours. According to Phillips, Roosevelt was willing to accept "a recitation by the Russians of the Soviet laws" concerning religious liberty. However, Moore, Phillips, and Robert F. Kelley (a career foreign service officer and Chief of the Division of Eastern European Affairs) did not approve of this approach, believing instead that "an original statement from the Soviets to us is necessary, if only to give the appearance of new concessions."[75] From all indications, the State Department view prevailed; the Soviets pledged to guarantee the free exercise of religion, not just recite current laws.

Roosevelt was content to acquire any statement, and that written statement was issued on November 16, 1933, conveniently coinciding with the meeting of bishops of the American hierarchy which had convened the previous day. In the exchange of letters between Roosevelt and Litvinov, which comprised the public statement, Roosevelt emphasized that American citizens in the Soviet Union would enjoy the "free exercise of liberty of conscience and religious worship, conduct without annoyance or molestation of any kind religious services," and would "be given the right to have their spiritual needs ministered to by clergymen, priests, rabbis or other ecclesiastical functionaries who are nationals of the United States of America." Litvinov and the Soviet government guaranteed that "nationals of the United States shall be granted rights with reference to freedom of conscience and the free exercise of religion."[76] With the religious issue now settled, Roosevelt awaited the reaction and the judgment of the Catholic community, particularly the bishops of the church hierarchy.

Although the visit by Al Smith to the White House in the midst of the negotiations on November 14 was reported "as having no connection with the disclosure of the President's position on the religious question," Smith did speak in support of the President on the day of the release of the religious agreement.[77] Roosevelt must have been overjoyed by the reaction. Cardinal Hayes believed that Roosevelt was "most gracious" to have invited Smith to the White House and observed that Smith's speech was "inspired" by the conference with Roosevelt.[78] An aide to Cardinal Hayes also wrote that "the Cardinal is very happy with what you have achieved. He has not yet heard any opinion from other sources. As soon as official commentary is available, I will see that it is sent to you."[79] Roosevelt was pleased to hear from Hayes, responding that "we have really accomplished much in regard to the difficult question of religion in Russia. I would be so interested to know what you hear officially."[80]

If Smith was echoing the words of the President in attempting to maintain the continued support of Catholic-Americans, Father Maurice S. Sheehy and Bishop John Ryan of Catholic University of America were likewise extremely interested in the President's strategy directed toward the Catholic hierarchy. Both of these men assisted Roosevelt during the period of the negotiations with the Russians by convincing members of the Church hierarchy to avoid any disapproval of the recognition of the Soviet Union, thus "leaving the President's hands free" to deal with Litvinov.[81] In addition, the noted syndicated columnist, Raymond Clapper, recorded that Cardinal O'Connell of Boston confided that Roosevelt had Catholics invited to the White House "to get them quieted and clear way for recognition."[82] Even Father Walsh said that "he had no comment to make on the religious clauses in the agreement," emphasizing that "the success or failure of the Russo-American agreement... rests with the Soviet Union."[83] The release of fourteen Catholic priests from Soviet prisons on November 19, (a proposal advocated by Walsh in his memorandum of October 31) in exchange for twenty-six Communists imprisoned in Lithuania, could very well have been a sign of Russia's good faith, or an action demanded by Roosevelt to insure Walsh's silence, or a secret agreement not contained in the public statement.[84] Roosevelt had his victory.

In negotiating the religious question, Roosevelt was emphatically concerned with Catholic-American opinion and the effect that the recognition of Russia would have on it. As one historian has written, "Roosevelt's charm" brought the Catholic-American community into line. "The switch of Catholics reflected their desire to avoid a break with Roosevelt, their belief that he would improve religious conditions in the Soviet Union, and Roosevelt's flattery of Walsh, which threw this Catholic leader off balance for a brief time."[85]

In recollecting the lessons he had learned as a result of the establishment of diplomatic relations with the Soviet Union, George F. Kennan observed the tendency of a leader in Roosevelt's position to color his statements and take actions so that they would have a significant effect "on those echelons of American opinion, congressional opinion first and foremost, to which the respective statesmen are anxious to appeal. The question, in these circumstances became . . . how do I look, in the mirror of domestic American opinion, as I do it?"[86]

Roosevelt did attempt in this and later dealings with the Soviet Union to negotiate for religious freedom in the Soviet Union. However, one clearly must conclude, in agreement with Kennan, that the President "exchanged these promises with Litvinov 'only' because of their psychological impact on the American people and was not worried about their later effectiveness."[87]

During the period following the announcement of recognition, hostility was turning into praise. In the Catholic press, editorial comment was "for the most part temperate" and concerned with the possibilities for the future. "Roosevelt's insistence upon the guarantee of religious liberty was praised . . . [and] when it was found that two fifths of the matter in the notes concerning recognition dealt with freedom of worship, it was believed that considerable good might be brought out of an otherwise regrettable situation."[88] Similar reactions made their way from around the country to the White House. "One of the largest and most influential Catholic clubs discussed the matter [recognition of Russia] about ten days ago. One of the speakers was cheered when he said, 'Roosevelt has put God back into Russia.' This statement is going to over five hundred leading secular papers."[89] And, finally, from the influential *Brooklyn Tablet* came the observation that "seldom—probably never before—in American diplomatic correspondence has so much space been given to the discussion of the fundamental principal [of freedom of religious worship]." Hopefully, the exchange of notes would be construed that "Russia is quite as willing to modify its anti-religious policy as it had modified its policy regarding communistic propaganda."[90]

Roosevelt had correctly perceived the situation regarding Catholic-American opposition. Whether or not he was instrumental in having Father

Walsh, without notice, travel to confer with Pope Pius XI about the recognition agreement will not be known. However, no statement was made concerning his visit to the pontiff. But it was understood that he "made a report on the recent recognition of the Soviet Union by the American Government."[91] Walsh had previously announced that, while the negotiations were in progress, "comprehensive and formal guarantees of an unprecedented character in several fields were made by the Soviet government prior to recognition." These guarantees, Walsh believed, were a "significant abandonment of the previous Soviet policy, which uniformly demanded recognition first, and detailed discussion and mutual guarantees to follow."[92] To surmise that the trip was the final piece of handiwork of the President to maintain the support of *all* Catholics would not be unfair; it would be a maneuver that, in the handling of ethnic groups, could be labeled typically Rooseveltian.

2

The Church in Mexico

The recognition of the Soviet Union was not the only issue that occupied the attention of America's Catholics. Almost as soon as the ink dried on the Soviet-American accord to establish diplomatic relations, Roosevelt was confronted with a ground swell of Catholic-American pressure aimed at changing his policy toward Mexico. A wave of anticlericalism had swept across Mexico. Churches were closed, priests were forbidden to conduct worship services, and church-operated schools came under the control of the government. News of this persecution of the Church spread quickly throughout the United States.

The cornerstone of Roosevelt's Good Neighbor policy toward Latin America was non-interference in their internal or domestic affairs. Publicly, Roosevelt adhered to his policy. Even privately, he at first hid behind the Good Neighbor policy and sat idly by while religious freedom was denied to Catholics in Mexico. But, as the Catholic-American hierarchy, press, and parishioners, in conjunction with a significant bloc of congressmen, appealed to the administration for action, Roosevelt set a program in motion. And, so as not to appear to be coercing the Mexican government, Roosevelt's actions took place strictly in private.

Ever since the Catholic Church was disengaged from the political life of Mexico and its religious functions narrowly restricted by the Mexican Constitution of 1917, "American Catholics...[kept] an anxious eye on Mexico."[1] The constitution prohibited clerics from criticizing Mexican law. Church members could neither vote nor hold office, nor assemble in places of worship for political reasons. Religious publications had to exclude any mention of political affairs, and the actions of government officials could not be questioned or criticized.[2] Even with the advent of the 1930s, when the Church began to become more democratic—elevating Mexican-born priests to posts in the hierarchy, organizing to eliminate luxury in the Church and misery in the ranks—another wave of anticlericalism in 1934 rolled over the Church, this time led by Mexico's president, Plutarco Elias Calles.[3]

General Calles, President of Mexico and head of the National Revolutionary Party from 1929 to 1935, turned on the Catholic Church while president and condoned "state governors who all but eliminated Catholic institutions and influence in many provinces of Mexico."[4] The renewed hostility toward religion and the Church by Calles evolved when student strikes broke out in the fall of 1933 in the various institutions of learning. Calles charged that the clergy were responsible for the uprisings.[5] Therefore, at the convention of the National Revolutionary Party in January of 1934, the party adopted a statement by Calles, known as the Six-Year Plan, which pledged the party to amend the Mexican Constitution to only permit the state to operate primary and secondary schools and to teach in these schools the "postulates of the socialist doctrine to which the Mexican Revolution gives support." Under this plan religious instruction and religious influence would be excluded from all primary and secondary schools in Mexico.[6]

In addition, the plan called for the following action to be taken. Under the constitution, priests were to be labeled as professionals. As stated in the Six-Year Plan, the state could establish laws detailing the conditions under which persons could exercise their professions, and could likewise organize a police force to watch any professional and prevent him from violating any federal, state, or municipal law. Publicly, Calles had declared his hostility toward the Catholic Church in Mexico and pledged to suppress any opposition to his government, placing at the top of his list the clergy and the Church.[7] Roosevelt had not yet moved into the White House when in February of 1933 the Catholic bishops in the United States issued a strong protest against the sustained persecution of the Church in Mexico, "thus providing a warning that not all of the new President's problems would concern domestic matters."[8]

Catholics in America saw the restrictions or the outright ban on religious activities in Mexico as obvious persecution. The questions of how many priests and churches were to function and who was to control education were critical. To the church hierarchy, the Mexican government's decision to secularize education, traditionally in the hands of the Church, was of utmost concern. The Six-Year Plan called for the erection of six thousand new schools—both primary and secondary—by 1940, and that all schools would be under the control of the government.[9] These apprehensions exhibited by America's Catholics held particular significance for Father John J. Burke.

In the spring of 1934 in an interview with the American ambassador to Mexico, Josephus Daniels, former Secretary of the Navy and confidant of Roosevelt, Burke summarized and expressed the minds of the bishops of Mexico and of the Holy Father regarding the situation in Mexico. Catholics, Burke said, were resigned to stay out of politics and accept the Calles regime, but would not relinquish their demands for religious liberty, for the opportunity to educate their parishioners, as well as to build up the native priesthood. No demonstrations reflecting the desires of the Catholic community, however, would take place prior to the upcoming presidential election in Mexico. Such actions were always interpreted by the government as evidence of political aggression, and Daniels agreed that no Catholic claims should be pressed at that time.[10] Then, on July 26, 1934, Daniels delivered a lecture.

At a seminar on education in Mexico City, Daniels praised President Calles's views on education, "expressing appreciation of the attitude of Mexico in recognizing the great work of Horace Mann and quoting General Calles as favoring the education of children."[11] Daniels was never more astounded when he discovered how infuriated America's Catholics had become over his remarks. To Catholics, Daniels seemed to support the Calles type of education which emphasized that, for the future of Mexico, "we must enter and take possession of the mind of childhood, the mind of youth." Aware of the educational system in the Soviet Union, America's Catholic community looked upon the Mexican system as a direct copy of Russia's atheistic and socialistic educational philosophy. And if Daniels condoned such a system, Catholics reasoned, Roosevelt should recall his ambassador immediately and discharge him.[12]

Not only did Daniels's speech cause an outcry for his recall, it provided the spark that motivated Catholic-Americans to organize a campaign to convince the Roosevelt administration that some form of intervention in Mexico by the United States was necessary. Diocesan newspapers, Catholic magazines (including *The Catholic World, America,* and *Commonweal*), and Catholic clubs and societies demanded action. The radio priest, Father Charles Coughlin, said that, in addition to Daniels, "American presidents for the last two decades had aided and abetted the rape of Mexico."[13] Francis C. Kelley, Bishop of Oklahoma City, advocated that Catholics should bring pressure to bear on the government through the Senate and the House, ignore the State Department, and stir up "a revival by Catholics of the agitation that I stirred up beginning with 1914."[14] The National Council of Catholic Women sent a resolution to the White House in October of 1934 deploring Daniels's approval of Mexico's antireligious school system.[15] By December of 1934, the State Department was flooded with mail and petitions, Hull directing his staff not to answer most of it. Over the next six months more than ten thousand communications reached the State Department dealing with the Mexican religious controversy, most demanding the removal of Daniels and an American protest. In addition, from New York to Spokane, Washington, Catholic groups organized boycotts of Mexican goods.[16] Burke realized that owing to the impact of the Daniels speech, the Mexican Six-Year Plan, and the prospect of the termination of religious liberty in Mexico most apparent, he must obtain an interview with Roosevelt at the earliest possible moment. The ground swell of Catholic opinion was mounting.

Father Burke was certain that, regardless of Catholic-American pressure, Roosevelt would never commit an armed force nor sever diplomatic ties in order to convince Mexico to grant religious liberty. The United States had just recognized the Soviet Union, and only recently Roosevelt and Hull had declared that the United States would "never again send its troops in any hostile way into any of the Latin-American countries."[17] Furthermore, Burke believed that Roosevelt would have to be very careful not to provoke the people of Mexico if he desired to intervene. If they learned that the American government was hostile to their political system, Mexico would be strong enough to defy or oppose the United States.[18] Nevertheless, Burke was convinced that Roosevelt had profound religious convictions, was devoted to aiding oppressed peoples, and under pressure from the Catholic community could be moved to intervene in Mexico.[19] However, that intervention would have to occur only through private, discreet channels.

Burke met with Roosevelt on October 22, 1934, and the attitudes and policies of the Roosevelt administration and Catholic-Americans toward the Mexican situation were discussed at the highest level for the first time. After a brief discussion of several minor matters, Roosevelt wanted to know about the latest developments in the religious controversy. Burke mentioned the Six-Year Plan, stressing particularly the desire of the Mexican government to prohibit any education except that "which was godless, and indeed positively atheistic." He cautioned Roosevelt that many American Catholics looked upon the United States as granting its unspoken approval to the actions of the Calles regime.[20] Daniels's speech was a prime example. Although Roosevelt had dismissed talk of recalling his ambassador to Mexico at a press conference on October 17, 1934, both Roosevelt and the State Department were well aware of the repercussions in the Catholic community. When Undersecretary of State William Phillips telephoned Daniels on October 17, requesting permission to quote Daniels's version of his statements of July 1934, Phillips emphasized that he wished to quote Daniels owing to the political strength of all consolidated facets of Catholic-American opposition.[21]

Burke continued. Whether Daniels intended to support the Calles educational program did not matter. What did matter was that Daniels gave the impression, both in Mexico and in the United States, that "he stood back of Calles' program," and that "exceeded his position and privileges as Ambassador."[22]

Roosevelt agreed that something ought to be done. He promised Burke that a statement would be issued from Mexico City, stating that the United States would never encourage a program that served atheism. To Burke's charges that the Mexican government was determined to drive out the bishops and decrease the number of priests allowed to minister, eventually confiscating churches and religious schools, Roosevelt promised even more. "I think I should informally send a message to Calles," Roosevelt declared, "saying that I think if the Mexican Government proceeds with a program of exiling the Bishops and priests and introducing an atheistic program, Mexico would make of itself a spectacle before the civilized world." Burke was elated. However, Roosevelt cautioned Burke "not to mention Mexico in any way... to the newspaper men." Roosevelt would proceed privately in his attempt to change Mexican policy.[23]

What Roosevelt promised Burke, however, and what he accomplished were two different things. After receiving word from the Mexican Embassy and discussing the matter of a further statement by Daniels with the State Department, Roosevelt decided that no statement should be made. He maintained that Daniels had explained all that was necessary and that to issue additional statements would only tend to stir up more hostility in Mexico. Such a course the United States naturally could not take, Phillips recorded in his diary, even though the "American Catholic Church wants us to take a strong hand in preventing the Mexican Government from driving the Church out of Mexico."[24]

Needless to say, Burke was disappointed, but nevertheless he met again with Roosevelt for the last time in 1934 on November 12. Roosevelt wanted to know the latest information pertaining to the situation in Mexico. Burke explained that the persecution of Catholics was even more ruthless than before, with many Catholics being driven into exile. Hopefully, Burke pleaded, the American government would at least intervene informally with the Mexican government. Roosevelt agreed, saying that he thought that "this might well be done." If he was the ambassador to Mexico, Roosevelt said, he "would speak very plainly to the Mexican Government."[25] Roosevelt promised Burke that he would discuss the matter with the Secretary of State. If Burke had some feeling of progress from this encouraging session with Roosevelt, his euphoria must have soon vanished, for no word came from the White House for the next three months. It would take greater pressure on behalf of the Catholic-American community to move the President, and that pressure was not long in coming.

Both Roosevelt and the State Department believed that the protest over the Mexican controversy, including the speech of Daniels, was only relegated to "a small segment of our Catholic friends." In writing to Daniels, Hull revealed that "a small but vociferous element which in the main has been keeping up this comment will soon tire of its undertaking to injure you."[26] A close friend of Roosevelt and one of the most influential Catholic laymen in America, Michael Francis Doyle, also recorded in December of 1934 that Roosevelt "was pleased to hear this expression... that the complaints which had been made did not reflect the general attitude of the Catholic-Americans."[27] Even as Catholic pressure intensified during January and February of 1935, the Roosevelt administration remained calm and "carefully refrained from taking any action respecting this Mexican domestic question which could cause the Mexican Government any embarrassment."[28] With such inaction on behalf of the Roosevelt administration, the Catholic community in America began an active campaign to involve the American government, and one of the first manifestations of this campaign began in the Senate.

Various protests made their way to Capitol Hill. Senator Robert F. Wagner of New York put on record a series of resolutions by the Knights of Columbus demanding that the United States sever trade and tourism with Mexico. Catholic groups in Massachusetts petitioned Congress for action, and the New York State Senate sent a resolution to Washington urging the United States to condemn the Mexican government's religious policy.[29] Finally, on January 31, 1935, Senator William E. Borah of Idaho introduced a resolution in the Senate calling for the Senate Foreign Relations Committee to conduct hearings on the persecution of the Church in Mexico. Borah believed that the Senate could obtain enough evidence of religious persecution that the Senate would be able to take the lead in the protest movement.[30] To verify its impact, Key Pittman, Chairman of the Senate Foreign Relations Committee, wrote Hull that "without executive opposition . . . it is possible that the resolution will be favorably reported by the Committee on Foreign Relations and adopted by the Senate of the United States."[31]

While the Borah Resolution gained ground in the Senate, a similar movement began in the House of Representatives. Secretary Hull, in a letter from Congressman Maury Maverick of Texas, was informed that numerous congressmen had started a movement to have the House criticize Mexico. Maverick revealed that he was in a very perplexing position owing to the fact that 75 percent of his constituents were Catholics, "hundreds of whom have written me, asking me to support such a rebuke for the Republic of Mexico."[32]

As the protest from the House grew to greater proportions, Assistant Secretary of State William Phillips remarked that members of Congress are "seizing the opportunity to attack the Department and the government, not on behalf of the Church, but purely on behalf of their own selfish future. The Knights of Columbus have joined in the fray."[33]

The Knights of Columbus, representing one-half million members and purportedly all twenty million American Catholics, began a nationwide protest, the purpose of which was to bring the situation in Mexico not only to the attention of official Washington, but also to all segments of the American population.[34] Supreme Knight Martin H. Carmody informed Roosevelt in January of 1935 that a committee from the Supreme Board of Directors of the Knights of Columbus adopted a resolution concerning the policies of the Mexican government in suppressing religion and, at the earliest possible moment, would like to meet with him.[35] Roosevelt did not see the group, but did suggest that they present their resolutions to the Secretary of State. Although the committee from the Knights of Columbus saw Hull, Carmody felt rebuffed. For the first time in twenty-five years, Carmody said, the "doors of the White House have been closed" to the Knights of Columbus.[36]

In addition to Carmody and the Knights of Columbus, Father Burke and the NCWC also launched a concerted effort to impress Roosevelt with the seriousness of the Mexican situation. Throughout the numerous dioceses in the United States, hundreds of thousands of protests and petitions were written and signed and then presented by the NCWC to Roosevelt. The National Council of Catholic Men and the National Council of Catholic Women (both lay organizations of the NCWC) sent information on the Mexican question to their affiliated organizations in the United States. And the NCWC News Service gave eyewitness reports to the Catholic and secular press concerning the activities of the Mexican government.[37] Needless to say, these reports filled the columns of the publications daily.

With this assistance by the NCWC, the Catholic press joined the protest in the spring of 1935. An article on Mexico in *America* charged that the Mexican government was preparing for "the Dictatorship of the Proletariat." The author, the Most Reverend Francis Clement Kelley, Bishop of Oklahoma City and Tulsa, added that "Bolshevism is...battering at our doors."[38] *The Baltimore Catholic Review* contained the most outspoken remarks of any bishop in the United States, Archbishop Michael J. Curley of Baltimore, who blamed Roosevelt for trying to halt the protests against the persecution in Mexico.[39] On March 28, the *Review* published the stinging remarks of Bishop Curley, delivered at a meeting of the Sodality Union of Washington.

Curley wanted Roosevelt to alert the American people to the violation of fundamental human rights in Mexico. As bishop of Baltimore, he would no longer remain silent or "kotow" [sic] to the Roosevelt administration. Roosevelt could not ignore twenty million Catholics, Curley said, nor the Knights of Columbus, "the millions of sodalists, [nor] the 2,000,000 Holy Name men in this country in this year 1935." Millions of Catholics would be voting in 1936, Curley warned, and they might see fit to express "their opinion of this present Administration's determination to block all legislation in behalf of Mexico."[40] Echoing Curley's remarks, *The Brooklyn Tablet* urged Catholics to write and wire the President and members of Congress, specifically encouraging them to pass the Borah Resolution.[41]

The inaction of Roosevelt toward the anticlerical policy of the Mexican government now, after several months of Catholic pressure, took a turn toward direct and discreet action. Roosevelt, in accordance with his policy of avoiding a public protest toward Mexico, and with the sanguine approval of Burke and the administrative Committee of the NCWC, engaged in a successful attempt to defeat the Borah Resolution. Previously, Burke had agreed with Roosevelt that nothing should be done publicly regarding the Mexican question. If a public policy of protest was enunciated, Burke reasoned, the persecution of the Church in Mexico would only increase.[42] Therefore, with the hearings about to begin on the Resolution in late February in 1935, the administration urged the Senate Foreign Relations Committee to postpone any consideration of the Resolution. Hull viewed the Resolution as an attempt on the part of the American government to dictate the laws governing the internal affairs of another country. Engaging in a public discussion should be avoided at all possible costs.[43]

With the administration's viewpoint known to the Senate Foreign Relations Committee, Borah reconsidered his position. Borah confided to his friend, Bishop Kelly of Idaho, that it became "necessary therefor [sic] to consult with friends before determining upon our course. To urge the Resolution at that time would have undoubtedly resulted in its defeat."[44] Consequently, the Resolution remained pending before the Committee on Foreign Relations, being postponed from week to week, and eventually relegated to the position of being permanently tabled.[45]

Actually, the Borah Resolution was never designed to be passed. When Burke met with Senator Walsh and discussed the Borah Resolution and the fact that public and particularly political action be made subject to the approval of the American bishops, Walsh revealed that the Resolution "was introduced to arouse public attention and to promote publicity," rather than to be approved. It was for "show" purposes only.[46]

Although Burke, the Apostolic Delegate, and the Administrative Committee of the NCWC frowned upon such public protest as the Borah Resolution involved, they soon began to ascertain the impact of the outspoken faction of the Catholic community. For all intents and purposes, such a split among Catholic-Americans existed. However, the extent of the influence of the Knights of Columbus, Archbishop Curley and Father Charles Coughlin, coupled with the supporters of the Borah Resolution, led Roosevelt again to consult with Burke and the American bishops in order to inform them of his plan (which was in agreement with what the Administrative Committee of the NCWC had demanded of the President) privately to intervene in the internal affairs of the Mexican government.[47]

On March 5, 1935, the Roosevelt administration, represented by the Secretary of State, entertained at the State Department the Mexican ambassador, Francisco Castille Najera, calculating to use the occasion to open a frank discussion of the Catholic situation in both Mexico and the United States. The administration hoped that Mexico would be willing to cooperate in some way to help alleviate or reduce the cause for Catholic opposition toward the administration in the United States. Hull admitted that he was the "target of terrific denunciation" by America's Catholic population, who were demanding some kind of government interference in the religious situation in Mexico. As politely as possible, Hull recommended to the ambassador that he convey the wishes of the Roosevelt administration to his government that Mexico avoid or minimize "any utterances or actions in Mexico which were calculated to feed the agitation and violent utterances that were taking place in the United States."[48]

Najera, Hull recorded, entirely and wholeheartedly understood his motives and purposes and agreed "to cooperate 100 per cent." Sympathizing with the unfortunate situation in the United States involving Catholics and the Roosevelt administration, he informed Hull that he would go to Mexico City as soon as possible to acquaint his government with the situation. As they parted, Hull emphasized the unofficial nature of their meeting and looked with anticipation toward the invoking of "such cooperative efforts on the part of the Mexican Government as would make my difficult task less difficult and in that way redound to the good of Mexico."[49]

After Hull's interview with Najera, Roosevelt instructed one of his friends and governor of the Philippines, Frank Murphy, to see Burke. Murphy told Burke that Roosevelt intended to send a private message to the Mexican government. Personally, Murphy thought that Roosevelt should send a message, "but that he should do so publicly."[50]

Reversing his previous position, Burke agreed with Murphy. A public message should be sent as soon as possible. When Murphy "hinted" that Burke help in framing the message for the President, Burke replied that he was "at his service day or night," adding that "I must not be asked to go to the White House or to the Department of State, but that some non-public place should be chosen for any meeting."[51]

Roosevelt, however, did not like Burke's recommendation that a public statement be sent to Mexico in lieu of the hopeful sign that Najera, at the behest of the Roosevelt administration, might initiate cooperation on behalf of his government. Returning to Burke after meeting with Roosevelt, Murphy said "that Secretary Hull—and President Roosevelt—were both opposed to the writing of such a note concerning Mexico and freedom of religious worship, as had been discussed in our previous conversation." According to Burke, Murphy indicated that the decision was final. Primarily, it was Hull who opposed such a note, for whether the note be public or private, Hull believed that it would not only offend Mexico, but also the vast majority of Protestants in the United States.[52] Although Roosevelt was feeling the pressure of the Catholic community at this time, his desire to act was temporarily restrained by the arguments of the Secretary of State.

While Hull might have been convinced that Roosevelt placed the utmost of faith in the manner in which the Secretary of State was handling the situation in Mexico, Roosevelt actually decided to bypass Hull. Roosevelt wanted to intervene privately and make contact with Calles. Consequently, as he would do on various occasions during his presidency, Roosevelt had Undersecretary of State Sumner Welles act as his personal representative on the Mexican controversy. Welles told Burke that, regarding Mexican matters, there was no one else to whom he should speak. Hull was not "in" on this controversy. Welles said "that it was peculiarly the President's own work and that he [Welles] was attending to it at the request of the President."[53] Thus, from the spring of 1935 to the death of Father Burke prior to the presidential election in 1936, a close collaboration began between Roosevelt, Welles, and Burke in order to alleviate the cause of religious persecution in Mexico.

In April of 1935, one month after the Roosevelt administration contacted Najera, Burke met privately with Welles at his home in Washington. Welles told Burke that he had contacted the Mexican ambassador and found him agreeable to "deal with somebody who would be responsible from the point of view of the Catholic Church," and, when Welles mentioned Burke, the ambassador replied that he would be very willing to see him and to discuss the situation in Mexico with regard to the Church.[54] While no meeting occurred between Burke and Najera because of a protocol technicality on the part of the Mexican embassy, Najera did propose to make several recommendations to his government. First, he would encourage his government to give some evidence of goodwill toward the Catholic Church. Najera proposed a meeting between himself and Archbishop Pascual Diaz of Mexico City. "With the explicit approval of the Mexican Government," Diaz would forward to the Supreme Court of Mexico a petition of protest against those Mexican States which had refused to allow priests to worship. Then the Supreme Court would order the States to permit the priests to minister and hold public services. And as a guarantee, Najera pointed out that the "Mexican Government would see that a favorable decision was given to this petition." Najera was certain that his government would work with Diaz and make him "the confidential agent of such a petition."[55]

Burke was encouraged and gratified over the turn of events. However, his only disappointment lay in the fact that Roosevelt had not given an adequate answer to the demands of the bishops of the United States, which were presented by Burke to the President in November of 1934. The Administrative Committee of the NCWC had urged Roosevelt to do something to show America's disapproval toward the attitudes of the Mexican government to the Catholic Church. With the Administrative Committee of the NCWC conducting its annual meeting in Washington on May 1-3, 1935 (and specifically devoting this meeting to the Mexican situation), Burke asked to see Roosevelt personally. On May 2, they met.[56]

Perhaps the prime motive for the interview with Burke and Roosevelt's eventual decision to act on the proposals of the American Catholic community was best revealed in a letter written to Roosevelt by Bishop John F. Noll, a member of the Administrative Committee. Noll emphasized that "it would be difficult to keep the Catholics quiet if the Catholic hierarchy, which represents all the Catholics of the nation, is completely ignored. The Catholic Hierarchy," Noll continued, "has declined to endorse the Borah Resolution, the petition of the Supreme Officers of the Knights of Columbus, and others, principally to give your Excellency an opportunity to do something with less embarrass-ment."[57] Roosevelt agreed that the request of the bishops deserved his attention. After receiving thousands of petitions and protests, he wrote to Noll and promised to do all that his office as Chief Executive could encourage "to promote the principle of the freedom of conscience and the exercise of religious liberty."[58] Roosevelt was anxious to talk about the Mexican situation when Burke arrived at the White House and, as Burke was led to the President's own study, Roosevelt said he was glad that Burke had come and thought that he "would have come earlier."[59]

Burke opened the interview by speaking of the meeting of the Administra-tive Committee of the NCWC; that the Administrative Committee had directed him to see the President personally in their name; and that he had not been down to see him, or ask for an interview, because of the unhappy situation with regard to newspaper stories concerning the Catholic body and their attitude on the Mexican situation. Burke reviewed the petition of the NCWC and the need for the United States government to do something to show its disagreement with the Mexican government. He reminded Roosevelt that he had promised the NCWC that something would be done and that "because nothing was really being done... there were more and more demands and greater indignation among the Catholic people of the country, and surely some answer was required."[60]

Roosevelt said that "he had given a great deal of thought to the situation, that he was very anxious to do something in order to help the Catholic Church in Mexico, and have the Mexican Government assume a fairer attitude towards religion and religious worship." Burke mentioned the difficulty concerning the appointment of an apostolic delegate to Mexico and the fact that the Vatican desired a non-Mexican rather than Archbishop Diaz. Hopefully, Burke went on to say, the President could use his good offices to have the Mexican government consent to the appointment of a foreign apostolic delegate, thereby "giving recognition to the corporate character of the Church."[61]

The entire discussion of the Mexican situation continued, going into a great many details, and the outcome of it was that Roosevelt positively assured Burke that he "would send for the Mexican Ambassador; that he would have a very earnest talk with him; that he would make it the position of the United States Government itself that the Mexican Government meet this request and be willing to accept and to negotiate with regard to further guarantees of religious liberty in Mexico, and the greater freedom of the Church in Mexico."[62] Unlike the results of previous interviews with Roosevelt in the fall of 1934, the President immediately acted on his promises, and instructed his staff to have the Mexican ambassador report to the White House within the next few days.

A few days after Roosevelt spoke to Burke, the President asked Welles to inform the Mexican ambassador that he wished to see him. This was done and shortly thereafter the Mexican ambassador, accompanied by Welles, visited the President. At the outset of the interview, Roosevelt emphasized the pressure that Catholic-Americans were exerting on his administration and his hope that Mexico could initiate some action so as to eliminate the causes of the Catholic protest. Roosevelt told Najera that he was upset about Mexico's denial of religious liberty to her citizens. More importantly, he was annoyed because of the "bad will, the dissatisfaction, the extended protests which such action on the part of the Mexican Government was creating and furthering in our own country."[63]

Najera outlined for Roosevelt the plan that had been previously agreed upon: to have Archbishop Diaz petition the courts that priests be allowed to go into those States where they were prohibited, and the intent of the Mexican Government to have the Supreme Court decide favorably on the petition. Roosevelt appreciated this step (which was never used), but asked, "could not the Mexican Government go further?" Roosevelt wanted the Mexican government itself to move to alleviate the restrictions and persecution directed at the Catholic Church. In addition, Roosevelt echoed Burke's other request for Mexico to recognize an apostolic delegate from the Holy See.[64]

According to Welles, Roosevelt spoke strongly and fully throughout the interview on all areas of Catholic-American interest, and the Mexican ambassador was very much impressed. Welles thought that Roosevelt had gone "as far as a President of the United States could go." Several days after the interview, Najera informed Welles that he had communicated with his government and that he was going to Mexico shortly to bring back the answer of his government to the President's desires.[65] The administration—and Father Burke—waited in hopeful anticipation.

During this period of waiting for the Mexican ambassador to return, Roosevelt instructed Daniels privately to discuss the attitudes of the Roosevelt administration toward the religious persecution with the leadership of the Mexican government. Daniels also knew of Roosevelt's interview with Najera and of the fact that "the President had spoken very fully and very emphatically; that the President was much distressed over the situation in Mexico, and he

[Daniels] was himself."[66] Roosevelt was obviously determined to work in private to influence the Mexican government. Now, with Daniels also about to return to Mexico "to make known to the Government our earnest desire to .promote freedom of religion," Roosevelt had another voice with which to convey the American position.[67]

Meanwhile, amid increasing pressure from congressmen and the Catholic community in the United States, the Roosevelt administration was tempted to make a public statement on the Mexican question even before Najera returned. Hull was advised by Assistant Secretary of State R. Walton Moore, after meeting with several congressmen, that if the United States failed to make a statement of its position vis-à-vis the Mexican persecution of the Catholic Church, "the political effect may be injurious in many localities."[68] Also, Roosevelt's secretary, Marvin H. McIntyre, went to see Burke, suggesting that Roosevelt thought of informing Carmody of the efforts that he was making with regard to the Mexican situation.

Burke disagreed. He advised McIntyre to tell Roosevelt to wait. The Church hierarchy was the official authority for the Church, and to make the Knights of Columbus the "repository of those confidences" which should be reserved for those who speak officially for the Church—the hierarchy—was inadvisable. McIntyre agreed, and Roosevelt waited.[69]

Najera returned to the United States on June 24, 1935, after a one-month absence, and on the following day revealed to Welles the bizarre activities that had occurred within the Mexican government. Upon his arrival in Mexico, Najera went directly to see the former president of Mexico, Portas Gil, who was the present foreign minister. According to Najera, Gil was the dominant power in Mexico, having more influence with President Lazaro Cardenas than any other member of the National Revolutionary Party, including General Calles, the leader of the party and virtual dictator of Mexico.[70] Najera told Gil of his meeting with Roosevelt and the President's strong feelings about the religious situation in Mexico, and its repercussions in the United States. They talked over the matter "fully," and also went over the whole situation at great length with Cardenas.[71]

At the same time, Ambassador Daniels also had several conversations with Gil as Roosevelt had directed, during which he emphasized that Mexico had lost prestige in the United States because of the fact that churches were closed and that priests were being denied the opportunity to officiate. Gil told Daniels that Cardenas was giving the religious question the utmost consideration and that a decision would be forthcoming.[72] What did occur rocked the Mexican political scene.

Immediately after the visits of Najera and Daniels, a break occurred between Cardenas and Calles. All of the cabinet members were asked to resign,

Cardenas replacing most of the Calles men with his own "sincere partisans."[73] Najera told Welles that Calles was definitely out of the picture in Mexico and had been forced out of the leadership position in the National Revolutionary Party mainly because he "showed himself very vindictive against the Church."[74] Cardenas and Gil had announced that a more moderate attitude on church questions would emerge, confiding to Najera that the reopening of churches and the right to worship publicly would begin as soon as the "political situation made it possible."[75] A similar commitment was also made to Daniels.

That the intervention of Roosevelt helped to force the change in the Mexican cabinet—thereby rendering the outlook for religious freedom in Mexico a real possibility—should not be underestimated. It was only after Najera presented the message of President Roosevelt concerning religious persecution in Mexico to Cardenas and Gil that Calles was forced out. Meeting with Calles after the political shake-up, Najera told Welles that he found Calles "more vehement against the Catholic Church and more opposed to any arrangement between the Mexican Government and the Catholic Church than at any time in the past."[76] In a letter to Roosevelt, Daniels similarly concluded that "the representations we have made of the concern our country has in situations that jeopardize the most friendly relations had made an impression. I hope for better days and better conditions."[77] The Roosevelt administration and America's Catholics did not have to wait long for better days and better conditions.

It was primarily Portas Gil who wanted to put an end to the religious persecution and have the Mexican government come to some permanent understanding with the Church. So while Najera was reporting the new attitude of the Mexican government to Welles, Gil and Cardenas were acting. Their first step was to replace the Secretary of Agriculture, Garrido Canabal of Tabasco—a rabid anti-Catholic—with Governor Cedillo of San Luis Potosi, known throughout Mexico for his affinity with the Catholic Church during the height of the persecution. This first piece of concrete evidence by the Cardenas government "to adopt a liberal policy towards the Mexican Catholics," as Najera characterized it, was immediately followed by the announcement that churches were being reopened in the State of Colima and shortly thereafter in Queretaro.[78]

In a long-distance phone call to Najera in late June of 1935, Gil outlined several additional steps of the new plan, which were likewise to be transmitted to Roosevelt. In Mexico City, more priests were permitted to officiate at church services, and all restrictions were lifted on orderly demonstrations by Catholics. It was the intention of the government, Gil said, gradually to extend this policy in all of the Mexican states. Regarding the appointment of an apostolic delegate to Mexico by the Vatican, Gil reported that an exchange of views had already begun between Archbishop Diaz of Mexico City and the

Mexican government. Gil ended by hoping that a complete settlement of the religious situation would be achieved by September.[79]

Overall, Roosevelt and Welles were delighted by the results of American intervention in the Mexican question and the eventual effect it would have on the Catholic-American community, namely, that the Mexican government would enter discussions over the appointment of an apostolic delegate (another issue that would continue to involve the United States in Mexican affairs), and that the Cardenas government would change its laws against the Church and permit the Church a far greater liberty of action than she ever enjoyed in Mexico. As Welles revealed, the "condition of Catholics in Mexico created a very serious problem for us here."[80] Now, the noted improvements would hopefully be followed by an even more moderate policy. One did not have to wait very long.

Press reports emanating from Mexico in July of 1935 told of cheering Catholics in Mexico City, applauding among other things the lifting of the religious ban on the use of postal facilities for the transmission of religious matter, and the granting of amnesty to political refugees.[81] These pronouncements by President Cardenas were followed by reports that, in States where they had been barred, priests were being permitted to return to assume their normal duties.[82] The beginning of the new policy of moderation was more than encouraging to Roosevelt.

Father Burke was also decidedly encouraged. In a highly secret confidential report to the hierarchy of the Catholic Church in the United States in October of 1935, Burke told of how Roosevelt—with the assistance of Welles—opened contact with the Mexican government and applied pressure. He advised the hierarchy that, since negotiations were still going on between the United States and Mexican governments, the Mexican government was "unwilling to have it known publicly that it...[was being] influenced by the Government of the United States or by the Holy See." Therefore, Burke cautioned the hierarchy (as well as the Knights of Columbus and other groups associated with the Church) to avoid any public outbursts that would disrupt the confidences that had been secured by the Roosevelt administration.[83] Even when Cardinal Hayes expressed to Burke his "keen regret" that Roosevelt "had not seen fit to intervene in the matter of religious freedom in Mexico," Burke wrote him a confidential letter in which he informed the Cardinal what Roosevelt had done and of his continuing interest in the solution of this problem. Hayes "regretted his misapprehension of the facts" and expressed his appreciation of Roosevelt's actions.[84] Burke would have agreed with Roosevelt, who in 1941 explained to Myron Taylor—the President's personal representative to the Vatican—the overall position and attitude of the United States government toward the Mexican controversy. Roosevelt observed that, eight or nine years ago, most of the churches in Mexico had been closed and that hostility in the United States called for military intervention into Mexico so that the churches could be reopened. "The Government of the United States," Roosevelt noted, "took the position that by constant peaceful pressure the churches could be re-opened. As is well known, this has taken place from small beginnings until today the Mexican Government itself no longer adopts an attitude of atheism."[85]

From this point, until the presidential election of 1936, Roosevelt hoped to avoid any public condemnation of the Mexican government. The new policies in Mexico, he believed, were his best bet to avoid any continued hostility on behalf of the Catholic-American community. He knew that if any public congressional action was taken, all chances of additional advances in Mexico "might go by the board."[86] His goal was to render the Mexican religious controversy a dead issue well before the election of 1936 and, to accomplish the task, he had to appease the discordant elements in the Catholic community and their allies on Capitol Hill.

Having such a favorable response from his private intervention with the Mexican government, Roosevelt decided to meet with the two most vocal antagonists of his policy toward Mexico—the Knights of Columbus and the Congress of the United States. According to Hull, the administration was having great difficulty in attempting to please congressmen and the Knights of Columbus in regard to the Mexican situation.[87] The major protagonist, however, was Carmody. Previously, Carmody and a committee from the Knights of Columbus sought an interview with Roosevelt in January of 1935, but Roosevelt refused to see them.[88] Now, in July of 1935, Roosevelt gave his consent. The Knights of Columbus was primarily upset about the fact that Roosevelt had not replied to a letter addressed to him by Carmody, protesting against the religious persecutions by the Mexican government and inquiring as to why the government of the United States did not exercise its good offices in Mexico. Its members were further disappointed by the fact that the Senate Foreign Relations Committee had failed to invite the Knights of Columbus to testify on behalf of the Borah Resolution.[89]

Father Burke had previously told Roosevelt that Carmody need not be given an explanation of the President's efforts regarding Mexico. And Burke "knew of no reason why they should know." Actually, Father Burke, desiring to maintain a united Catholic front on the Mexican question and avoid the charge that Catholic pressure and influence caused the intervention by the United States government in Mexico, wanted all public and political activity to be approved by the bishops.[90] That included the Knights of Columbus. Roosevelt, however, believed the time was opportune to attempt to silence all public outbursts and allow the Mexican government ample time to implement its new policy.

As the consummate politician, Roosevelt wanted the Knights of Columbus and the Congress to know of his close association with Burke and the hierarchy, and of his concern for the Church in Mexico, without publicly elaborating on his action. At the interview with Carmody and his delegation on July 8, Roosevelt listened quietly while the group spoke of their concern about the apparent inaction of the United States in "failing to use its good offices to bring about a termination of the established anti-religious policy of Mexico." They emphasized the fact that they voiced the sentiments of millions of Catholics who deplored the closing of churches, the banishment of priests, and the "immoral and communistic national educational system."[91]

When they finished, Roosevelt began to discuss the many phases of religious conditions in the world, connecting them to the problems in Mexico. Then, he emphasized that what he was about to state to them regarding Mexico was to be held confidential. Roosevelt told them of his close communications with the Vatican and of his "almost daily contact with members of the Hierarchy of the United States and with Father Burke." According to Carmody, Roosevelt wanted it known that the "position and attitude of the government with reference to Mexican affairs was fully understood by and was in accord with the views of those representing the Church."[92] Then, Roosevelt ended the interview with the promise that, in his next public address, he would make a statement concerning the Mexican situation.[93]

After his meeting with the Knights of Columbus, Roosevelt met one week later with a congressional delegation, led by co-chairmen John P. Higgins and Clare Gerald Fenerty. The delegation presented a petition—signed by 250 members of Congress—to Roosevelt, urging him to end America's official silence on the Mexican situation and publish to the world "our deep concern in this question." Specifically, the delegation wanted the Roosevelt Administration to open an inquiry—an investigation—of the domestic affairs in Mexico.[94] Of course, Roosevelt had no intention of implementing such a proposal, but he did understand their motives because his motives were the same—to keep America's Catholics on the Democratic Party line.

Roosevelt had learned from the Secretary of State that these same congressmen, in previous meetings at the State Department, had similarly demanded an American investigation into the internal affairs of Mexico. Even at that time they were told by Hull that such an inquiry would only tend to "aggravate the conditions of the Catholics in Mexico," but the congressmen persisted.[95] They really persisted, according to Phillips who participated in these sessions, not because they cared about the situation in Mexico, but because they wanted the administration "to go on record in such a way that the Congressmen will gain the support of their Catholic voters at their next election."[96] The influence and pressure from the Catholic-American community had spread to the other end of Pennsylvania Avenue as well, and Roosevelt knew it.

So, at the conclusion of his interview with the congressional delegation on July 16, Roosevelt promised—as he did with the Knights of Columbus—to release to the press an official statement of America's concern for Catholics in Mexico. That statement read that Roosevelt was "in entire sympathy with all people who make it clear that the American people and the Government believe in freedom of religious worship, not only in the United States but also in all other nations."[97] With the delegation encouraged and satisfied by the President's statement, congressional pressure on the administration virtually came to a halt.

For the time being, Roosevelt had curtailed the public outbursts over the Mexican situation against his administration, but his concern for the influence engendered in the discordant elements of the Catholic community, particularly the Knights of Columbus and those that urged armed intervention in Mexico, continued. Up to the election in November of 1936, Roosevelt's concern over the possible loss of Catholic support caused him to maintain constant pressure on Mexico to end its campaign against the Church. Ambassador Daniels confirmed as much when he wrote years later of how serious the situation had been in Mexico and how deeply Americans felt. "At one time it looked like certain leaders of the Knights of Columbus could and would control a big vote against Roosevelt because we had not been able to do anything about it."[98] However, under the influence of the Roosevelt administration, a good start had been made with the Mexican government by the summer of 1935. Over the next year and one-half, the news from Mexico only got better.

Under Roosevelt's guidance and insistence, Daniels and Welles continued to intervene in the Mexican situation. Daniels initiated several conversations in July with President Cardenas and Gil to—in his words—"quietly convince the authorities that the first thing to do is to permit churches to be opened and priests to officiate in those states where churches are now closed." Daniels wrote Roosevelt that he "sought in every unofficial way, and sometimes near-official, to show how deeply you feel about the situation and will continue to do so as occasion offers." Likewise, Daniels hoped that, because of his efforts in Mexico, Roosevelt's wise and moderating influence would "calm our Catholic friends in Congress and that there will be no political repercussions that will give trouble next year." Subsequently, Cardenas informed Daniels that, as a result of preliminary investigation, several additional States, particularly Zacatecas, Colima, Guana Juato, and Jalisco, were about to reopen more of the churches in their territory.[99]

Welles also received some very welcome news in July. The Mexican ambassador reported that, if the Vatican appointed Archbishop Diaz as Apostolic Delegate instead of Archbishop Ruiz y Flores, the Mexican government would give Diaz "complete lattitude to reorganize the Church in the Republic and to exercise the necessary authority over the Mexican bishops and priests." The Mexican ambassador gave Welles the clear understanding that, if this step were taken, the state governments of Mexico "would be encouraged to show increasing leniency to the Catholics." Welles was thoroughly excited.[100]

At their next meeting, Welles told Burke that, if the Holy See appointed Diaz, the Mexican government "would live up to its promises to have priests restored to the States now forbidding them." Welles was very cautious and careful in giving Burke this news, with Burke recording that Welles gave it "under the greatest secrecy." To Burke, the Vatican—by appointing Archbishop Diaz—virtually would end the uproar in the United States over the Mexican situation. The appointment of Diaz would be "recognition of the corporate Church in Mexico, and may lead to a better day." As for Welles, it looked as though the Mexican question—as far as the United States was concerned—was practically settled.[101]

It should be noted that the Vatican—now that such encouraging word was received from Mexico through the auspices of the Roosevelt administration—was placed in a crucial role in the settlement of the Mexican controversy, and to the dismay of the Roosevelt administration and Father Burke, did not appoint an apostolic delegate to Mexico until February of 1937. In a private memorandum, Burke revealed his innermost dissatisfaction. He observed that the Vatican had witnessed the driving out of Calles—"the Archenemy of the Church"—from Mexico, and was aware of the stability of the Cardenas government. Also, that the Vatican had asked and had received "favorable action of the President of the United States, [namely] that the Mexican Government agree to the appointment of an Apostolic Delegate to Mexico, and lighten its attitude of persecution against the Church." Roosevelt had acted, but now "the Holy See won't use the open door." To Burke, it was very evident why the Vatican did not move on this matter. Those who had the opportunity of expressing the authority of the Holy See regarding Mexico were "indirectly giving support to the 'physical force advocates,' to those who say no compromise at any cost: to those who have publicly put themselves in opposition to President Roosevelt."[102]

At the end of July, during another meeting with the Mexican ambassador, Welles was informed that the Mexican government would finish the work it had begun in the States of Tabasco and Colima; that priests would be allowed to return.[103] Similarly, the Roosevelt administration also received word from two prominent American visitors to Mexico who made known the fact that progress was being made with Cardenas.

William Franklin Sands, professor of Public Relations at Georgetown University and a member of the Committee on Religious Rights and Minorities sent to survey the religious situation in Mexico, told the American press that government officials had assured him that Daniels had never let up for a minute stressing the importance of a solution to the religious problem and that President Cardenas had stated that there would be no religious persecution.[104] Frank Tannenbaum, a Columbia University economist and authority on Latin America, also interviewed President Cardenas. Tannenbaum had been disturbed because of a fear that attempts would be made to organize America's Catholics to oppose Roosevelt in 1936. In his conversations with Cardenas, Tannenbaum stressed the fact that the friends of Mexico in the United States desired to "counteract the unkindly propaganda against Mexico which has developed on account of the religious controversy." He emphasized that Catholics in the United States could make "serious political use of Mexico's religious problem, and that Mexico's internal religious policy might in the long run endanger liberalism and liberal politics in the United States, which by implication would have serious consequences for Mexico itself." Therefore, Tannenbaum urged Cardenas to permit him to take back a message "to the effect that churches would be open in Mexico in all the States within six months." The reply from Cardenas was most interesting. For various political reasons, Cardenas said he could make "no definite commitment," but he would take into consideration all that Tannenbaum had said and "would so conduct the government that these serious grievances would be mitigated to the effect that the Mexican internal religious policy will not be a cause for attack against the liberal policies of the President of the United States."[105] Before the new year arrived on January 1, 1936, a major incident occurred that upset the optimistic feeling prevalent in Washington toward the Mexican government—Cardenas decreed a program for the nationalization of all church property.

The Mexican government issued its decree on the nationalization of church properties on August 31, but news of the decree was not immediately reported in any of the Catholic papers. It was published, however, in the newspapers associated with International News Service, which according to Colonel P.H. Callahan—an influential Catholic layman, former executive of the Knights of Columbus, and vigorous supporter of President Roosevelt—meant William Randolph Hearst. Callahan frequently corresponded with Roosevelt and the State Department and knew that no other group, like Hearst and his associates, understood the Catholic pulse more or realized that public knowledge of "such a step by Mexico would cost Roosevelt a million or two votes."[106]

Roosevelt and the American people also learned of the fact that a petition had been addressed to President Cardenas in the fall of 1935 by the bishops of Mexico—supported by thousands of laymen—to repeal the nationalization law and to amend those provisions of the Mexican constitution which empowered the government to "carry on a persecution of religion as drastic as that of bolshevist Russia."[107] The petition met with the outright refusal of Cardenas. News of these actions in Mexico travelled quickly to Chicago, where, in early October, the Knights of Columbus was holding its quarterly meeting of the supreme board of directors.

At this meeting, the board decided to make another protest to Roosevelt on the Mexican situation. In a letter signed by Carmody, the board reviewed the events regarding the Mexican question since their meeting with Roosevelt on July 8, when Roosevelt promised to take advantage of his first public address to condemn Mexico's religious intolerance. It was pointed out that he not only failed to fulfill his promise after their July interview, but that he made no reference to Mexico in his most recent speech on October 2 in San Diego. "Have you shut your eyes to the sufferings of those millions of oppressed people who are our immediate neighbors in the South?" they pleaded. The responsibility for inaction and failure, they concluded, would be his responsibility.[108]

Roosevelt had made a statement on July 17, and, on October 2, he did travel to San Diego, California, to deliver another public address on the theme of religious freedom. Mexico was never mentioned. Carmody and the Knights of Columbus agreed with one correspondent of *The New York Herald Tribune* that Roosevelt's words were but a "small sop to the Catholics." But a spokesman for the NCWC News Service defended the President and advised the Knights of Columbus that no other newspaper but the *Herald Tribune* belittled the President's speech. In fact, he said, *The New York Times* called Roosevelt's San Diego speech "forceful" and the Associated Press labeled it "timely and perhaps history-making."[109] After seeing Carmody's letter, Roosevelt and his advisors decided to respond publicly.

In writing to Carmody, Roosevelt did not reveal the actions that he and his administration, under the influence of the Catholic community, had initiated toward Mexico nor how Mexico was responding. Knowing that Burke, in a secret, confidential report to the hierarchy in the United States in late October of 1935, had revealed the extent of the influence of the Catholic-American community and the actions of the Roosevelt administration regarding Mexico, Roosevelt felt no need for a public pronouncement. As Roosevelt previously revealed to Burke, "if it were publicly known, it would cause nationwide protests on the part of the Protestant body."[110] Roosevelt also knew that the Mexican government would cease to cooperate if it was revealed that American and Catholic-American pressure influenced their domestic affairs. Consequently, Roosevelt, knowing that continued progress by the Mexican government in the religious situation was his best hope in eliminating this question as a campaign issue, responded to Carmody that he abhorred "religious intolerance, whether at home or abroad. For my own part, however, I decline to permit this Government to undertake a policy of interference in the domestic concerns of foreign governments and thereby jeopardize the maintenance of peaceful conditions."[111]

Predictably, the Catholic press reacted almost unanimously in its criticism of Roosevelt's reply to Camody. Several papers, including the *Baltimore Catholic Review, The Brooklyn Tablet,* and the *Providence Visitor,* labeled Roosevelt's comments as supporting tyranny in Mexico, giving comfort to those who hated religion. *America* saw the Mexican government becoming more hostile to the Church now that Roosevelt had announced his policy of non-intervention.[112] Father Coughlin declared in a radio address to millions of Americans that Roosevelt had given "an invitation to Cardenas and the rest of the Communists in Mexico who control the money, the munitions and the arms to do whatever they want to religion and its followers."[113]

One student of this period concluded that it appeared that Roosevelt would not be able to mollify this segment of the Catholic community. This group "insisted that what they wanted was not intervention, but a cessation of the interference taking place. Unfortunately, they could point to no specific action by the Roosevelt administration, save Daniels' statement, which would be termed intervention."[114] The Roosevelt administration similarly concluded that Roosevelt's letter to Carmody had met with the enthusiastic approval of all elements in the United States "except those relatively small elements of the Catholic Church which have been pressing for a renewal of physical violence in Mexico and except for those other elements, still fewer in number, which are perniciously partisan."[115] However, Roosevelt did not take lightly the so-called "small elements of the Catholic Church." It was primarily the Knights of Columbus, the outspokeness of Archbishop Curley of Baltimore, and the radio addresses of Father Charles Coughlin that threatened to upset the progress of the Roosevelt administration regarding Mexico. Keeping in mind, then, all factions and opinions of the Catholic-American community, Roosevelt actually accomplished a great deal—more than he dared reveal publicly—in his continued private, behind-the-scenes intervention with the Mexican government in the fall of 1935. And it is this story that must be told.

In November, when Cardenas refused to act on the petition of the Mexican bishops regarding the nationalization of Church property, Roosevelt instructed the Mexican ambassador, Najera, and the American ambassador to Mexico, Daniels, to see Cardenas and other high officials in the Mexican government to effectuate a change in this policy. Najera left for home immediately, and after a one-month stay, returned to Washington to report on the result of his mission. At the same time, Daniels had a long interview in Mexico with Portes Gil, in which he pleaded very strongly for cessation of the religious persecution and for a qualification of the programs on social education.[116] Najera reported that, while in Mexico, he had three long conversations with Cardenas. In these conversations, Najera told Welles, he "urged the President to ease up on the religious situation." Cardenas told Najera that he was endeavoring to bring under the Federal government the regulations in the States about opening of churches. This was a difficult process mainly because it was against the present constitution, but Cardenas was using his influence with the state governors to have them agree to this policy.[117]

"Most important of all," Welles noted from his interview with Najera, "the Ambassador stated to me that in his presence President Cardenas had given orders that the nationalization of church properties was to remain a dead letter." As far as Cardenas was concerned, government authorities would "close their eyes to the retention by the Church of all properties which were actually in use in accordance with the state laws."[118] Roosevelt's quiet diplomacy had succeeded. However, of greater significance concerning the influence of the United States on Cardenas and the religious situation, was that Najera informed Welles that Cardenas held that "the opinion of the United States should be for the Mexican Government the keystone of their [Mexico's] both foreign and domestic policy."[119]

Throughout his discussions with Cardenas, Najera stressed the state of Catholic opinion in the United States. In response to the interest shown by the Catholic Church in the United States, urging that the archbishop of Orozco be permitted to officiate at Mass, Cardenas agreed to grant his petition. With regard to the opening of churches, Najera reported that churches were now opened "in every one of the Mexican states except in Tabasco, where the churches have been closed for approximately ten years and where the situation was delicate and would require some delay before the churches could be opened."[120] Najera also informed Welles of the appointment of General Eduardo Hay—a practicing Catholic—as the new Secretary of Foreign Affairs. And finally, Najera learned from Cardenas that "several Bishops of Mexico were now in frequent friendly conversation with the Mexican Government."[121]

Roosevelt, Welles, and Father Burke beamed at these most recent accomplishments by the Cardenas government. Cardenas had assured the United States government that he would continue to follow his policy of encouraging gradual relaxation of State restrictions on the Church as he had been for the past six months. It would take time, but, according to Najera, Cardenas "was determined to adopt a course which would lead to religious liberty within the existing restrictions of the Constitution."[122] While the actions of the Mexican government looked brighter and brighter, however, Roosevelt never resisted an opportunity to curtail or counteract any unfavorable activity toward the administration here in the United States. Playing a key role for Roosevelt in this regard was his friend and one of America's most prominent Catholic laymen, Michael Francis Doyle.

Doyle—in addition to Father Burke—availed himself of every opportunity to silence public denunciations on the Mexican situation. After the unfriendly outbursts by some Catholics over Roosevelt's published letter to Carmody in November of 1935, Doyle wrote the White House that, at a meeting on November 18 and 20 of the Catholic hierarchy attended by ninety bishops, an organization was established to aid religious freedom in Mexico. The organization was called the Catholic Bishops Commission for Mexican Relief. Doyle stated that he would do everything in his power to see that "this movement is not used for any political purpose," and he offered to keep in touch with the President.[123] Roosevelt immediately told McIntyre that he "would like to see Doyle...sometime soon for fifteen minutes."[124]

Roosevelt had cause to worry about the impact of this new organization to aid Mexico—the Vatican was contributing to its mission and its membership would eventually total over two million. Doyle notified the State Department of its formation and of his concern because of the fact that it would be headed by Archbishop Curley and Bishop Kelly, "both of whom have strongly criticized the National Administration." Doyle promised, however, that such criticism would not continue and that he was giving his services with that idea in mind. "The entire Catholic Church in this country is now being organized to back up the work of this Commission," Doyle wrote. Even Al Smith had donated office space in the Empire State Building. But, Doyle would not allow the organization to be utilized in any anti-Roosevelt movement. He had contributed a great deal to further the interests of Roosevelt over the past five years, but noted that nothing was "more important than what I am doing in this matter."[125]

Doyle's effort proved to be significant. In April of 1936, Roosevelt learned of Doyle's actions at the annual meeting of the Catholic Association for International Peace, at which the Catholic Bishops Commission for Mexican Relief also met. At Doyle's suggestion, the Mexican question was eliminated from the program. "This was done to prevent any criticism of the Administration's policy," Doyle said, and even Archbishop Curley concurred. Only a project to erect a seminary was discussed.[126] By the spring of 1936, then, public outbursts of condemnation toward Mexico's religious policies had, to a large degree, abated. Happily for Roosevelt, the news from Mexico was having the desired effect.

One of the key issues in the Mexican religious controversy and the solution thereof was that the Vatican and the Mexican government could not agree on the appointment of an apostolic delegate to Mexico. The American hierarchy and the Vatican had urged Roosevelt to use his good offices to settle this issue—which he did—but over the past year the intervention of the administration in this dilemma proved fruitless. However, in the spring of 1936, a breakthrough occurred. Roosevelt and his administration convinced Mexico to agree to meet a special representative from the Vatican, who would "endeavor to secure unity among the Mexican bishops and at the same time take the necessary steps to reestablish some discipline among the Mexican priests."[127] Najera promised to meet the representative in Mexico City and work to secure the success of his mission. Furthermore, it was understood that if the mission proved successful, the way would be paved "for an agreement by the Mexican Government that a permanent Apostolic Delegate of Mexican nationality be appointed to reside in Mexico City."[128]

Monsignor Piani, the apostolic delegate to the Philippines, was selected for the mission to Mexico. Upon his arrival in the United States, he read all the files of the Apostolic Delegation in Washington with regard to the Mexican question. He told Father Burke that he "was amazed . . . at all the United States Government was doing and was apparently willing to do to promote the interests of religious liberty in Mexico."[129] After Monsignor Piani left for Mexico, Amleto Cicognani, the apostolic delegate to the United States, and Burke went to see Welles to thank him "for his help and courtesy and asked Mr. Welles to thank the President." Welles assured Cicognani that what he had done was "by the order of the President; that the President was eager to do all in his power to have the Mexican Government extend religious liberty." Cicognani and Burke promised to reciprocate by communicating the actions of the President confidentially to the members of the American hierarchy.[130] Roosevelt's private diplomacy was producing ample dividends.

Unfortunately, as previously mentioned, Archbishop Ruiz was not allowed to return as apostolic delegate to Mexico until February 5, 1937. The effort by Piani to secure an apostolic delegate for Mexico had failed.[131] While the appointment of an apostolic delegate would have helped to solve the Mexican controversy for the Roosevelt administration, Roosevelt did not lose hope nor restrict his activities and intervention. Ambassador Daniels became his prime conduit for conducting one last flourish of private persuasion before election day in November.[132]

The religious situation in Mexico, Welles wrote Daniels, was not receiving "any unfavorable comment" in the United States at that time. In fact, the Associated Press carried reports in April that "thousands" of churches in Mexico had been opened. Likewise, *The New York Times* revealed that the Mexican government had no intention of interfering with the actions of governors in reopening churches nor in permitting priests to officiate.[133] Even the front page articles in *The Brooklyn Tablet* during the spring of 1936 reflected what Roosevelt had accomplished and had learned of privately—that "more churches are permitted to open," that a "moderating anti-religious program" had federal approval throughout Mexico, and that the overall picture "shows some gains have been made."[134] The members of the hierarchy of the Catholic Church in the United States were "greatly encouraged" in the early months of 1936 not only by the train of events that had occurred in Mexico, but also "by the general trend" which the religious situation was taking.[135] Roosevelt hoped to read more of the same right up to the elections in November.

Although the religious situation was improving, Daniels continued to see Cardenas for Roosevelt. In May, Daniels asked Cardenas—at the request of Roosevelt—if he would not grant a greater measure of religious liberty to Mexico's priests. As the Catholic press in the United States had correctly stated, the churches in Mexico were opening, but the priests were not being permitted to officiate in their churches as rapidly as could be the case. Cardenas agreed, hoping that his efforts to grant the liberty of religious worship would "lift the religious issue out of Mexican politics."[136] At this meeting Cardenas and Daniels also discussed the Yucatan area, and as a result of these talks the State Department concluded that the "bettering of the religious situation" which had occurred "in the Yucatan consular district [could be] attributed to the President of Mexico, influenced by the American Government."[137] However, one of the major areas of interest for improvement of the Mexican religious situation, in the eyes of the Roosevelt administration, was in the State of Veracruz.

Throughout the summer and fall of 1936, Daniels met on several occasions with Cardenas about the situation in Veracruz. Daniels pointed out that Veracruz was "the show window of Mexico," the "richest section outside of Mexico City," and as such, Americans and others visiting Mexico by sea were confronted immediately by barred churches. Therefore, "Mexico is given a bad name at the start."[138] Also, Daniels went on, Catholics there—who were very numerous—were told when they applied to the State governments for permission to open churches that it "was a matter to be taken up with the President in Mexico City, and when they would take it up in Mexico, they would be told that the Constitution gave exclusive right to each State to regulate the number of churches and priests."[139] Neither would shoulder the responsibility. Daniels wanted some movement from Cardenas.

Daniels knew that Cardenas "was anxious to do everything that would ease the situation," that he had "the greatest admiration for President Roosevelt and said that so far as he was concerned whatever he could do to be helpful he would do."[140] Consequently, one month later, Cardenas informed Daniels that the situation in Veracruz had been difficult, but a new governor would be in office by December 1, and he intended that the "more moderate course pursued in other States would be followed in Veracruz." Laughing, Cardenas informed Daniels that the shade on the show window of Mexico was being pulled down.[141] On December 1, 1936, Daniels recorded that a new governor was inaugurated and, as Cardenas had told him, Daniels could now observe that "in nearly every State in which a new Governor, in sympathy with his policy, had been inaugurated, his taking office was soon followed by the opening of churches which had been closed and marked by a spirit of moderation."[142] Now, prior to the election of 1936, Roosevelt and his advisors carefully watched for the Mexican religious situation—greatly improved by their handiwork—to be thrust into the political arena.

As it turned out, Catholic opposition over the Mexican question never did materialize. Various leaders in the Catholic community attempted to "keep alive, and if possible increase, their attacks on the Roosevelt administration."[143] According to Secretary Hull, "the extreme partisan republicans, especially in the Knights of Columbus," were watching every opportunity to exploit the Mexican situation, but like the "increasing number of the higher and more influential members of the Church," they were becoming "less vocal."[144] In fact, just prior to the election, Michael Francis Doyle reported that he met very few members of the Knights of Columbus who were going to vote against Roosevelt because of the Mexican question.[145]

In October of 1936, a Gallup Poll discovered that 78 percent of the Catholic-Americans interviewed would support Roosevelt.[146] The religious conditions in Mexico had definitely improved. Religious harassment had abated and with the decline in anticlericalism, Catholic-Americans, "like other Americans, became more interested in their own pressing social and economic problems than in a foreign religious dispute."[147] Yet, as one student of the period wrote, "had the elections taken place some eighteen months earlier at the height of the uproar, Roosevelt would have lost some votes, or perhaps would have been forced to modify his stand against U.S. intervention."[148]

As we know, Roosevelt did modify his stand on intervention—and did intervene privately to persuade the Mexican government to end its policies of religious persecution—because of the influence and pressure from the Catholic-American community. Although Father Burke died before Roosevelt's reelection, Burke no doubt would have agreed that, through the Roosevelt administration, all factions of the Catholic community in the United States helped to alleviate religious persecution and bring about an improved religious condition for the Catholic Church in Mexico after 1935.

3

The Spanish Civil War

With the elimination of the blatant religious persecutions in Mexico, pressure from the Catholic-American community subsided and was not to be felt again by Roosevelt until he was well into his second term. At that time, the issue involved another predominantly Catholic country and provoked one of the most bitter controversies that Roosevelt ever faced during his entire tenure in the White House. It was the Spanish Civil War, and the question confronting the Roosevelt administration and America's Catholics was whether or not the United States should send arms, ammunition, and implements of war to the Republican government of Spain in its struggle against the Nationalist or Fascist forces of General Francisco Franco. By the early months of 1938, Franco's forces were seemingly on the verge of victory.[1]

Throughout the Spanish Civil War from 1936 to 1939, Franco's forces received from Hitler and Mussolini substantial military aid, primarily planes, tanks, and various technical equipment. The Loyalist government, seeing the arm of Fascism extending into Spain, appealed to the rest of the world for similar support, but met only the policies of non-interference and non-intervention from Great Britain, France, and the United States. However, it was the Soviet Union that eventually assisted the Republican government with planes and tanks, as well as technicians and advisers.[2] Nevertheless, Franco's support far exceeded that of the Loyalist government, and in part accounted for his eventual victory in the spring of 1939.

It was this influence and intervention by the Soviet Union in Spain that provoked the cries of many in the United States, primarily the Catholic-American community, that the Loyalists were aiding in the establishment of communism in Spain. It should be noted, however, that the Communist Party by no means dominated or controlled the Republican government; in fact, the "violence perpetrated by extremists on both left and right before the outbreak of the civil war was of Spanish origin."[3] Still, the Catholic hierarchy, influential Catholic laymen and congressmen, Catholic organizations and the Catholic press, firmly believed in the possibility of communist hegemony in Spain and throughout this controversy proceeded to support America's neutrality stance, thus aiding Franco.

On January 8, 1937, an embargo was placed on the shipments of arms, ammunition, and implements of war to either side in the Spanish Civil War. And, on May 1, 1937, as the old Neutrality Law of 1935 was about to expire, Roosevelt signed the new act, primarily designed to isolate the United States from any future war. This new law automatically put into effect—when a state of war or a civil war threatened the United States—an embargo on arms shipments. In addition, the legislation banned loans to belligerents and prohibited travel on belligerent ships. Also, American merchant ships could not be armed and could not carry arms to governments or representatives friendly to the belligerents.[4] If Roosevelt had his way, he would have desired to have greater discretion in applying these restrictions, but the predominantly isolationist Congress insisted that the restrictions be mandatory, thereby indicating to the President and the nation the growing power of Congress over America's foreign affairs.

The leading isolationist and initiator of neutrality legislation was Senator Gerald P. Nye of North Dakota. Nye subscribed to the view that wars were caused by bankers and industrialists, the same people who precipitated America's domestic problems. Nye became a leader for mandatory neutrality legislation when his Senate committee, investigating the munitions industry, revealed that a strong link existed between the munitions industry in the United States and America's entry into World War I.[5] However, when Italy and Germany intervened in the Spanish Civil War in 1937 and began to supply Franco, even Nye—as well as the isolationist Congress—began to have second thoughts on the fairness of the arms embargo toward Spain. In March of 1937, Nye introduced a resolution, calling upon the United States to drop the arms embargo against Spain and begin to sell arms to the Loyalist government. If the embargo was to be used, Nye reasoned, it should be directed at Italy and Germany, not Spain.[6]

Nye's resolution—which was eventually tabled by the Senate Foreign Relations Committee—was most unacceptable to Roosevelt; as unacceptable as would be the more formidable attempt by Congress in May of 1938 to lift the embargo. Throughout his first administration, and as he now began his second term in office, it was obvious to Roosevelt that to lift the arms embargo he would have to be willing to lose the support of the Catholic-American community. And this he had no intention of doing.

As already pointed out, Roosevelt had a good track record for abiding by the demands of the Catholic community, specifically during the negotiations concerning the recognition of Russia and during the anticlerical movement in Mexico. He became indebted to the Catholic-American community during the election of 1936 for its effort, in conjunction with the leadership of the Democratic Party, to eliminate the implication that he was a communist or sympathetic to communist principles.[7] It was Father Coughlin who was Roosevelt's nemesis. Coughlin's radio addresses, coupled with his publication, *Social Justice,* reached the ears of millions of America's Catholics. Roosevelt's Catholic friends, both in and out of the hierarchy, orchestrated the counterattack.

Working with the knowledge and support of James A. Farley— Roosevelt's superb chairman of the National Democratic Committee—Father Maurice Sheehy of Catholic University of America set out before the election to visit the cardinals and bishops in the United States. After acquiring their support, Sheehy then published and had released throughout the country their statements of support for Roosevelt. Roosevelt was also informed that Sheehy had gotten most of the Catholic publications "in line"; that they were going "down the line" for the Democratic Party.[8]

Of great importance to Roosevelt and his chances for reelection was the support rendered by George Cardinal Mundelein of Chicago. As a prominent supporter of Roosevelt, "Mundelein was eager to help erase the impression that the Catholic Church was speaking through the voice of Coughlin.... In September of 1936 Mundelein publicly expressed his support for the Roosevelt administration and emphasized the prosperity which it had returned to the United States."[9] Edward J. Kelly, mayor of Chicago, told Roosevelt that the influence of Mundeleins's endorsement would produce a most beneficial effect, for "His Eminence is loved and revered by millions of Catholics in this great area, and he is also held in very high esteem by many thousands of non-Catholics as well."[10]

Mundelein not only publicly supported Roosevelt, but privately gathered allegiance through the church organization. Prior to the election of 1936, Mundelein summoned all of the priests under his jurisdiction and told them that he wanted to talk to them politically. According to Father Sheehy, who was present at the meeting, Cardinal Mundelein wanted his priests to refute Coughlin. "Within five minutes," Sheehy said, "Cardinal Mundelein completely destroyed Coughlin."[11] During the campaign, Roosevelt made a point of seeing Mundelein when the election train arrived in Chicago. Roosevelt recorded that Mundelein had been "perfectly magnificent all through the campaign," and this support, coupled with the Cardinal's endorsement of Roosevelt in December of 1935 at Notre Dame during the anticlerical controversy in Mexico, showed Roosevelt that Mundelein had a "decidedly beneficial effect" on the Catholic-American community, and therefore possessed enormous political influence.[12]

Catholic support for Roosevelt in 1936, then, was highly significant. Through the election of 1936, Roosevelt "forged a new political coalition firmly based on the success in the great northern cities, and led in Congress by a new political type: the northern urban liberal Democrat."[13] A student of this period discovered that one poll concluded that "81 percent of all Catholics who voted supported Roosevelt. Both the Gallup and Roper polls indicated that Roosevelt had received substantial support from Catholics, Gallup estimating it at over 70 percent." Similarly, in the larger cities of the United States, "where most Catholic votes were congregated," Roosevelt won handily.[14]

As a consequence of the election, in relation to neutrality legislation and the Spanish Civil War, "a stampede to Washington" occurred, led by pacifists, "groups which had been outraged by the treatment of the Catholic Church in Spain," and those who demanded neutrality.[15] In light of this strong Catholic support and the significance of the Catholic vote toward further New Deal success, Roosevelt had to face the possibility of losing it if he erred in the formulation of his foreign policy, particularly regarding Spain. So, by the time that Nye introduced his resolution in March of 1937 calling for the United States to embargo arms to Italy and Germany and suggesting that arms be sold to the Loyalists in Spain, Roosevelt already knew the pulse of the Catholic community, and the diagnosis revealed that no change in the present procedure was needed.

Father Burke, General Secretary of the NCWC and former barometer for Roosevelt of the attitudes of America's Catholics, died in the fall of 1936, and Roosevelt began to rely on Mundelein to give him the Catholic view. It was clear that Mundelein occupied such a pivotal position. For example, when Norman Thomas, the perennial Socialist Party candidate for President and one who urged Roosevelt on several occasions to lift the arms embargo against the Loyalists, met with Roosevelt in 1937 after a visit to Spain, he recorded the influence that Mundelein and the Catholic vote had on Roosevelt. Thomas, like Roosevelt, sympathized with the Loyalist government in Spain. But, unlike Roosevelt, he believed that the embargo should be lifted. When he pushed Roosevelt, Roosevelt began to tell Thomas "what a great man Cardinal Mundelein was."[16] Thomas got the distinct impression from the interview and was convinced that "the major thing in Roosevelt's mind was not so much foreign policy but a belief that in his *whole* policy, domestic and foreign, it was necessary to carry along the Catholic Church." For Thomas, America's Spanish policy was being made by the Catholic Church.[17]

Before the Spanish embargo controversy reached a fever pitch in May of 1938, Roosevelt urged Mundelein to ask the Vatican to use its position to arouse a worldwide "moral indignation" against the Fascists in Spain.[18] The answer was received by Roosevelt and Mundelein in May of 1938. The Vatican announced that it recognized the Franco government as the legitimate government of Spain.[19]

Although Mundelein occupied a favorable position with the President, Roosevelt was also made keenly aware of the public opinion of the Catholic community regarding Spain by "Catholic politicans like John McCormack of Massachusetts, Catholic organs such as *America* [the Jesuit weekly magazine], the 'opinion makers' at the Catholic University of America, and the leaders of the National Catholic Welfare Conference."[20] Several incidents reflected the growing influence of the Catholic-American population on the Roosevelt administration and on the Congress before the arms embargo controversy in May of 1938. One such incident in 1937 involved a plan by a group of Americans to form a Board of Guardians for Basque Refugee Children. They hoped to bring five hundred young Basques to the United States and care for them throughout the Spanish Civil War.[21] Homes had been found for the children in the United States, and the State Department had anticipated that the plan would be implemented. Of assistance to the committee was Eleanor Roosevelt, and upon her advice United States Ambassador to Spain, Claude Bowers, was named as chairman. Almost immediately, Catholics opposed the program. The most pressure on the White House and the State Department came from McCormack, who believed that "the scheme was intended for use as Communist propaganda." Catholic opponents saw the Board of Guardians as mainly individuals who were pro-Loyalist and, furthermore, believed that the children could be better taken care of closer to their homes.[22]

Roosevelt consulted the State Department and Undersecretary of State Sumner Welles advised that, since jurisdiction over the admission of these refugees was a function of the Department of Labor, Frances Perkins (Secretary of Labor) should act. But Welles advised her that the children should not be brought into the United States. If they lived in countries in Europe closer to their parents, organizations in the United States could send money and contribute in various ways.[23]

Welles's opinion and the final disposition of this incident reflected the opinion of outspoken Catholic critics. Cardinal O'Connell of Boston firmly opposed the plan as did the Massachusetts Knights of Columbus, which saw the plan as a danger to America's neutrality policy.[24] Welles also told the White House that McCormack discussed the question with the Department and was advised that the question was one that would be resolved by the Secretary of Labor.[25] With such pressure exerted, no Basque children ever entered the United States.

In January of 1938, Catholic-Americans again showed their hostility and opposition toward any favorable action directed at the Loyalist government in Spain. Sixty members of Congress sent their congratulations to the Loyalist Cortes meeting in Valencia for their fight to preserve democracy.[26] Almost immediately, most of the "congressmen quickly repudiated their signature and explained them away after being pressured by a number of Catholic leaders— among the latter, the irate David I. Walsh, Democratic Senator from

Massachusetts."[27] The NCWC, various bishops, and Catholic organizations condemned the message, and when the NCWC news agency surveyed the sixty senators and representatives some charged that their signatures were obtained by trickery, and that they did not mean to favor the Barcelona Government.[28] If they had questioned Roosevelt, he too would have responded in a similar manner.

Privately, Roosevelt was sympathetic to the Spanish or Loyalist government. However, one must agree with the observation of Eleanor Roosevelt that "Franklin frequently refrained from supporting causes in which he believed because of political realities." As in the case of the Spanish Civil War, this annoyed her immensely. The United States "had to remain neutral though Franklin knew quite well he wanted the democratic government to be successful."[29]

Publicly, Roosevelt never depicted the influence of the Catholic-American community or the loss of the Catholic vote as one of the reasons for not lifting the Spanish arms embargo. He always cited Franco's dominance of the seas, the practical hopelessness of a Loyalist victory, the policy of non-intervention by the League of Nations—primarily England and France—in the Spanish Civil War, and the strong isolationist feeling in the United States and in the Congress. Even prior to the introduction of Nye's resolution in the Senate on May 2, 1938, calling for the lifting of the arms embargo for the Loyalist government only, Roosevelt told Mrs. Roosevelt that, although he was in agreement with the Loyalist cause, he maintained "that it would be absolutely impossible to repeal the Neutrality Act, because the people of this country feel that it was designed to keep us out of war, and, on the whole, it is the best instrument to accomplish that end." Roosevelt felt certain that he "could not get the people to change this point of view without a period of education and perhaps from experiences which they have not as yet had."[30] Perhaps Roosevelt had in mind the opposition of the Catholic-American community, for according to a public opinion poll in February of 1938, 75 percent of the American people sympathized with the Loyalists.[31] Almost a year later the same poll revealed similar results, but by religion the outcome showed 58 percent of the Catholics favoring Franco and 83 percent of the Protestants supporting the Loyalists.[32]

One noted historian of this period concluded that Roosevelt had changed his mind in the spring of 1938 and decided to support the Nye resolution, but the opposition from the Catholic community was so overwhelming that Roosevelt quickly moved to dismiss any inkling of administration support.[33] And yet, recent studies show that Roosevelt never did change his mind on lifting the arms embargo. He and the Congress knew "how explosive the issue was" and best described it in "terms which Harold Ickes could best appreciate when he told him that members of Congress were 'jittery' about the Catholic vote and that they wanted to drop the embargo issue . . . there is no doubt of the accuracy of his remark."[34] However, it can now be noted that neither view is totally accurate. Roosevelt and his administration did fear the loss of the Catholic vote and the influence of the Catholic community if the arms embargo was ever lifted. Similarly, Roosevelt did understand the pressure that could be brought upon his administration or the Congress by America's Catholics if a recommendation was given to lift the embargo. Consequently, when Nye introduced his resolution in the Senate in May of 1938, forcing the Roosevelt administration—not the Congress—to bear the brunt of the opposition from a decision to either support or reject the resolution, Roosevelt and his administration decided to plant a story in the news media.

Although in part accurate, the story was that the administration was contemplating the lifting of the arms embargo by urging a congressional review of America's neutrality legislation. The major reason to plant the story, however, was solely to provoke a resurgence of Catholic opposition directed toward the Congress in order to defeat any debate on the Nye resolution. It was a masterful maneuver to use the concerted influence of the Catholic-American community to defeat a piece of foreign legislation that, for all intents and purposes, placed the Roosevelt administration in a politically disastrous position. Roosevelt never desired to revoke the embargo, and the unfolding of the events involving the embargo controversy in the spring of 1938 can only lead to such a conclusion.

Breckinridge Long, a close associate of the hierarchy in the State Department and former United States Ambassador to Italy, was retained by the Loyalist government of Spain to present their view of the operation of America's neutrality policy vis-à-vis that government.[35] Although influential, Long was but a part of the overall pro-Loyalist pressure that was mobilized in March and April of 1938 in order to motivate the President, the Congress, and the State Department to lift the Spanish arms embargo. As Moffat recorded in his diary, these were the days of "a big drive on the part of all Loyalists or Loyalist sympathizers for us to remove the embargo on Spain partly to enable Barcelona to get airplanes, partly to mark a definite sign of encouragement. Among the latest to put pressure on us was Breckinridge Long."[36] It is important to follow Long's activities during these several months because, through the use of his diary, he described the actions and attitudes of certain key persons in this controversy.

When Long visited Roosevelt on March 24, the President remained non-committal on the arms embargo and suggested that long see Cordell Hull. After a one-hour conversation, Long noted that he was "sympathetic but noncommittal and referred me to Moore, Dunn and Moffat." They also were non-committal, but definitely opposed to any change of policy.[37] Actually, Long was hoping that the State Department would "find some way by indirection to wink at transshipments of military equipment" to the Loyalist government, and thereby a debate to revise the neutrality laws would not be necessary. But, Long "recognized that to withdraw the embargo resolution would produce a violent political fight and would bring many forces into opposition with the Administration."[38] It was quite obvious to Long that the State Department, as represented by Moore, Dunn, and Moffat, did not wish to have the administration become the "whipping boy" for those who opposed the lifting of the embargo, namely the Catholic-American opposition. Whether they intended it or were just quoting to Long the law, Moore, Dunn, and Moffat concurred that any change in the neutrality law rested with the Congress, and hence the Congress, not the administration, would have to answer to the opposition. As Moffat noted, he and the others "went round and round in circles until finally we were able to convince him [Long] that unless there was Congressional action there was nothing to be done that would not be a violation of law."[39]

Having been so informed by these three officials of the State Department, Long nevertheless decided to continue to press Hull and Roosevelt one more time before he went to Congress for a reversal in policy. On March 25, Long met Hull again and with him for a time, Moore. He presented Hull with a memorandum, in which he proposed a change in policy and outlined the extent of the material and military support given to Franco.[40] Similar work for the Loyalist government was also being conducted at the White House, where Donald Richberg—called by Long as "the number one boy of the White House"—represented the Spanish government and worked through James Roosevelt, the President's son and secretary.[41] Although Long disliked the fact that his work conflicted with the policy of his own government, he continued to press the demands of the Loyalist government and finally was given some assurances by Hull that the Roosevelt administration might reconsider its neutrality policy.[42] Hull told Long that if sufficient proof of an Italian and German invasion was received, possibly such information would provoke Roosevelt to reconsider and then revoke the embargo.[43] Long must have been encouraged for, on the following day, he secured a promise by James Roosevelt that the Spanish problem would be brought to the President's attention and hopefully placed on the agenda for the next Cabinet meeting.[44]

On April 10, however, Long finally received word of the administration's position on reopening debate on the neutrality policy. The answer—as Long reiterated to Miles Sherover, the American purchasing agent for the Spanish government—was no, not now.[45] Prior to learning of this position, Long had conversed with Hull and did ascertain that the administration was very reluctant to aid the Loyalist cause, primarily because it looked "as if the Loyalist government was collapsing under pressure of big guns, tanks and aircraft superiority."[46]

Roosevelt and Hull, throughout this period, believed that the Loyalist government was virtually defeated. In March, when Roosevelt urged the State Department to have America's ambassador to Spain, Claude Bowers, then living in France at St. Jean de Luz, make periodic visits to Barcelona in Spain, the State Department discovered that only two roads were still open from France to Barcelona and they were constantly under fire. Under the circumstances, Roosevelt agreed to wait for several weeks before issuing instructions. For Moffat, Franco's victory seemed evident and the Loyalist cause in a state of demoralization.[47] Even in mid-April, after Roosevelt told a private press conference of newspaper editors that France controlled Spain's seaports, he explained to Ickes that, if munitions were shipped, they would not reach the Loyalists because of Franco's control of the sea.[48] And, when Roosevelt returned from a Caribbean fishing trip at the height of the controversy over the arms embargo, he again told Ickes that he was "opposed to doing anything about it."[49] From all indications Roosevelt and Hull, aware of the international situation in Spain, of the Vatican's support for Franco, and of the opposition of the Catholic-American community toward lifting the arms embargo, never contemplated a change in the embargo. However, a small group of careerists in the State Department, including R. Walton Moore, the counselor, were understood to say by some congressmen and others like Breckinridge Long that the reason the administration could do nothing regarding Spain was because of the lack of congressional action to repeal the embargo. Thus, a congressional initiative was mounted and reached its peak while Hull was on vacation and Roosevelt was fishing in the Caribbean.

No evidence exists to suggest that several careerists in the State Department— namely Moore, Dunn, Green, Moffat, and others—deliberately sought to reverse the policy of Roosevelt and Hull concerning Spain by encouraging a congressional initiative. True, they were upset—as Moffat called it—from "the organized pressure of the Left Wing" in the press, and they were giving the Spanish question a great deal of thought.[50] But this did not mean that, due to such pressure, these men had a "change of Heart" and encouraged the Congress to act, presumably with the approval of the administration. Such was not the case. What they did do was to reiterate "out loud" to several members of Congress—and particularly to Breckinridge Long—that although the administration was opposed to a repeal of the arms embargo, the Congress, under the neutrality law, could if it so desired change the neutrality act and treat both sides alike, thereby maintaining America's neutrality. By maintaining the present embargo on Spain, most members of Congress reasoned that the United States was acquiescing in a victory for Franco. Since this was an emotional issue, some congressmen and others, specifically Breckinridge Long, took this attitude to mean that if the Congress decided to reconsider neutrality legislation, the administration would not hinder such action. Consequently, the fight to reverse the arms embargo toward Spain moved to Capitol Hill.

Breckinridge Long understood the opposition that existed in the United States on both sides of the embargo controversy, and no doubt also understood that the Roosevelt administration did not wish to bear the brunt of the opposition by having to take a stand on such a divisive issue. Therefore, from his discussions at the State Department, he believed that if both parties in Congress desired to reconsider the neutrality legislation and at the same time bear the brunt of the opposition, then the administration would support such a change. In early April, Moore implied just such a policy, which was to be looked upon by Hull and Roosevelt as a major blunder by the State Department on this issue. Moore "informed Congressman Jerry O'Connell that, contrary to some press reports, Hull had not said that he did not desire Congress to reconsider neutrality measures."[51] Similarly, before Long was told by Hull on April 10 that the administration would not change its policy vis-à-vis Spain, Long too was under the impression that Hull might reconsider the neutrality legislation if evidence was provided that revealed an invasion of Spain. Moffat also recorded that on March 24, Long was told at a meeting at the State Department that unless there was Congressional action, nothing could be done by the administration.[52] Even James Roosevelt, who at that time was the Secretary to the President, sent a letter on May 5, 1938, drafted by the State Department, which emphasized that the United States would continue its neutrality policy "until the Congress, in whose hands the matter rests, either amends or repeals the existing statutes with regard to the shipment of arms, ammunition and implements of war to Spain."[53]

Although these officials of the State Department were merely stating how the neutrality act could be changed, most pro-Loyalists, including Long, misinterpreted the intent of their remarks to mean that a congressional initiative would be welcomed. Thus, on April 5, Representative Byron Scott introduced a resolution to repeal the arms embargo.[54] At about the same time, Alvarez del Vago, the Spanish Foreign Minister, was even informed, probably by Long, that Roosevelt and Hull were inclined to eliminate the Neutrality Act, but Hull refused to act because he believed the Loyalist position was hopeless.[55] Moffat did record that "most people think the Secretary is secretly for the Nye Resolution," and possibly this attitude by Hull also can be faulted as leading to a misinterpretation on the administration's position by pro-Loyalists. For the first part of April, Long definitely believed Hull might reconsider the embargo act. Moffat was quick to add, however, that Hull actually felt just the opposite. Hull thought that Congress was attempting to upset the power of the President. Moreover, for the first time Hull "showed a certain testiness toward Judge Moore for having said the State Department disinterested itself in whatever legislation Congress chose to pass."[56]

From all indications, then, the statements issued by these various officials of the State Department helped to exacerbate an issue which Roosevelt and Hull had just curtailed, or so they thought. Prior to the resolution introduced by Representative Byron Scott on April 5, his colleague, Jerry O'Connell of Montana, had introduced a resolution proposing to amend the Neutrality Act. Under his proposal, aggressors would be denied aid and victims of aggression would receive aid. Also, O'Connell called for the arms embargo against Loyalist Spain to be lifted. Chairman of the House Foreign Affairs Committee, Sam McReynolds, agreed to begin hearings on the resolution on March 29. He also confided that Hull had no objection to holding the hearings. But, just before the hearings were to begin, McReynolds announced that the committee had reconsidered its position on O'Connell's resolution. According to James Roosevelt, the State Department caused the hearings to be stopped because they did not want a public discussion of the embargo situation. It should be noted that a Gallup Poll showed, at that time, about two-thirds of the American people supporting the Loyalists.[57] However, the damage had been done and a new method of dealing with the furor in Congress had to be found.

Before Roosevelt and Hull began their separate holidays in late April and early May of 1938, both were well aware of the increased agitation over the arms embargo. On April 27, McIntyre, secretary to the President, "informed Roosevelt of reports that Senator Pittman and others were disposed toward some action on the Spanish question."[58] While on their holidays, events took a new turn. Although the administration had stopped the hearings on the arms embargo in the House Foreign Affairs Committee, the Senate now began to urge some action on neutrality legislation. And, on May 2, 1938, Senator Nye introduced his resolution which proposed to lift the arms embargo *only*, however, for the Loyalist government in Spain; *not*, to the surprise of Breckinridge Long, to undertake a reconsideration of the neutrality legislation.

Knowing that the Roosevelt administration opposed any change in American policy toward Spain, Long had taken his case to the Congress, encouraged by the words of Moore and others in the State Department that only Congress could change the Neutrality Law. Apparently believing that his desire to repeal the Neutrality Law, through the introduction of a resolution to that effect, would be advocated in the Senate Foreign Relations Committee, Long listened carefully to Nye's resolution. Nye's resolution, however, was not Long's resolution. Nye changed it, according to Long, at the last moment and "so phrased it that it applies only to Spain—not to the general neutrality law; and proposes to authorize the President to revoke the embargo—instead of repealing the provisions of law on which the embargo rested." Long knew that Nye had changed the resolution "to suit his own political partisan purposes and to place the President in the position of acting affirmatively and to take all the opposition attack—to bear the brunt of the blame and opposition—whereas a repeal of the civil war parts of the Neutrality Act, with all political parties cooperating, would share responsibility."[59] With the Nye resolution Long saw the lines now drawn for the administration—not the Congress—to incur the wrath of the opposition. When Hull returned to Washington one week before Roosevelt, the administration was faced with the choice of either repudiating America's liberals or America's Catholics.

Since the outset of the Spanish Civil War, Roosevelt—attuned to the position of the Catholic-American community through the intercession of the hierarchy, influential laymen, and the press—would not countenance the lifting of the arms embargo. Like others who talked of the importance of the Catholic vote, "Roosevelt was only one of the many politicians who believed that there was such a vote, and acted accordingly."[60] Roosevelt and Hull did not need to be told, as they were in this instance, that "the backbone of the Democratic Party throughout the entire North is the Catholic vote. If that is alienated, the party in the North is finished. If the administration should now lift the Spanish embargo, it would be difficult to convince the Catholics of the country that the purpose of so doing was not to aid the enemies of their Church."[61] Contrary to what some historians have written, namely, that Roosevelt and Hull considered raising the arms embargo toward Madrid in the spring of 1938, Roosevelt and Hull planned to offer nothing but sympathy.[62] It was the misinterpretation of the views of these careerists at the State Department that lent encouragement to Long and many members of Congress. Years later, Claude Bowers, the United States Ambassador to Spain during the Spanish Civil War and a staunch Loyalist, revealed that Roosevelt's sympathy was with the Loyalists and "that the President 'squirmed' a great deal over the American policy."[63] When he was relieved of his post in 1939, Bowers met with Roosevelt and was told by him that the United States "made a mistake. You've been right all along."[64] Later on in his life, Bowers stated that Roosevelt had to conform with the attitude of the Catholic community regarding the Loyalists because his domestic programs would have suffered.[65]

   That Roosevelt was primarily concerned with losing the Catholic vote and support over the Spanish question seems clear. As mentioned above, Roosevelt was constantly aware of Catholic-American opinion on this issue, and he abided by it. In March of 1938, Cardinal William O'Connell of Boston stated that Franco deserved the title of "defender of Christianity" for he was fighting to preserve Christian civilization.[66] Eastern newspapers immediately printed headlines of O'Connell's position. One student of this period—upon reading the issues of the *Boston Pilot*, the diocesan newspaper which O'Connell saw as his personal newspaper—revealed that, for the civil war years in Spain, "one is struck by the three themes; its overwhelming concern for the persecuted

Spanish Church, its repeated warnings about the evils of communism, and its constant attempt to defend General Franco."[67]

In April of 1938 in a letter to James Roosevelt—at that time Secretary to the President—the correspondent enclosed a confidential report from Washington that purported to be the administration's attitude toward the Spanish question. It stated that Roosevelt was the principal obstacle to the repeal of the arms embargo, and that "Cardinal Mundelein, who always publicly professes friendship for Roosevelt, has advised the President that any move toward lifting the embargo would arouse Catholic opposition throughout the country, and that this might seriously cripple Roosevelt's domestic economic measures." While Cardinals O'Connell, Hayes, and Dougherty openly supported Franco, the report concluded, Mundelein attacked covertly.[68]

Upon consultation with James Roosevelt about this incident, Roosevelt said that he "did have conversation with the President on these matters" concerning the lifting of the arms embargo. And, he continued, "although in their hearts and emotionally I am sure both my parents' sympathy was with the Republican government in Spain...the President most certainly was concerned with the Catholic-American community and tendency to vote en bloc during his Presidency." Roosevelt concluded by pointing out that "Mundelein was considered by my father to be an effective and charming person for whom he had a sincere regard and respect, and it would seem only natural that the Catholic hierarchy and press should apply pressure to have their views understood and supported."[69] Joseph Lash—as yet another person close to the Roosevelt family—later wrote that Roosevelt was not only fearful of isolationist sentiment during the arms embargo controversy, but was "even more fearful of the loss of the Catholic vote which had been strongly New Deal."[70]

Catholic-American pressure, then, did not force Roosevelt "to keep an embargo that he personally disliked."[71] Such pressure was not necessary. Roosevelt had no intention of losing the support of the Catholic-American community by favoring the lifting of the arms embargo, as reported by *The New York Times* on May 5. On the contrary, Roosevelt sought to arouse the Catholic-American community to such a pitch against the Congress that the Congress, not the administration, would back down from the seemingly overwhelming support that the Nye resolution was evoking in the Congress. Consequently, Roosevelt desired to terminate a movement in the Congress to force the administration to take a position on the arms embargo that could be politically disastrous. The planted story, the "leak," to Arthur Krock, chief of the Washington bureau of *The New York Times*, which alleged that the administration favored the lifting of the arms embargo, was a calculated political maneuver of enormous significance by a master politician: it contemplated, and accomplished, the motivating of the Catholic-American community to force Congress to back down from a policy that would have, if enacted, seriously fragmented the Democratic political machine throughout the country. The evolution of the strategy of the Roosevelt administration to combat the passage of the Nye resolution began the day Hull returned from his holiday.

Roosevelt was fishing in the Caribbean when Hull arrived in Washington, D.C. on May 2, the same day Nye introduced his resolution. Although Senator Vandenberg commented that Nye's resolution should not be taken seriously, Pittman differed completely.[72] Pittman said that such a powerful lobby urging the lifting of the embargo was rarely seen in Washington, and he wanted the State Department to answer several questions for the committee before it announced its position.[73] Moffat, in his diary, confirmed the fact that lobbyists both for and against the embargo increased their pressure every day, and since most senators favored Nye's resolution, Moffat concluded the resolution would pass "overwhelmingly."[74]

The passage of the resolution was the last thing that Hull wanted to contemplate. Hull was clearly upset about the German and Italian intervention in Spain, but was determined that the United States would not be drawn into the war.[75] Both Hull and his advisors realized that the Nye resolution was—as Breckinridge Long similarly described it in his diary—a resolution which "did not merely authorize the President to lift the embargo against Spain but was a distinctly unilateral proposition authorizing the President to lift it against the Loyalists only."[76] And, Pittman would not block discussion or hearings on the resolution in the Senate Foreign Relations Committee as Congressman McReynolds did in the House Foreign Affairs Committee.

Pittman, like most members of Congress, wanted the administration to render its decision first. Pittman pointed out to Joseph P. Kennedy—America's ambassador to Great Britain—on the very day Nye introduced his resolution, that the resolution provided another burden for those Democratic congressmen who were running for reelection in 1938.[77] When a similar initiative toward Spain was begun in the Congress in January of 1939, R. Walton Moore revealed that Pittman still believed that a discussion of the embargo question would ignite a religious controversy in every state of the union with unforseeable results,and, as in May of 1938, most senators wanted Roosevelt to state his position first—rather than reveal their own—and then attack it.[78] Consequently, with political pressure reaching a boiling point, most senators favored Nye's resolution only if they did not have to go on the record.[79] So, to Hull and his staff, the embargo question became simply a problem as to "who'll take responsibility."[80]

Upon his return, Hull was also enraged about the press attacks on his subordinates. In his influential, syndicated column, *Merry-Go-Round*, Drew

Pearson charged the careerists at the State Department with blocking the lifting of the arms embargo.[81] Specifically, Hull was concerned with the charges that he could not keep order in his own house and, as previously discussed, Hull was upset that Moore and others had intimated to Long and other members of Congress that the intitiating of neutrality legislation would not be opposed by the administration. Therefore, on May 3, Hull held several conferences at the State Department, with the primary purpose that America's policy of neutrality be understood by all and was not reversible.[82]

It must be pointed out that the various meetings at the State Department between Hull and his staff regarding the Nye resolution on May 3 and 4, revealed that Hull was indignant, particularly with Judge Moore, for the Department conveying the impression to the Congress that "the State Department disinterested itself in whatever legislation Congress chose to pass"[83] For example, at an afternoon conference on May 3, Hull was informed by Moore that he, Dunn, and Hackworth—in response to Pittman's questions—could safely say that they found no objection to the Nye resolution. Moore added that the Department should not be unduly concerned about the terms of the resolution.[84] Similarly on May 4, Hull discovered that most of his advisors did believe that if the arms embargo was lifted, it should be lifted for both sides. Moffat added a personal note in his diary that he too had "hopes that if the embargo is raised it will be raised against both and thus preserve our neutrality."[85]

Hull now realized the causes for the dilemma which presently weighed heavily on the administration. He also understood why Breckinridge Long and many congressmen had a revived enthusiasm for lifting the embargo even after Hull informed Long that the administration would not change its policy vis-à-vis Spain. And, with the Nye resolution stressing the lifting of the embargo in favor of the Spanish Loyalists only, Hull saw developing the political and religious controversy that Pittman confidentially described occurring over this issue to Ambassador Kennedy. Liberals and Catholics both supported New Deal legislation and were essential to Roosevelt's coalition, but the former liked the Loyalists and the latter sided with Franco.[86] Aware of the factions involved and of the fact that, if the administration publicly took a position on the Nye resolution, the Roosevelt administration alone would incur the brunt of the opposition, Hull decided to telephone Pittman—in response to his inquiry for expression of the position of the administration—and tell him that several more days were necessary to work out a reasonable reply.[87]

Much of what occurred next in this episode has been confusing because of the conjecture posed by Moffat in his diary, which incidentally has been the best record to date of what did occur in the State Department on this matter. Moffat recorded that apparently Pittman took Hull's reply that he needed more time to "workout" an answer to mean that "the Secretary ultimately would be with him." Moffat then assumed that it was Pittman who conveyed to the press that the administration supported Nye's resolution and the fact that it would pass "overwhelmingly," even though Moffat knew that Hull's view was just the opposite.[88] Consequently, with *The New York Times* publishing Arthur Krock's story on May 5 that "Roosevelt Backs Lifting Arms Embargo on Spain," Moffat's conclusions seemed accurate. However, on the same day that *The New York Times* published this headline, Moffat was informed by William Stone of the Foreign Policy Association that Pittman was not the person who informed *The New York Times*, and therefore Pittman should be "absolved . . . from double-dealing."[89]

What did occur was that Hull or Welles gave Krock the information on which Krock based the story, and the purpose of the planted story was to cause the arousal of the Catholics in the United States so that they would cause an uproar against helping the communist-supported Loyalist government.[90] By the initiating of a "planned leak" about how the administration felt on the arms embargo (which the various officials at the State Department did espouse and did actually convey to Long and numerous members of Congress), Hull and/or Welles, and most assuredly with Roosevelt's approval (even though he was fishing in the Caribbean), foresaw that the opposition from the Catholic-American community would be so great that Congress would have to back down from approving the Nye resolution. As a result, therefore, the administration would not have to intercede to prevent the passage of the resolution.[91] Ickes also recorded that he was told that the story was a deliberate plant to stir up America's Catholic community, and with such pressure on the Congress, Roosevelt could sit back, take no position, and watch Congress squirm.[92] And, when asked if this position was in actuality the new American policy toward Spain, Hull could call the story a rumor, a misrepresentation of official State Department policy, and, as he did mention on May 6, that the United States had plenty to do looking out for problems of more immediate danger.[93] The Roosevelt administration, through the press, had created a political crisis of such magnitude that the Nye resolution would never reach the floor of the Senate.

It should be noted that Roosevelt and Welles could have planted this story with Krock without the knowledge of Hull. As Krock revealed years later, "when it came to really doing the maneuvering on the great chessboard of diplomacy, he [Roosevelt] never let Hull have much to do with it at all. He would send for Sumner Welles to come over to the White House, and it was with Sumner that he would say, 'Now look, don't let old Hull know about this, but you and I will do so and so.' "[94] Indeed, as previously described in this work, Roosevelt and Welles did collaborate on the anticlerical situation in Mexico without Hull's knowledge, and since Welles was Roosevelt's State Department link to the NCWC and the attitudes of the Catholic-American community—

particularly the hierarchy—Welles could have informed Roosevelt by wireless of the opposition building among America's Catholics over the possibility that Congress might lift the arms embargo. Consequently, with the desire to resolve this dilemma, Roosevelt and Welles could have decided to plant the story with Krock. The storm of controversy Roosevelt hoped to generate became a reality. Upon his return to Washington on May 9, the leading members of Congress met with him to confirm the impact of the Catholic pressure.

That Krock's article in *The New York Times* on May 5 stirred up the Catholics in America and in turn the Congress was clearly evident. The article delineated that different policies existed toward the Spanish situation and the Sino-Japanese conflict and that the administration either wanted to amend the Neutrality Act to give Roosevelt discretionary power in applying the law, or repeal it. The article continued by stating that the Senate would vote for Nye's resolution by wide majority with the administration favoring it. With the House leadership saying that they could secure approval of any Senate action, the Senate Foreign Relations Committee decided to meet and report favorably on the resolution. Finally, the article ended by saying that one could assume that Roosevelt would lift the embargo against both factions in Spain, and that if he did it would end a period of experimenting with statutory neutrality.[95] The Catholic community reacted quickly and several days later, with Catholic opposition moving in high gear, Moffat noted that "the bitterness inspired by this Spanish strife among the Left Wingers on the one hand and the Catholic conservative elements on the other surpasses anything I have seen for years."[96]

It was reported in the *Washington Times* in May of 1938 that widespread sentiment existed in Congress to lift the embargo. However, with the Catholic Church taking such a determined position in favor of Franco, the *Times* added, any move to lift the embargo would meet with outright opposition from that religious bloc. One observer of Catholic pressure at that time wrote that Catholics have adopted the Franco cause as the cause of all American Catholics, and, at every opportunity, use the fact that there are twenty million Catholics in the United States who would oppose any change in American neutrality policy.[97] In addition, *The Brooklyn Tablet*—upon learning of the supposed position of the Roosevelt administration—immediately urged its readers to write to Roosevelt and their senators and congressmen, urging them to "maintain the embargo on munitions to Spain [and to] boycott the munition makers."[98]

Throughout the week after the publishing of *The New York Times* article, the White House, the State Department, and members of Congress received thousands of messages denouncing any attempt to lift the embargo. *The Brooklyn Tablet* noted that the protest was succeeding and that the government was now equivocating in its previous determination to change the embargo policy.[99] The *Tablet* continued to appeal to America's Catholics to keep protesting; the pressure was obviously bearing good fruit.

In the midst of the Catholic protest, Jay Allen, a foreign correspondent for the *Chicago Daily Tribune* and one who covered the Spanish Civil War, told Ickes that he was outraged at the position of the Catholic Church. Most American correspondents in Spain, he said, sympathized with the Loyalist government and deplored the fact that the Catholic Church was involved in this question.[100] Allen noted the impact of the Catholic opposition movement by revealing that the passage of the Nye resolution was a foregone conclusion before the "deluge of protests brought about its defeat."[101] The later Vice President of the United States, Henry Wallace, also wrote that the Catholic Church had a very profound effect on American foreign policy, particularly influencing "the attitude of the United States toward Loyalist Spain."[102]

James A. Farley, Postmaster General and chairman of the Democratic National Committee, joined the Catholic protest, but knew it was not necessary to pressure the President. Farley understood that there was "no doubt about it that Roosevelt was concerned about the Catholic vote." Until his dying day, Farley expressed his admiration of Franco and the belief that Franco "saved Spain from the Communists in the 1930's."[103] Alvarez del Vago, the Foreign Minister to Loyalist Spain, recently attested to the influence of Farley on Roosevelt. Although his informant was dead, del Vago was told in detail of Farley's pro-Franco maneuvers, and how he convinced Roosevelt that "if he lifted the embargo he would lose the Catholic vote and consequently the next election."[104] Vago believed that the Franco sentiment in the United States was obviously the work of the Catholic hierarchy.[105]

The Nation also reported that the hierarchy was speaking for the more than twenty million Catholics in the United States and using its potential political power to influence Roosevelt's policy toward Spain. To the editors of *The Nation*, Roosevelt would never risk losing votes around Boston, New York, Chicago, Detroit, and Baltimore.[106] On Capitol Hill, one student of the period has written that the influence of the Catholic Church was well developed by spring of 1938 and that Catholic politicians, like John McCormack of Massachusetts, in conjunction with the leaders of the NCWC and the Catholic press, were lobbying with vigor.[107] McCormack, for one, not only favored aid to Franco because Communism would be impeded by aiding Franco, not the government of Spain, but also did all he could to "promote Franco in the United States."[108] When Roosevelt returned from his fishing holiday, congressional leaders quickly made their way to the White House to inform Roosevelt of the impact of the Catholic-American protest on the Congress.

Roosevelt returned to Washington on Monday, May 9, and refused to answer questions from the press on the Spanish situation, particularly avoiding Nye's resolution.[109] Although it was known at the State Department that Nye claimed that his resolution would pass with ease—coming out of committee with a four-to-one favorable margin—Roosevelt knew that the Congress, being so inundated with protests from the Catholic-American community for the past week, would never get the opportunity to vote yes or no.[110] The planned "leak" to Arthur Krock had worked. Before meeting with Roosevelt at 12:30 P.M. on Monday, Hull telephoned Pittman. Pittman said that only two senators—Nye and Borah—were now pushing to pass Nye's resolution, and therefore the committee would probably support Roosevelt's position.[111] Undoubtedly, Hull transmitted the contents of his conversation with Pittman to Roosevelt.

Likewise, on Monday morning Ickes met with the President and raised the embargo question. Roosevelt told him that he opposed any action on the embargo. Even if ammunition could get into Spain across the French border, Roosevelt would not act. After several pleas by an adamant Ickes, Roosevelt revealed the real reason why he never favored the lifting of the arms embargo and why the Nye resolution would not be considered at this time. Ickes recorded that Roosevelt had brought up the matter with congressional leaders that morning. "Speaker Bankhead, Majority Leader Rayburn, and Congressman Ed Taylor had been in to see him just before I went in. He said frankly that to raise the embargo would mean the loss of every Catholic vote next fall and that the Democratic Members of Congress were jittery about it and didn't want it done." To Ickes, Roosevelt let the cat out of the bag, and it was "the mangiest, scabbiest cat ever. This proves up to the hilt what so many people have been saying, namely, that the Catholic minorities in Great Britain and America have been dictating the international policy with respect to Spain."[112]

Later, after his meeting with Roosevelt, Ickes told Thomas Corcoran, Roosevelt's aide and confidant, about Roosevelt's reason for not lifting the embargo. Corcoran said that "he had talked it over with a high Catholic ecclesiastic whom he had told that if the Catholic Church kept on as it was going, there would be a wave of anticlericalism that would sweep the country. He added that he didn't know but that he would be one of the leaders in the movement."[113] Corcoran confided to this author that Roosevelt "always considered the impact of ethnic groups in his decisions," and that they "truly play an enormous role in foreign policy decisions." During the arms embargo controversy in the spring of 1938, Corcoran continued, Roosevelt "had to consider the influence of Catholic-Americans; no doubt about it as a major factor in not lifting the embargo."[114]

When the meeting between the congressional delegation and Roosevelt was concluded on Monday morning Rayburn came out of the White House and told reporters he was against any change in the neutrality laws.[115] As Arthur Krock rightly reported in *The New York Times* several days later, the domestic political situation in the United States greatly influenced the final decision on the arms embargo.[116] Even Miles Sherover, the purchasing agent and general manager in the United States for the Spanish Loyalist government since 1936, confirmed to the noted historian of the Spanish Civil War, Hugh Thomas, "that Roosevelt anyway gave [me] to understand that it was the catholic vote which affected him."[117]

After his meeting with the President, Hull returned to the State Department with instructions for his staff to begin drafting a reply to Pittman opposing the Nye resolution. By working on the letter to Pittman on May 10, Moffat learned of and confirmed the impact that the Catholic community had made on the Congress. Moffat was right when he wrote on May 9 that the Spanish embargo question became more and more a case of "who'll take responsibility"; for on May 10, various senators told Hull that they wanted him to take more responsibility for the views of the American government on this issue. Moffat concluded by noting how politically dangerous it was for politicians with Left Wingers pulling on one hand and Catholics tugging on the other.[118]

While Hull and his staff, as instructed by Roosevelt, drafted a negative reply to the Senate Foreign Relations Committee, Roosevelt, from the moment of his return from his holiday, publicly maintained a non-committal attitude on the Nye resolution. At a press conference on May 10, Roosevelt told the reporters to consult the State Department when asked whether the United States planned to change its policy of an arms embargo toward Spain, or whether the lifting of the arms embargo was something that only Congress could determine.[119] Even Breckinridge Long on May 11 noted that the Spanish embargo question was discussed by Roosevelt at a breakfast meeting, but no decision was rendered.[120] However, on May 11, when Hull presented Roosevelt with his draft reply to be sent to the Senate Foreign Relations Committee advising against lifting the Spanish embargo, Roosevelt gave his consent, and on May 13 the letter was made public.[121] Upon its receipt in the Senate Foreign Relations Committee, each senator quietly read it and voted seventeen-to-one to postpone indefinitely any consideration of Nye's resolution.[122]

When the State Department was informed of the vote in the Senate Foreign Relations Committee, Hull summoned those who worked on the Spanish situation to his office. Moffat noted that Hull "looked about five years younger and was evidently pleased at having gotten out of one of the tightest corners he has been in with ease and dexterity."[123] Later, Pittman was to see Breckinridge Long about the Spanish controversy and they agreed that nothing could be done in Congress at that time, but possibly some revision of the Neutrality Act could be proposed next year.[124] It was not until the winter of 1938 and the early months of 1939, then, that the Roosevelt administration and the Congress would again witness the extent of the influence of the Catholic-

American community. The issue and the result, however, would remain the same.

The contemplated change in the Neutrality Law of 1937, due to expire in May of 1939, was to call for a repeal of the arms embargo and an extension of cash-and-carry to all belligerent trade.[125] Not desiring publicly to commit his administration to neutrality revision, Roosevelt decided to have Pittman press for neutrality revision in Congress.[126] Pittman announced on January 11, 1939, that the Senate Foreign Relations Committee would begin hearings on neutrality revision at the end of January. Eight days later, however, Pittman surprisingly announced the postponement of those same hearings.[127] The Catholic-American community was again on the move.

The Catholic-American community, which viewed the revision of the Neutrality Law of 1937 as an attempt to permit arms to be shipped to Spain, swarmed on Capitol Hill as Congress opened its doors for business in January. The "Keep the Spanish Embargo Committee" began the Catholic barrage by organizing a meeting in Washington, D.C. on January 9. It consisted of twenty Catholic lay groups representing over four million Catholics, and was led by Louis Kennedy, president of the National Council of Catholic Men and actively supported by the Knights of Columbus. Approximately four thousand people attended the meeting and listened to national figures praise the arms embargo. At the same time, the NCWC had organized a national campaign to flood Washington with petitions favoring the embargo. By January 14, over four hundred thousand cards and letters were on the desks of congressmen and senators. No doubt the Congress understood that such a campaign had the support of the Church hierarchy which controlled the NCWC.[128] As Michael Francis Doyle confirmed for Roosevelt, "bishops throughout the country" were directing their people to sign protests, letters, and petitions, and mail them to the Congress.[129]

Father Charles Coughlin added to the movement to increase the pressure on the Congress. On January 15, Coughlin told his radio audience—estimated at over three million—that hundreds of groups were in Washington pressuring the government to lift the embargo and aid the Spanish Loyalists.[130] Coughlin's impassioned remarks resulted in another mammoth mail delivery to Congress immediately after the broadcast.[131] By February 5, it was estimated that over 1,750,000 signatures supporting the Catholic position had made their way to Capitol Hill.[132]

While Roosevelt, publicly uncommitted, observed the impact that the Catholic opposition exerted on the Congress, he and his administration clearly understood that any change in the Neutrality Law in January would never reach fruition until the Spanish Civil War ended or opposition to the arms embargo subsided. Indicative of the opposition and in response to inquiries made by the NCWC, various congressmen and senators responded by expressing their dedication to the embargo and their promise that they would exert every effort to preserve it. Representative John McCormack of Massachusetts replied that any change in policy now would only aid the communist-dominated Loyalist government; and Senator Pat McCarran answered one NCWC inquiry to the effect that "any attempt to tamper with the embargo would be met by senatorial opposition that would be long remembered."[133] Of greater importance, Pittman advised the administration that a discussion of the Spanish embargo would "stir up a religious controversy in each of the forty-eight States with political results that no one could foresee."[134]

Louis Fischer, the prominent journalist for *The Nation* who lived in and reported from Spain during the war, observed that the Catholic opposition in the United States "terrorized many politicians who in private favor the lifting of the embargo. Last May the Catholics plus the British Embassy prevented the embargo from being lifted . . . the opposition has altered little since May."[135] As in May of 1938, the religious reason—the Catholic-American community— reigned as the foremost cause for inaction on this politically sensitive issue. Moffat was correct when he recorded Pittman's words that the protests from around the country made senators aware of the fact that they were on a "hot spot," and "the sooner they could get off it by avoiding the issue, the happier they would be."[136] Thus, the hearings on the neutrality proposals were terminated by Pittman on January 19, and were it not for the fact that Franco's forces eventually crushed the Madrid government on March 28, the neutrality revisions would probably have met with continued inaction on behalf of the Roosevelt administration and the Congress.

In January, Roosevelt and the State Department agreed with Pittman that since Franco was about to consolidate his victory, the administration would postpone any discussion of neutrality revision until the Spanish question abated.[137] As various sources reported, Catholic-American pressure dictated American foreign policy. Ickes wrote of how "so many high stationed Catholic clergymen [were] ready to pour the vials of their wrath upon the Loyalist cause whenever the Spanish issue [was] raised."[138] Ambassador Bowers, who was quickly relieved of his post on March 1, 1939, so that the Roosevelt administration could recognize the Franco government on April 1, 1939, explained that the attitude of the Catholic hierarchy in the United States was "bitterly resented" in Spain and that their methods of influencing the American government had caused great harm to the Catholic Church.[139] Moffat confirmed the fact that in the discussions between Roosevelt, Hull, and Pittman to drop the neutrality revision hearings, the domestic political picture played a large role. Hull concluded that it would be "a mistake to risk the transfer of the venom existing between Catholics and Left Wingers on the embargo to the broader subject of revising our neutrality legislation."[140]

So, one must agree with the conclusion of Ickes who wrote that after three years of the Spanish Civil War, "it is fear of the Catholic sentiment in this country which has prevented the lifting of the embargo which might have saved the Spanish situation months ago, or even more recently."[141] Years later, Vice President Henry Wallace also recorded in his diary a conversation with Paul Appleby, his publicity man and confidant, about the arms embargo controversy during the Spanish Civil War. Appleby said that when the American people eventually find out "what the Catholic Church has been up to in international politics there will be a very strong anti-Catholic feeling sweep across the country." Neither man had any strong prejudices against Catholics, but both felt that the Roosevelt administration would be in great jeopardy if the truth ever came out.[142] If Roosevelt had kept a diary, he too might have recorded such sentiments.

II

Italian-Americans

The real reason why the Pittman-McReynolds' neutrality bill was abandoned . . . was not emphasized in the press at the time. I was in very close touch with the House Committee on Foreign Affairs during the consideration of the bill and I attended most, if not all, of the meetings at which the Committee considered it. The reason why the bill was abandoned was perfectly clear to me. It was simply and solely that the organized opposition of groups of Italian-Americans, who sent their spokesmen day after day to speak before the Committee and to make the rounds of the offices of members of Congress, was so strong that practically no member of Congress who had any considerable number of Italian-Americans in his district dared to proceed with the bill. This opposition was, of course, founded on the belief that the bill if passed would operate to the disadvantage of Italy in the Italo-Ethiopian war. In my opinion, this reason for the abandonment of the bill not only predominated, it was the only efficient cause of the abandonment. This was the best example I have ever witnessed of the power of an organized minority to influence important legislation.

Joseph C. Green to Carleton Savage,
July 27, 1944

4

The Italo-Ethiopian War

During the Spanish Civil War, Roosevelt had no trouble from the Italian-American sector even though Mussolini maneuvered troops and munitions on Franco's behalf throughout Spain. At that time Italians in America donned their other hat as Catholics. And in addition, America's neutrality posture offered no conflict of interest to them in their relationship to and love of the old country. But, in the fall of 1935 when Mussolini invaded Ethiopia to avenge Italy's humiliation of 1896 at Adowa, Italo-Americans confronted the Roosevelt administration with a furious backlash as the administration sought to alter its neutrality stance vis-à-vis Italy. When the smoke settled around the White House, the halls of Congress, and the offices at the State Department, the American government realized that it was the Italian-American community—represented by various groups of influential leaders—who helped to alter the foreign policy of the United States government during the Italo-Ethiopian War.

On October 3, 1935, word was received in the United States from Rome that Mussolini had begun the penetration of Ethiopia. Roosevelt immediately invoked the Neutrality Act of 1935 and announced an arms embargo on both belligerents. Although the embargo reflected the isolationist attitude prevalent in Congress, it was far from actually providing equal treatment. Since Italy had produced a stockpile of arms and munitions, the embargo did not affect her; but Ethiopia—devoid of adequate war material—was forever doomed from future acquisitions.[1] More importantly, the arms embargo did not apply to American trade and exports of raw materials to Italy, particularly oil and iron ore. America's neutrality policy was, for all intents and purposes, not neutral, and Italy seemed to have garnered an ally from across the Atlantic while the League of Nations, which had labeled Italy an aggressor and had levied economic sanctions, fumed over America's unwillingness to cooperate wholeheartedly.[2]

In order to counteract any unfair advantage that Italy acquired as a result of the application of the Neutrality Act, Roosevelt and Hull decided to announce—over and above the Neutrality Law—a moral embargo, urging Americans to cease and desist from trading with either nation or from traveling on belligerent ships. Reflecting American public opinion that Italy's action was an unwarranted aggression, Roosevelt hoped that the moral embargo would curtail Italy's aggressiveness and contribute to an early settlement of the dispute.[3] Since the administration had no legal right to embargo raw materials to belligerents, the moral embargo appeared to offer the best solution. Moreover, even some die-hard isolationists who opposed presidential discretion in the implementation of American foreign policy, supported the moral embargo.[4]

The philosophy of Roosevelt and his Secretary of State toward American neutrality and its implementation were clearly revealed during this period. Neutrality meant the absence of American military involvement and presence in world affairs. However, their neutrality stance demanded that the United States not sit idly by and observe a growing conflict, but pursue an interventionist and, to a degree, an internationalist posture. The hope was that, by exercising such power and influence through this posture, the incidents that could cause United States involvement in a foreign conflict would be eliminated.[5]

Roosevelt concurred with Hull's concept that America's neutrality legislation should not restrict the President from using it as a foreign policy tool; that is, Roosevelt believed that wide discretionary powers should be granted to and exercised by the President, as in the case of the moral embargo. For example, although Roosevelt was referring to the possibility of a European War—not the Italo-Ethiopian War—and the probability of the United States entering into an economic boycott of various countries, this entry in the diary of Robert W. Bingham, American Ambassador to Great Britain, clearly indicates Roosevelt's concept of American neutrality. According to Bingham, Roosevelt believed that he had the power "to bring our country into such economic boycott by Presidential proclamation without having to secure the approval of Congress." Bingham regarded this view of utmost significance and importance, and when he asked if he could make this statement to the British authorities, Roosevelt told him by all means to do so. The fact that Roosevelt claimed he had this power, Bingham concluded, and that he was "willing to exercise it, and that I can give a direct assurance to this effect, may actually be the means of preventing war in Europe."[6]

Hull also believed that the President should not be handicapped by neutrality legislation, but should have wide discretion in determining what goods and raw materials are or are not articles of war.[7] In reference to the Italo-Ethiopian situation, Roosevelt and Hull—as they revealed at a Cabinet meeting in September of 1935—wanted to classify certain raw materials as articles of war and prohibit their shipment to Italy.[8] To Hull, importing cotton for explosives, steel for military equipment, and oil for the army, was more important to a country like Italy which could manufacture its own munitions than to import foreign armaments.[9] For all intents and purposes, then, the Roosevelt administration—by invoking the moral embargo—was asking the American people to stop doing business with Italy.

According to the 1930 census, Italian-Americans had become the largest single foreign-born group in the United States and while they were not high on the social and economic ladder, they were nevertheless exercising significant political influence. In the case of the New York City mayoral campaign of 1933, Fiorello La Guardia used his Italian heritage to acquire approximately 90 percent of the Italian vote.[10] Over one million Italian-Americans lived in New York City, more than any other ethnic group, and in the United States approximately five million Americans of Italian descent had either been born in Italy or had at least one Italian-born parent. Overall, 12 percent of all foreign Caucasians were of Italian descent.[11] With the advent of the Italo-Ethiopian War during the summer and fall of 1935, Italian-Americans reacted favorably and with loyalty toward their mother country and the exploits of Mussolini, and also became a problem for the Roosevelt administration.

Initially the Italian-American community had no problem accepting the Neutrality Act of 1935. However, when it became obvious that Roosevelt objected to Mussolini's African adventure and announced the moral embargo, Italo-Americans countered with "maximum pressure."[12] Roosevelt actually became aware of the growing tide of opposition forming in the Italian-American community prior to the establishment of the moral embargo on October 5th.

It was during the summer of 1935 that tension mounted over the Ethiopian crisis. Since Black-Americans identified closely with the plight of Ethiopia, they and Italian-Americans clashed on several occasions in New York City. Street brawls erupted and Mayor La Guardia had to assign 1,200 extra police to patrol Italian neighborhoods where Blacks smashed windows in Italian stores.[13] If Black-American hostility toward Italy was not enough, the Roosevelt administration also had to deal with the Italian population.[14] Italy's consular officials and Italo-American social and cultural centers began to publicize widely the exploits of Mussolini. Propaganda from Italy also poured into the United States and excited the latent patriotism and nationalism of the Italian immigrant.[15] The State Department observed that "unquestionably any anti-Italian action based on alleged American sympathies for the Abyssinians would provoke strong reaction from American-Italians who are following developments with 'fervid patriotism.'"[16]

In addition, various Italian-American groups, clubs, and associations began to urge Roosevelt to adopt a favorable attitude toward Italy. The

President of the Italian-American Federation of Societies and Clubs, John De Pastine—on behalf of American citizens of Italian extraction—made known to Hull his resentment that the United States would support Britain in its efforts to enforce League of Nations sanctions against Italy.[17] Likewise, a similar message from the Italo-American Employers and Workers Association of New York professed that they were desirous of having the United States adopt a more sympathetic attitude toward Italy.[18] Thousands of Italian-Americans revealed that they shared these views by attending numerous rallies in New York, Chicago, Philadelphia, and Boston, at which they pledged money, gold, and other personal valuables for Italy's war effort.[19]

After the proclamation of the moral embargo, Italian-Americans quickly realized that the moral embargo was actually an attempt by the Roosevelt administration to intervene in the Italo-Ethiopian War by curtailing only Italian trade. Generoso Pope, publisher of *Il Progresso Italo-Americano*—the foremost Italian daily in the United States—gave Roosevelt's pronouncements on the moral embargo front page coverage, reporting that the embargo on trade would be disastrous for New York and American commerce.[20] The Italian ambassador to the United States, Augusto Rosso, similarly claimed that the United States was going to cripple Italy's efforts in Ethiopia and was not, by any stretch of the imagination, exercising a policy of neutrality.[21] And typical of the responses arriving at the State Department was the message from the Italian Chamber of Commerce of Chicago, purporting to represent the sentiments of over three hundred thousand Italian-Americans "in and around Chicago." Enforcing sanctions, they reasoned, was obviously taking sides; it was following the policy of the League of Nations—even though the United States was not a member—and would ruin legitimate trade between Italy and the United States for all Americans.[22] Roosevelt and Hull, nevertheless, held to the moral embargo.

As a matter of fact, Roosevelt publicly warned the American people on October 30, as did Hull, against profiteering during the war. *The New York Times* reported that this strongly worded statement was "tantamount to declaring for the cessation of all American trade with Italy." Roosevelt wanted American businessmen to know, the *Times* contested, that "the warning was no idle gesture," and that he might enforce the embargo if the war was prolonged by the desire of a few Americans for increased profits. Concurring with the President, Hull reiterated Roosevelt's statement of October 5 by emphasizing to the American people not to trade with either side. Hull hoped that an early peace would restore "normal business and normal business profits."[23] Although both men were intent on discouraging all trade with Italy, they did not admit at a press conference the following day whether they meant all trade or just abnormal trade, or what measures the government would take if the American people violated the moral embargo.[24]

Despite efforts by Roosevelt to affect the course of the war, oil sales from the United States increased and American firms continued to do business with Italy. In addition, the United States Treasury reported to Roosevelt that the Italian Embassy, collaborating with various companies in the United States, was beginning to export goods to Italy.[25] On November 15 the administration acted again. Wishing to avoid any tie to League sanctions against Italy and yet reassure them, Hull warned that the shipping of exports of oil, copper, trucks, tractors, scrap iron, and scrap steel—"this class of trade"—was definitely contrary to American policy. In this statement, Hull did not differentiate between normal or abnormal amounts of exports. It would not be until after the uproar from the Italian-American community following this statement that the administration would modify its position on November 26, stressing that "this class of trade" was not prohibited, only abnormal amounts of the same.

Italian-Americans immediately took to political action as never before. Prior to Hull's statement of November 15, correspondence with the Roosevelt administration generally favored American policy, but as one student of this period noted, those letters "received after mid-November ran five-to-four in opposition, and 90 per cent of the majority were from Italian-Americans." Generoso Pope had organized the campaign to flood Washington with over one million letters.[27] Indicative of the attitude among Italian-Americans who wrote the administration were the remarks of the editor and publisher of the San Francisco *Daily L'Italia,* Ettore Patrizi. He urged Washington to avoid the views of the League of Nations, particularly concerning an oil embargo. He argued that the League just wanted to draw the United States into the war and hinder American trade and friendship with Italy.[28] The portent of the future was reflected by an anonymous letter from "Italians," claiming that if the administration banned oil shipments to Italy, neither Roosevelt nor the Democratic Party would "get an Italian vote next year, and there are millions of Italian votes in the U.S."[29] And on November 22, the Italian ambassador again made known his opposition to the moral embargo and the unfriendliness of this position toward Italy.[30]

During this period Roosevelt still insisted on taking appropriate action to hinder trade with Italy. At one point, when Roosevelt learned of Standard Oil of California and of New York possibly establishing the Standard Oil Company of Switzerland, he instructed Hull that "if it is for the facilitating of exports of oil from this country to Italy, I strongly recommend that you tell the story to the Press."[31] Similarly, when the *U.S.S. Ulysses,* a privately owned oil tanker contracted to deliver oil from the United States to Italy, was about to begin its voyage, Roosevelt intervened and stopped the ship from sailing. He even wanted to go so far as to threaten to publish a black list of persons trading with Italy, but the State Department intervened and prevented such a public disclosure.[32] By the end of November, the State Department realized that another public statement was necessary, and Roosevelt—finally sensing the scope of the opposition at home—eventually agreed.

Assistant Secretary of State R. Walton Moore, concerned about the approaching election year, corroborated the fact that in November the administration was proceeding very cautiously over the Italo-Ethiopian conflict, hoping to avoid any mistake in foreign policy that could be used as an election issue.[33] Joseph Green, in the Division of European Affairs, an associate of Moore and one of the Department's officials who attempted to steer the administration's neutrality bill of 1936 through Congress, could not have stated it better. He wrote that politics had invaded the State Department. Questions like how the administration would be affected, or what would be the impact on the party or the campaign were constantly posed and discussed at great length, particularly by Hull and Moore.[34] But it was Dr. Edwin M. Borchard—Professor of International Law at Yale University and an expert on American neutrality policy—who at a meeting of the Senate Foreign Relations Committee actually summarized the correct attitude at the State Department; the administration had to modify its policy and stress the distinction between normal and abnormal trade in order to appease the Italian-American community and soften their objections. He observed that, until mid-November, no emphatic distinction was made between normal and abnormal trade. A close examination of the press at that time verifies this view. To Borchard it seemed a rather "sudden inspiration" on behalf of the administration to stress this position on November 26.[35] Consequently, on November 26, Hull met the press and although he reiterated the intent of the moral embargo and America's neutrality policy, he also stated with emphasis that American policy did not prevent normal trade with the belligerents, only abnormal exports of certain war commodities.[36]

Roosevelt had in fact backed down from his attempt to wield a big stick over American foreign policy. Breckinridge Long, America's ambassador to Italy, was "much relieved" with the modification, noting in his diary that the "American Government now is not to embargo shipments to Italy but to limit shipments to the same amount as in recent normal times."[37] At home, Roosevelt emphasized that his hands were tied by the neutrality law—he had no discretionary power to embargo various raw materials—and normal trade to Italy was permissible. He even withdrew his previous objection to the sailing of the oil-laden *U.S.S. Ulysses,* and the cargo made its way to Italy. Roosevelt publicly professed that his decisions were based on his desire to avoid war in Europe and the constraints of the neutrality law, and no doubt this was true. But privately his actions conformed to the warning of caution by the State Department; that domestic opposition, led by the Italian-American community, had to be his foremost concern. Thus, with the Congress about to convene in January, Roosevelt planned to untie his hands and propose that the

Congress change the neutrality act to read that the President could exercise discretionary power over the export of war materials. However, the Congress was receptive to the Italian-American community, and their influence and pressure would help defeat and alter the intent of the proposed Neutrality Act of 1936.

Congress had only January and February of 1936 to formulate a new neutrality policy, for the Neutrality Act of 1935 terminated on February 29. At the outset, Roosevelt made known his desire for wide discretionary power and his wish to be able to determine what constituted normal quantities of commerce. When Congress convened, the President exhibited his hostility to the Italian adventure in Ethiopia and his program to counter it.[38] Roosevelt spoke to Congress on January 3, and, after denouncing Italy, he asked Congress to continue the arms embargo and to give him the power to decide what commodities should be denied to a belligerent who was prolonging or maintaining war.[39]

The administration's bill in its final form was drafted in conferences between the President, Pittman, Judge McReynolds (Chairman of the House Foreign Affairs Committee), Secretary Hull, and Moore. Joseph Green of the Division of European Affairs, who worked closely with Hull and Moore on the neutrality legislation, provides perhaps the best and most informative description of events and motives involved in these deliberations. His letters to Jay Pierrepont Moffat, at the American embassy in Australia and former head of the Division of European Affairs at the State Department, give a clear and objective view of the attitudes of Roosevelt, the State Department, and the extent of the influence of Italian-Americans on this legislation.

By proposing the items mentioned by Roosevelt, the administration actively spawned a compromise. Appealing to the isolationist desire of Congress to avoid foreign entanglements, an extension of the arms embargo and a ban on credits to belligerents was advanced. To adhere to Roosevelt's concept of using neutrality legislation to influence foreign policy, the clause granting discretionary power to embargo "certain articles or materials used in the manufacture of arms, ammunition, or implements of war, or in the conduct of war" was likewise inserted.[40] The primary consideration by the administration, regarding the content of this neutrality bill, was to avoid a fight during an election year between the administration and the isolationists in the Senate. As Green observed, the direction of American foreign policy and the welfare of the country were "subordinated to considerations of domestic politics."[41]

And, for all intents and purposes, it seemed as though the administration had succeeded in writing an acceptable bill. The prominent isolationist, Senator Nye, telephoned Green to "express his delight" with the bill; Pittman had worked on it and was to introduce the bill to his committee (no bill could be navigated through the Senate without his endorsement); and it appeared to be a sure thing to go through the House "without difficulty."[42]

Upon hearing the President's speech on January 3, 1936, Italian-Americans began to organize and embark on a two-month program of pressure politics in order to change the President's proposed bill. Italian-Americans considered the speech an insult and began to flood the White House and Congress with letters.[43] Within ten days, over twenty-five hundred letters from Italian-Americans made their way to the State Department.[44] Typical letters protested American ties to League policies or approval of the new neutrality bill, which to the Italian-American community sought to embargo oil and other essential merchandise necessary to maintain life and normal business ties with Italy.[45] However, it was primarily Section 4 of the Pittman-McReynolds bill—the proposed neutrality bill of 1936—that incurred the wrath of Italian-Americans. This section granted the President the discretionary power to embargo commodities, other than arms, ammunition and implements of war which he desired, and in effect permitted Roosevelt to exercise enormous control of all American commerce as he saw fit in any foreign conflict. As a student of this period discovered, over "90 percent of the opposition correspondence composed of form letters [came] from Italian-Americans."[46]

The letter and telegram campaign, as well as those who lobbied against the bill in Washington, emanated from numerous Italian-American groups which represented millions of Italian-Americans. One of the most important groups, the Friends of Italy, organized chain letters. The League for American Neutrality, whose "general committee consisted of more than 100 persons [with] nearly all of them bearing names of Italian origin," came into existence to influence Congress on the neutrality bill and could depend on the support of 150,000 Italian-American citizens of Massachusetts.[47] In addition, the Italian Union of America was comprised of over four hundred societies, claiming a total membership of 400,000, and, in April of 1936, this organization reported that it had held over one hundred conferences, arranged seventy-five radio addresses, sponsored one hundred and fifty articles, and distributed more than three hundred thousand pamphlets on the neutrality issue. The Order of the Sons of Italy, with a membership of over 300,000, was one of the Italian-American groups that testified before the House Foreign Affairs Committee.[48]

In Boston in January of 1936, the League For American Neutrality sponsored a meeting in Faneuil Hall. In a highly political speech, Governor Curley praised Mussolini, calling him "a lover of peace and savior of Christianity."[49] Salvatore A. Cotillo, a justice of the New York Supreme Court, put pressure on congressmen and sent a brief to every member of House and Senate which maintained that it would be un-American to grant the President discretionary powers.[50] In the Senate, Senator Borah received a typical letter that summarized Italian-American sentiment. Any attempt to hinder American trade to Italy, the writer said, must be viewed as an unfriendly act against Italy, far from reflecting a position of neutrality.[51] Even Pittman became the subject of hostility by Italian-Americans when a constituent informed him that his derogatory comments toward Italy in a recent speech were sent to every prominent Italian-American Democratic leader throughout the United States.[52]

The State Department was well aware that the pressure being exerted on the Senate by Italian-American communities throughout the United States was having some effect, the protests holding that the neutrality legislation should not apply to the Italo-Ethiopian conflict.[53] Congressmen and senators, especially from northern districts, reflected the effect of that pressure. Democrat Peter A. Cavicchia, an Italian-American congressman from Newark, New Jersey, believed that Roosevelt, armed with the discretionary power proposed by the new neutrality bill, would obviously help Britain, not Italy. Cavicchia wanted to supply Italy with whatever she needed except guns and ammunition.[54] Congressman George H. Tinkham of Massachusetts, which had a substantial Italian population, said he disliked Mussolini as much as anyone, but believed that the United States should be friendly toward Italians until they showed hostility toward America.[55]

Even though they detested what Italian-Americans were doing in Congress, several congressmen revealed the scope of the Italian-American operation. Representative Maury Maverick of Texas, on the floor of the House, said that he deplored the "powerful representations of the Italo-American groups who have protested the enactment of any bill. . . . Many of these who claim to lead millions of Italians, some of them who claim to control 'one, two, three, four or five million votes,' others who speak before congressional committees, with the obvious desire to put pressure on Congress asking preferential treatment for Italy, are doing themselves, their own people and the cause of peace a disservice."[56]

While Maverick believed that the Italo-American pressure on the Congress did not come from the majority of Americans of Italian descent, but from their leaders, Vito Marcantonio, the Italian-American congressman from New York City, disagreed. Marcantonio informed Roosevelt and the House that Italian-Americans were "not requesting special consideration. They are interested only in the welfare of the United States of America." He went on to say that Italian-Americans only want America's neutrality policy to be determined by the Congress, not the President.[57] Congressman Healey from Massachusetts agreed and stated that thousands of Italian-Americans from his area of the country were looking toward Congress for leadership.[58]

At the hearings on the neutrality bill in the Senate Foreign Relations Committee, Italian-American pressure was evident and of paramount importance. Senator Thomas Connolly from Texas noted that Italian-Americans were conducting meetings and "raising a great deal of fuss" about the fact that the United States might join in the application of sanctions against Italy.[59] Testifying at the Senate Foreign Relations Committee hearings on the neutrality bill in early 1936, Dr. Edwin Borchard seconded Connolly's observations and pointed out that Italian-American pressure was infiltrating the Congress primarily because of the administration's decisions in October and November to depart from real neutrality. By attempting to embargo certain war materials that obviously would damage Italy more than Ethiopia, the administration invited retaliation from the Italian-American community on the one hand and from groups who approved administration policy on the other.[60] With the onslaught on Capitol Hill by Italian-American groups opposed to this neutrality bill, Borchard warned that the result might just be that no legislation would be passed to meet situations similar to the Italo-Ethiopian War which involved American interests.[61] The Roosevelt administration, however, adhered to no such prophesy of doom. At least, not yet.

Roosevelt was beginning to sense the pressure of Italian-Americans when he received a memo from a member of the House Foreign Affairs Committee. Some Democrats on the House Foreign Affairs Committee were wavering. Amendments to the neutrality bill were being offered which eliminated the section granting the President discretionary power, and, because their districts contained "heavy foreign populations [Italian-Americans]," they were contemplating—though not deliberately—a change in their vote.[62] Roosevelt immediately contacted Hull and told him to "straighten the matter out."[63]

Likewise, Assistant Secretary of State Moore informed Roosevelt that significant opposition had developed toward the neutrality bill "by the hyphenated Italians in this country, which evidently disturbs some members of the Senate and House."[64] Moore believed that the Italian opposition was designed and directed by the Italian embassy, and, for all intents and purposes, the Italian embassy's final report for 1936 verified Moore's contention. The report cited the work of the Italian-Americans who opposed the administration's neutrality bill and the effort promulgated by the Italian diplomatic and consular staffs. The staffs used newspapers, movies, mass meetings, radio and direct pressure on members of Congress—those of Italian origin and those who had large Italian constituencies—to invoke sympathy to their cause.[65]

Evidently, Italian-American pressure was significant enough for Moore to have recommended that, through covert measures, Black-Americans could be recruited to counteract the efforts of the Italo-American community. According to a prominent student of this period, "nothing came of the idea." In fact, Black-American groups engaged in no activity on this matter whatsoever.[66] As previously noted, Black-Americans did clash with Italian-Americans during the summer of 1935 over the Ethiopian conflict, and apparently the administration saw an opportunity to re-ignite that hostility in the attempt to secure the passage of their bill. However, as evidence will show, Roosevelt wished to avoid domestic and ethnic divisions during this election year, and, from all indications, vetoed such a plan.

Possibly one of the most significant factors in the Italian-American endeavor to change the neutrality bill, which would later cause Roosevelt to drop the controversial section on discretionary power to implement sanctions, was the activity and influence of Generoso Pope. Pope, proprietor and editor of *Il Progresso Italo-Americano* of New York, was reputed to be one of the wealthiest and most influential Italian-Americans in the country. He was also chairman of the Italian Division of the Democratic National Committee, and, in occupying these roles, he made it plain to Roosevelt that his newspaper would "spare no effort" to give its readers all the information Roosevelt desired.[67] They were friends and Roosevelt knew of Pope's well-known influence among Italian-Americans. Pope was the most prominent leader of the Italian-American community opposing the administration's neutrality bill and prior actions taken under the moral embargo. In this regard, he was in Washington lobbying against the bill. Because of Pope's activity the White House, the State Department, and the Congress were flooded with communications from Italian-Americans, and, according to Hull, they all urged the passage of an amendment to either exempt Italy as a belligerent if the bill passed or eliminate the section establishing presidential discretion over trading items.[68]

On January 30, 1936, Roosevelt consented to an interview with Pope, and they "talked cordially for about an hour almost entirely on the subject of American neutrality."[69] Pope corroborated what Roosevelt and the State Department already knew, that Italian-American pressure on Congress would have a marked impact and, from all indications at that time, would cause the defeat of the neutrality bill. Pope added to the President's apprehension over the possibility of the bill's passage by making Roosevelt aware of the views of other members of Congress who agreed with Italian-American opposition to the bill and who urged an extension of the present neutrality law to May of 1937. Pope told him of the desire of Congressman Sirovich to extend the present neutrality law and exclude an embargo on war commodities. McCormack opposed all restrictions on trade and believed Italy should be sold anything she wanted. In addition, several senators revealed that they would never support sanctions or curtail trade with Italy. Even the Speaker of the House saw no need for a new law and confided to Pope that, if the neutrality bill in its present form was presented, it would not be approved.[70]

At their interview at the White House on January 30, Roosevelt told Pope that he (Roosevelt) disapproved of the Pittman-McReynolds Bill—his own neutrality bill![71] The President said that the United States desired to be neutral, and he wanted Pope to "tell the Italians that our neutrality will never imply a discrimination against Italy in favor of other nations . . . Italy may continue her trade as in the past, she may buy what she wants, except for commodities defined as contraband of war." In other words, the President said that Italy could buy all the materials it desired from the United States at normal levels, as long as the United States would not be drawn into the war. When Pope suggested, then, that the neutrality bill be dropped and that "a year's extension of the present law, which has effectively protected American peace," be substituted instead, "Roosevelt replied: 'Perhaps that would be a good solution.'"[72] Roosevelt adopted the Italian-American position on his own neutrality bill and, of course, knew Pope would make the President's views known to Italian-Americans, which he did.

After his interview with Roosevelt, Pope—accompanied by Sirovich— went over to the State Department to meet with Hull. In the interview with Pope, Hull "expressed enthusiastic admiration for Italy, which he had visited many times. He pointed out that when Selassie granted big concessions to the subsidiaries of the Standard Oil, he had forced the concessionaires to give these up, winning for himself the resentment of the Ethiopians." Hull was trying to defend America's neutrality posture and even went so far as to say that he hoped for an increase in trade between Italy and the United States. Surprisingly, Hull agreed that an extension of the present neutrality law was highly feasible and ended the interview by praising the Italian people.[73]

As Pope and a host of newspapermen and photographers came out of Hull's office, Green and Moore rushed in. They asked Hull if he knew who Pope was and if he was aware of the fact that what he told Pope would certainly appear in print in the following day's papers. Hull was "manifestly worried." In fact, when Long telegraphed Hull from Rome on January 31, reproducing the interviews printed in the Italian papers quoting Roosevelt and Hull verbatim and citing their condemnation of the Pittman-McReynolds neutrality bill, Hull was "horrified." Green immediately obtained copies of *Il Progresso* and made translations.[74]

According to Green, Hull ordered that nothing would be done unless the interviews appeared in English in the American press. However, to be on the safe side, Hull had Green and other members of his staff compose repudiations of both interviews in case they were reproduced from *Il Progresso*.[75] After a long session with Hull, in which several changes were made, the final draft of the repudiation of the interviews read:

> Generoso Pope, accompanying a member of Congress, called at the White House and at the Department on January 30. He was received by the President and by me and both of us chatted with him on the subject of neutrality policy in which he is particularly interested. My statement was confined solely to an explanation of the Pittman-McReynolds bill. Neither

the President nor I had any idea that we were being interviewed nor did either of us authorize the publication of what we said to him, save a few sentences the Congressman wrote down in my presence. He has nevertheless published prominently in his paper IL PROGRESSO ITALIANO-AMERICANO accounts of his conversations with the President and with me. His reports of these alleged interviews are so inaccurate and so filled with misrepresentations of what was said that I shall not attempt to discuss them in detail. I have prepared a statement to the press disavowing the alleged interviews in toto, and stating that any published versions of our remarks on pending neutrality legislation which are not confined strictly to an explanation and support of the Pittman-McReynolds Bill are absolutely inaccurate.[76]

Roosevelt was then apprised of the statements and authorized their use if necessary. And if it became necessary to repudiate the interviews, Hull explained to Green, "the Democrats would probably lose most of the Italian-American vote in the forthcoming elections."[77] Fortunately for the Roosevelt administration, nothing materialized. Believing that the neutrality bill could still succeed in Congress in spite of Italo-American pressure and that overall American public opinion opposed Italy's war in Ethiopia, Roosevelt and Hull wanted to have the repudiation ready to counteract any adverse publicity. However, almost simultaneously, Roosevelt was to learn from the sponsors of his bill in Congress that Italian-American pressure had all but insured the defeat of the neutrality bill.[78]

Although there has been much speculation, the real reason for the defeat and abandonment of the administration's neutrality bill was based largely on the organized opposition provided by groups of Italian-Americans. From the opening day of Congress in January, Italian-American organizations had their members across the country send five letters each to Washington, directing them to the President, the Secretary of State, their two senators, and their congressman. Green noted that he alone handled at the State Department over ten thousand letters during the month of January. In addition, spokesmen for the Italian-American community descended day after day to lobby members of Congress and speak before the foreign affairs committees.[79] Because of the efforts of these groups, over 41 pages out of 254 pages of House hearings testimony were devoted to Italian-American witnesses.[80] In fact, one student of this period concluded that the Rules Committee in the House actually held up the consideration of the neutrality bill because it was "swayed by intense Italian-American pressure."[81]

Green was in a unique position to observe the onslaught by America's Italian community. From the outset, Hull, Moore, and Green in various combinations went up to Capitol Hill every day for three weeks to attend the hearings in the House and Senate foreign affairs committee rooms. It was Green who attended most, "if not all," of the meetings of the House committee, when the Italians were stressing that if the bill passed it would hinder the Italian effort in the Italo-Ethiopian War.[82] Green noted, as a witness to the fierce lobbying by Italian-Americans in the Senate and House office buildings, that senators and particularly congressmen—hailing from Massachusetts, Rhode Island, New York, Connecticut, New Jersey, Pennsylvania, Maryland, West Virginia, Ohio, Michigan and California—literally "trembled openly in their boots." Representatives who faced election in November spoke plainly to Green that they dared not consider or vote for the neutrality bill. No representative with a large Italian-American population in his district would proceed with the bill, as indicated by one congressman from Connecticut who told Green that he would not vote for the bill because of the fact that he had "40,000 Italians in his district."[83]

The moment of truth for Roosevelt came on February 7. Pittman and McReynolds went to the White House and told Roosevelt not to proceed with the bill. They had supported the administration's bill for as long as they could, but now the pressure from the Italian-American community made it necessary to scrap it. Pittman seemed "glad to have an excuse to get rid of it." A conference was then held among Roosevelt, Hull, Moore, Pittman, and McReynolds. The bill was abandoned, and a new bill was drafted. Roosevelt and Hull now knew that the repudiation of their interviews with Pope would not be necessary.[84]

Several days later at a Cabinet meeting, Roosevelt informed his advisors that he could not get from Congress the wide discretionary power he wanted, and therefore was dropping the controversial Section 4. The new bill just proposed an extension of the Neutrality Act of 1935 to May 1, 1937, coinciding exactly with the demands of the Italian-American community and leaving debate on a more far-reaching bill until after the November elections.[85]

Italian-Americans presented the Roosevelt administration with perhaps the best example of organized political pressure by an ethnic minority during his entire tenure in the White House. It was obvious to Green that the administration's neutrality bill would have passed "had it not been for the highly organized and highly effective opposition of the Italian-Americans."[86] To Green, the Italian-American effort to influence this important foreign policy legislation was the best he had ever witnessed.[87] Likewise, Moore noted that it was regrettable how Americans of Italian descent would desire to have the United States government give aid and support to one belligerent at the expense of another. He ended his memo on what to him was undoubtedly an ominous note, asking whether the time had come "when Congress is to yield to the pressure of minority groups and disregard the opinion of the great majority of our citizens whose sole desire in this case is that there may be legislation that will give some approximate assurance against our country being involved in any bloody conflict that may occur and of whatever extent."[88]

Upon his return to New York City from his lobbying efforts in Washington, rejoicing in the similarity between the new neutrality bill and the proposals espoused through Italian-American activity, Generoso Pope conferred with his readers. On February 20, 1936, referring to the defeat of the administration's neutrality bill, he proclaimed in *Il Progresso* that it was "perhaps the first time that a movement of our community has assumed such political importance and has received such prompt and equitable satisfaction. And it is a precedent we must not forget."[89] Neither would Roosevelt.

III

Jewish-Americans

I expressed to the President at once . . . the deep appreciation of all of us at what he and Secretary Hull had done in the matter of intervention re Palestine. His face lighted up. . . . I told him that my joy was shared by Justice Brandeis, Felix and Judge Mack, but he interrupted me to say, 'Grand man! You know, Stephen, we and the Inner Circle call him Isaiah.' Then, with the deepest interest in what he was discussing, he told that he had had word from Neville Chamberlain. 'I have had word from Neville Chamberlain (who will be the Prime Minister in succession to Baldwin) to the effect: We have given up the idea of suspension because of your (the American) interest.'

Memorandum of conversation between FDR
and Rabbi Stephen S. Wise, October 5, 1936

5

Palestine's Open Door, 1936

In 1936, while Italian-Americans were proudly associating with Italian exploits in Europe, Jews in America shuddered at the exploitation of their kinsmen at the hands of the Nazis. To motivate Roosevelt to intervene on their behalf, Jewish-Americans pressured him continuously throughout his four administrations, urging him to adopt a foreign policy that sought to rescue Jews trapped in Nazi Europe and that envisioned the conversion of Palestine into a Jewish State. However, the Jewish community was split. Zionists opposed anti-Zionists; Jews who wanted European Jews rescued and brought to the United States were aligned against those who desired rescue but limited access to asylum in America. Roosevelt nevertheless attempted to satisfy all factions, implementing policies when possible, placating and appeasing when necessary, and for the most part being helplessly defeated by events and attitudes that even he as President was unable to alter or abolish.

Much of what Roosevelt accomplished for Jews the world over and for Jewish-Americans had to be planned and executed in private. Public statements of policy favorable to Jews was construed by the opposition as evidence of a "Jew-Deal," and from such comments the ugly head of anti-Semitism rose over America as it had over every corner of Europe. Roosevelt sought to avoid this situation. He did not want a divided country during the war, nor a split in the unity of the Democratic Party coalition. Consequently, if a foreign policy demand stemming from the Jewish-American community reached fruition, Roosevelt did not wish it to be made public. He wanted all demands from Jewish-Americans to be made in private, with little if any public agitation. The success of any action or the impossibility of satisfying a demand would then be made known to those Jews who were representative of and most significant in the Jewish-American community, and the results would filter down. To show that Roosevelt earnestly and sincerely struggled to rescue Jews from Nazi-dominated Europe before and during the war, and that he attempted not only to save the Jews in Palestine from extinction but also Palestine itself for a future Jewish homeland, the story must of necessity begin in the election year of 1936, and of course focus on Palestine.[1]

From the time of Britain's Balfour Declaration (1917), designating Palestine as a homeland for the Jews, to the issuance of the British White Paper in May of 1939, severely limiting Jewish immigration to Palestine, Palestine was one of the few places in the world where Jewish escapees from the Nazis were welcome. Jews and Arabs lived side by side in Palestine, and it was Britain—having accepted a League mandate in 1922—which had to maintain the peace. It was not an easy task.

As far as the United States was concerned, the American government had no power under international law or agreement to enforce its will in Palestine. It looked to Britain to maintain order, protect American Jews in the area, and to be the ultimate authority in the region. However, the United States did have approximately five million Jews, and if a President or a political party, particularly the Democrats, wished to maintain Jewish support, the demands of the Jewish community had to be made known to the British. Hopefully, the British, not willing to risk a break in Anglo-American relations, would heed any suggestion by the American government and a favorable outcome to all concerned would emerge. The appeasement of the Arab community was essential for successful operations in World War II and for the survival not only of Palestine as a Jewish homeland, but of Jews already inhabiting the territory. Yet from 1936 to 1945, the British continued to incur the hostility of the Arab bloc.

In April of 1936, the Arab community in Palestine erupted. A general strike in Palestine was put into effect and a series of widespread attacks commenced.[2] At first, these attacks were launched against the British authorities, not against individual Jews and Jewish property.[3] In Jerusalem, at the request of the American government, the British furnished protection for nearly eleven hundred Jewish-Americans quartered in that city. However, by the end of the month the situation intensified.[4]

Telephone and telegraph communications were being severed, an armed attack by Arabs was launched on a British convoy near Haifa, and an ambush was successfully negotiated on several buses transporting Jews in Jerusalem. Two Jews were wounded. In addition, bombings, sniping, arson, and agricultural sabotage escalated. The British countered with reinforcements from Cairo. The most significant aspect of the uprising, which affected the British and American governments, was the Arab demand that Jewish immigration to Palestine cease and that further sale of land to Jews be prohibited.[5]

To ascertain what caused the disturbance in Palestine, the British government announced that a Royal Commission of Inquiry would go to Palestine and make a thorough investigation of the situation and report the facts. Future British policy in Palestine would be based upon their findings. However, what the British government proposed to placate Arab hostility toward Palestine caused an immediate reaction in Jewish-American circles and among the leaders of the American government. The British would only send the commission to Palestine when the Arabs clearly terminated their attacks and ended the general strike. The Arabs, however, refused to cooperate unless the British suspended Jewish immigration into Palestine. In attempting to break the deadlock, the United States learned that the British government was considering to react favorably on the Arab demands, and, once immigration was suspended, it was assumed that the attacks would cease and the Royal Commission would commence its investigation.[6]

When the disturbances began in April of 1936, the Roosevelt administration adopted the view of "watchful waiting." To interfere in this British sphere of influence seemed out of the question. The British were adequately protecting approximately ten thousand American nationals in Palestine, and the administration believed that to dictate a particular course of action from Washington might only result in a British refusal to assume the responsibility for those Americans. In addition, the British had the difficult task of holding two rival populations in Palestine together. If the United States interfered, the situation would only be that much more difficult.[7] Yet, as the administration became "aware of the widespread interest in Jewish circles in this country in the Palestine situation" in May of 1936 and throughout the summer months, great care and attention were given to this problem. In a telegram to the American Consul General in Jerusalem, the State Department impressed upon him the importance of acting quickly with the local officials if any American national was in obvious danger.[8]

Jewish-American interests in foreign policy were transmitted to the White House from various Jewish organizations and groups, but the most influential was a small, cohesive group of men who had the attention of the President. Roosevelt perceived this group to be the key to the attitudes of Jewish-Americans, the most powerful and the most essential to maintain Jewish support and especially the Jewish vote in not only the 1936 election, but throughout his tenure in the White House. Felix Frankfurter, professor of law at Harvard University and a future Roosevelt appointee to the Supreme Court, was a close confidant of the President and had unusual access to the Oval Office. Associate Justice of the Supreme Court Louis D. Brandeis—or the "grand old man" as Roosevelt referred to him—was the inspirational leader in the group. He was highly respected and affectionately known as "Isaiah" of Chatham, his residence in Massachusetts. Samuel I. Rosenman, presidential speech writer and editor of Roosevelt's public papers and addresses, was highly regarded by Roosevelt although not a Zionist as the others, and he had numerous political contacts in New York City, where the vast majority of Jewish-Americans lived. It was primarily through Rosenman that Roosevelt became cognizant of the division of Jewish attitudes toward Palestine and rescue activities. This division would later cause Roosevelt to vacillate between these segments of the Jewish community, attempting to satisfy, as far as possible, their foreign policy demands.

Finally, Rabbi Stephen S. Wise, president of the American Jewish Congress, claimed to represent approximately five million American Jews and was thought by Roosevelt to be the most influential liaison to Jewish political opinion and political organizations in America and Europe. Wise was persona non grata at the White House for most of Roosevelt's first term, although they had been close friends in years gone by. Louis H. Howe, Roosevelt's long time friend and political manager, did not forgive Wise for supporting Al Smith in the 1932 election, but with Howe's influence and health waning and his death expected, a Wise-Roosevelt reconciliation occurred during this international crisis. In fact, Wise was proud of the restoration of friendly relations between himself and Roosevelt and looked forward to the "direct and immediate access" to Roosevelt that he had once before. Moreover, he was certain—as he confided to Chaim Weizmann, president of the World Zionist Organization— that any fair and reasonable plan submitted by the Jewish-American community urging Roosevelt to put pressure on Downing Street regarding events in Palestine would succeed.[9] Wise assumed correctly, for it was through the efforts of Wise and these other leaders, representing the attitudes of Jewish-Americans, that a change occurred in the American government's attitude toward the Palestine situation, and which in turn manifestly influenced the implementation of British foreign policy in Palestine.

Wise first informed Roosevelt in May of 1936 about the concern manifested among Jewish-Americans over the blatant killing of Jews by Arabs in Palestine. Since Roosevelt frequently expressed his concern for the Jewish cause in Palestine, Wise wanted Roosevelt to invite the British ambassador to the White House and get a first-hand report on the situation.[10] Wise emphasized that not only were Jews throughout the world concerned, but especially American Jews. Roosevelt responded by reassuring Wise that the United States will "continue to watch the situation closely and that we shall not fail to take such action as may seem helpful and proper in seeing that American interests in Palestine are adequately protected."[11] However, no immediate intervention by the American government was undertaken with the British government in London. Roosevelt believed that the British were doing all in their power to maintain security and protect American life and property. In addition, he felt that recent British military reinforcements were more than adequate to control the situation.[12] The tension in Palestine continued unabated until July, when Jewish-Americans became horrified at the news that the British were about to suspend Jewish immigration to Palestine in order to appease the Arabs and end the violence.

Various members of "the group" approached the White House and urged action, while Rosenman transmitted an urgent telegram to Roosevelt from Simon Rifkind, Senator Robert Wagner's law partner in New York. Written in London with the assistance of Wise and Frankfurter—they were in England with Chaim Weizmann—the telegram confirmed the fact that the British Cabinet was near a decision to suspend Jewish immigration. Once invoked, they reasoned, suspension could prove difficult to life and might also cause the Jews in Palestine to react violently after years of restraint. These Jewish leaders wanted Roosevelt to pressure London informally and impress upon the British that Anglo-American relations would be injured. Wise and Frankfurter were convinced that Roosevelt would respond sympathetically and that American Jewry would likewise gratefully remember.[13] Rosenman agreed and urged Roosevelt to do all that was possible and proper.[14] Frankfurter and Brandeis— in separate communications—seconded Rosenman's advice. To Wise, no one had a greater influence on Roosevelt than Frankfurter, and in this crisis Frankfurter indeed had the ear of the President.[15]

Upon receipt of these messages from the Jewish-American community, Roosevelt took immediate action. Such action, of course, was carried out privately. No public announcement was to be made so as to avoid anti-Jewish and anti-British elements in the United States from mounting opposition to the president's reelection plans. Roosevelt asked Assistant Secretary of State R. Walton Moore to "look into this" and let him "know the answer" to this situation from an American foreign policy position. It was Roosevelt and Hull, however, who eventually agreed on a course of action. A telegram was quickly drafted to Robert Bingham, American ambassador to Great Britain. It pointed out that influential Jewish groups in the United States and their leaders were pressuring the administration and were upset about the possibility of the suspension of Jewish immigration, fearing that "such suspension may close the only avenue of escape of German and Polish Jews and that it may prove difficult to revoke."[16]

Hull and Roosevelt wanted Bingham to mention this matter personally and unofficially to Anthony Eden, British Foreign Secretary, emphasizing that he was not speaking on behalf of the American government and that in no way was he attempting to interfere with British policy regarding Palestine. However, they told Bingham to stress that "influential Jewish circles in the United States are deeply concerned," and that the British ought to give considerable attention to this fact.[17] No greater pressure was applied at this time, either by involving the name of the President or the administration. Bingham responded and mentioned that he discussed the matter with the proper British officials in a personal way, was thanked for the information, but was given no indication of a possible change in policy.[18] Here the matter rested until mid-August.

While the terrorism in Palestine continued and with the British Royal Commission of Inquiry still in London, a new dimension to the drama began to unfold for the Roosevelt administration. Sponsored by William Randolph Hearst, the newspaper publisher of one of America's largest chain of newspapers and anti-Roosevelt, a contingent of three United States senators, Royal S. Copeland from New York, Warren R. Austin from Vermont, and Daniel O. Hastings from Delaware, set out in mid-August for a two-week visit to investigate the Palestine situation. The American Consul at Jerusalem confirmed to Hull that this trip was financed by Hearst and that he was certain that Hearst initiated it "to appeal to Jewish vote in coming Presidential elections through pro-Jewish propaganda and neutralization [of] former Hearst Nazi-philia."[19]

Contrary to what Hearst had planned, the Roosevelt administration sought to avoid any public announcement stating that the reason for Britain's change in policy, if it eventually were proclaimed, occurred due to American public opinion. A split in Anglo-American relations was not desired. The goal of the Roosevelt administration was to get Britain to suppress the terrorism in Palestine and to continue to allow Jewish refugee immigration, as demanded by Jewish-Americans. Privately, Jews would be made aware of the role played by the administration. Moreover, Roosevelt feared not only a rise of anti-Semitism in the United States from such a public disclosure—thereby affecting the livelihood of Jewish Americans—but also the possibility that the work that the administration had accomplished for Jews would become public knowledge and figure "too prominently" in the presidential election.[20]

Confiding in Wise at Hyde Park, Roosevelt revealed his concern about the increase of anti-Semitism at this time in the United States and pointed out the importance of the Jews "lying low" for a time.[21] Likewise, Hull expressed the administration's interest in avoiding a rupture in Anglo-American relations when he told one of the senators who visited Palestine (Copeland of New York) that the British government might suggest that the United States assume responsibility for the Palestine Mandate if the American government publicly intervened over there. The British had suggested such a proposal once before.[22] So, even when Great Britain finally did change its policy in Palestine by postponing indefinitely the suspension of Jewish immigration and the Hearst papers intimated publicly that "the views of the American Senators who have recently been visiting in Palestine was one of the main reasons," Roosevelt offered no rebuttal.[23] Roosevelt knew, as did the leadership of America's Jews, that the change in British policy was due to the private intervention of the Roosevelt administration influenced by America's Jewish community. And that private intervention began as soon as Rabbi Wise returned to the United States from England late in the summer of 1936.

Upon arriving in New York on August 31, Wise and his colleagues from the Emergency Committee of the Zionist Organization of America went directly to see Jim Farley, National Chairman of the Democratic Party. Farley wanted Wise and other leaders of the Jewish community to campaign for Roosevelt in every major city east of the Mississippi River, and Wise agreed. In exchange for their assistance and in all probability the Jewish vote, Farley knew the price tag and therefore was "very ready and even eager to be of help," according to Wise, in motivating Roosevelt and Hull to influence Britain to resolve the crisis in Palestine. Farley immediately telephoned Hull and arranged for an appointment for Wise early the following day. Wise then asked Farley to send a telegram to Roosevelt, who was in Salt Lake City, urging him to tell Hull to do what Wise wanted regarding Palestine.[24]

In the telegram, Farley told Roosevelt of Wise's appointment with Hull and of the fact that Frankfurter and Brandeis had concurred with the proposals that Wise would make to Hull. Farley concluded that Roosevelt's help was extremely and "immensely important from every point of view."[25]

On September 1, Wise met with Hull in the Secretary's office and noted that Hull was very friendly and more than eager to be of assistance. Hull had spoken earlier to Roosevelt and had a thorough understanding of the Palestine situation. Wise then asked Hull to do two things. First, he wanted Hull to contact Roosevelt and get his permission to call London. And secondly, he desired to have Hull talk directly to Baldwin or Ormsby-Gore and explain how Roosevelt thought regarding the possible suspension of Jewish immigration and why it would be a disaster to the envisioned Jewish National Home which the Balfour Declaration guaranteed. Hull agreed.[26]

Wise proceeded to make it clear to Hull that, "if the Jews chose to bedevil Anglo-American relations, they could do it and do it well and effectively." Wise knew that the Roosevelt administration and London were "deeply concerned about anything that may be done to injure Anglo-American relations," and Hull quickly nodded in agreement.[27] After Wise left the State Department, Hull immediately telephoned Ambassador Bingham in London.

It was at 10:30 on the morning of September 1, 1936, that Hull made his call to London. Cautioning Bingham that the call was very confidential, Hull proceeded to explain the situation. Wise and other Jewish rabbis, he said, had just been in his office and were "exceedingly exercised" about the definite report that the British Cabinet at its meeting on September 2 would probably vote to suspend Jewish immigration into Palestine. Bingham was aware of the implications of such a policy, particularly the fact that Jews from Germany and Poland or any other part of the world would be denied the asylum that only Palestine could provide.[28]

Hull emphasized the point that, if the proposed action on suspension took place, Jewish-American relations could be upset for years and the repercussions from the Jewish community could be disastrous. "They are greatly excited over here," Hull said, "and, as you know, there are three or four million of them. You are also aware of the personal influence of these people who called upon me and their associates." To Hull, it was important that the Jews "over here" were reassured and knew that the administration was doing everything possible to influence the British Cabinet. And with the presidential election coming up, Hull advised Bingham, "this is a very acute period for the next two months on this side."[29]

In his next breath, Hull directed Bingham to intercede with the proper officials of the British government—namely, Baldwin, Eden, and Gore—and appraise them of "our fears." If necessary, Hull concluded, Roosevelt was prepared to telephone the same British officials and reiterate his desires. All of this effort, Hull said, was being initiated because Rabbi Wise had asked the administration to do so. Like an expectant father, Hull awaited Bingham's reply.[30]

Bingham returned the Secretary's call later in the afternoon and told Hull that he would have to see Baldwin and Eden tomorrow before the Cabinet meeting. Baldwin was out of town and Eden was not feeling well. However, he did convey all of Hull's concerns to the British Foreign Office, speaking directly to the Deputy Permanent Under Secretary. They understood completely, Bingham said, and in fact stated that "we have got to consider the same feeling, that same element, on our part here." Although Bingham noted that the Jews in England had not displayed any excitement over the suspension proposal, the Foreign Office nevertheless assured him that the Cabinet would be anxious to consider the wishes of the Roosevelt administration.[31]

Hull then decided to add more fuel to the fire and told Bingham about the activities of William Randolph Hearst. He said that the senators who were sent to Palestine were sent there by Hearst in order to provoke an anti-British situation and a pro-Jewish campaign in the United States. Hull said that the whole group was hostile to the administration and the British Cabinet should know about it. Bingham promised to also "give them that dope before the Cabinet meeting tomorrow."[32]

The conversation ended with Hull confiding in Bingham that he had talked with Roosevelt earlier in the day and that the President was keenly aware of the importance of the suspension situation. Bingham understood, and at the end of the Cabinet meeting on the following day he promised to contact Hull at once.[33]

While Hull waited for the decision from the British Cabinet, he decided to telephone Wise and inform him of the work of Bingham. In addition, Hull wanted Wise to know that he had again talked to Roosevelt and that the President had made further suggestions for Bingham, who "will follow things up and wait for any and every chance to advance our viewpoints. He knows that the President is very greatly concerned."[34] Wise was grateful and immediately informed Weizmann in London of the activities of the Roosevelt administration in their behalf.

Wise made it clear to Weizmann that anything that he would tell him could be used only in the most discreet manner. Wise stated that "both the president and the secretary of state did exactly what I wanted them to do. Of course I spoke for F.F. [Felix Frankfurter] and myself." Wise said that the administration had acted "ultra vires" and knew that, if the suspension of Jewish immigration into Palestine was enacted by the British, Anglo-American relations would be damaged and Roosevelt would be hurt in the November elections. Whether the efforts of the Jewish-American community would produce results in the British Cabinet, Wise confessed to Weizmann, he could not tell.[35] But, time did bring the desired response.

Fully aware of the views entertained in Jewish circles in the United States and the pressure extended privately by the Roosevelt administration, the British government postponed the suspension of immigration to Palestine. On September 3, the State Department obtained official confirmation that Weizmann had received a letter from Ormsby-Gore which indicated that the British government was not suspending Jewish immigration into Palestine, but was in fact sending additional military reinforcements to Palestine so that the total number of British troops there would reach approximately thirty-two thousand.[36] On September 4, Hull's office contacted Rabbi Wise with the good news.

Rabbi Wise was overjoyed. After contacting other Jewish leaders, Wise relayed to Hull a few days later how grateful they were and how they wanted Wise to thank Hull for the help he "personally gave us in the matter of the danger which threatened the Jewish National Home." Brandeis in particular, Wise said, rejoiced at the news that a postponement of the suspension of immigration occurred. And Wise promised to continue to spread the word privately as to how "the Administration rightfully over a period of months brought its influence to bear upon the Palestine situation."[37]

The reaction from the leaders of the Jewish-American community was perhaps best summed up by Brandeis, who believed that Wise had performed "a marvelous feat—nothing more important for us has happened since the Mandate, perhaps nothing so important as to make clear to Great Britain America's deep interest and particularly F.D.'s [Roosevelt] and Hull's views." To record the activities of the Roosevelt administration for the future and to conform to proper diplomatic protocol, Brandeis suggested that Wise obtain Roosevelt's permission to have an aide-memoire written depicting the administration's role and policy in this matter and have it sent to the British government. In that way, Brandeis argued, it would show the British that the

Roosevelt administration "means business."[38] Wise agreed and went to Hyde Park to see Roosevelt early in October.

Roosevelt's face lit up when Wise expressed "the deep appreciation of all of us" for all the assistance that he and Hull had given regarding the suspension problem. Roosevelt was also happy to hear that Brandeis and Frankfurter shared in the joy of the news from London. "Grand man! You know, Stephen," Roosevelt interrupted in reference to Brandeis, "we and the Inner Circle call him 'Isaiah'." Then, with great interest in the Palestine situation and well informed on the matter, Roosevelt proceeded to tell Wise of the British Cabinet's decision.[39]

Roosevelt said that he received word of the Cabinet's decision on suspension from Neville Chamberlain, who would shortly succeed Baldwin as prime minister. Chamberlain told Roosevelt that they had "given up the idea of suspension because of your [the American] interest." When Roosevelt finished discussing the matter and how the administration had intervened, Wise asked Roosevelt if he would agree to put the administration on record by submitting an aide-memoire to the British. Immediately, Roosevelt consented and added, "Steve, you tell Cordell that I want him to do this and to send over whatever you and Felix prepare."[40]

Wise made sure that other Jewish leaders in America, especially in this period prior to the presidential election in November of 1936, knew of the role of the President. Publicly, Wise told Roosevelt that Jewish leadership would make no use of the aide-memoire and would not say more "because of the reaction which might be hurtful and which might be used against you at this time by the other Party." But privately, wherever he would go and to whomever he would see, Wise would clearly emphasize the important contribution that the Roosevelt administration had made to all Jews.[41] And, in November of 1936, over 80 percent of the American Jewish community cast ballots for Franklin D. Roosevelt.[42] What he achieved in private for Jews in America manifested itself in an almost unanimous public endorsement by this very grateful segment of the American populace. With the reelection of Roosevelt and the certainty that the doors to Palestine would remain open to Jews, Roosevelt then embarked several months later on a rescue mission which would hopefully make those doors accessible to the many Jews involuntarily locked inside Nazi Germany.

Hitler's Outcasts

When the Schuschnigg government in Austria fell to the Third Reich on March 12, 1938, the Anschluss between Germany and Austria became a reality. Concurrent with this action, there occurred in Austria for the following two weeks—the period before the Roosevelt administration would announce its worldwide call for an international conference to rescue refugees from Nazi tyranny—the most blatant anti-Semitism that the world had seen since Hitler ascended to power. There were multiple arrests and humiliations, and the world press reported that Jews in Vienna were committing suicide at the rate of two hundred daily. In addition, Austria closed its frontiers to Jewish immigration, with Italy, Switzerland, and Czechoslovakia following in quick order.[1] These events caused the Roosevelt administration, in response to Jewish-Americans and other groups, to initiate a program of rescue.

What was to be called the Evian Conference, held in July in the French resort town of Evian-les-Bains, was planned by Roosevelt and announced to the world on March 25, 1938, at a press conference at Roosevelt's Warm Springs retreat in Georgia. Delegates from thirty-two nations would participate, including observers from Poland and Rumania, who primarily desired to deport Jews from their countries. Germany also permitted representatives of German and Austrian Jewry to go to Evian and present their plans to aid refugees. Actually, almost forty refugee agencies, mostly Jewish, submitted programs on how to proceed to end the refugee dilemma.[2]

In addition, Roosevelt established the President's Advisory Committee on Political Refugees in April of 1938, a national organization designed to assist the refugee agencies in the United States and to offer Roosevelt advice on how to assist refugees. Joseph Chamberlain, a confidant of Roosevelt and a professor of law, was the chairman. He was ably assisted by Samuel Cavert of the National Council of Churches of Christ, Archbishop Joseph Rummel of New Orleans, chairman of the Committee for Catholic Refugees from Germany, and Louis Kennedy, president of the National Council of Catholic Men. The other members included Henry Morgenthau, Jr., the secretary of the treasury, Bernard Baruch, the wealthy financier and presidential adviser,

James G. McDonald, former League of Nations High Commissioner for Refugees from Germany, and Rabbi Stephen Wise, president of the American Jewish Congress. The main task of the national committee was to obtain financial aid from private organizations in the United States that would be used by an intergovernmental commission, expected to be established by the Evian Conference. No public funds would be supplied by the American government.[3]

As with many other foreign policy initiatives, these proposals from the Roosevelt administration to rescue Jews stemmed from domestic political pressure, emanating specifically from the Jewish-American community. This is not to say that Roosevelt was forced into a position of advocating the rescue of Jews from Europe; far from it. As long as there were Jewish-Americans, he favored it. Although on numerous occasions he bowed to the wishes of the Jewish-American leadership, Roosevelt insisted that his work for Jews be done in private. And had it not been for the Anschluss, Roosevelt would have proceeded to search for refugee havens around the world—in private. By working in private for Jews, Roosevelt was merely attempting to avoid the opposition charge of a "Jew-Deal" and the rise of anti-Semitism in the United States. Overall, his approach was distinctly pro-Jewish; his motives clearly pro-Roosevelt. Now, with the Anschluss, Roosevelt faced a political delemma; should he continue to pursue Jewish goals privately—publicly avoiding a position on rescue efforts for refugees or on increasing immigration quotas— thereby mollifying the prominent isolationists and restrictionists; or should he adhere to things Jewish and call for a worldwide commitment to rescue those victims of Hitler's vengeance? To those who knew Roosevelt intimately, there would be no question that the story would begin and end with the latter.

As early as 1936, the plight of Jewish refugees in Europe concerned Roosevelt. At that time, he sent additional consuls to Germany to aid in issuing more visas and in less time. By 1938 and the advent of Anschluss, Roosevelt had moved in private to keep America's doors open to refugees when it appeared that American immigration quotas were in jeopardy of being made even more restrictive. Actually, since the beginning of Hitler's rise to power until early 1938, over 150,000 refugees, Jews and non-Jews, left Germany, and between 30,000 and 35,000 found their way to the United States. Next to Palestine, which had received 42,000 refugees, the United States placed second. There were problems on the horizon, however, for the refugee population.[4]

Frances Perkins, Roosevelt's Secretary of Labor, correctly observed that a powerful movement was underway in the United States, "among Jewish people particularly, to lift the immigration barriers and bring the refugees over here. There was equally strong opposition to it from those who didn't like them any better than the Germans liked them."[5] In Palestine, the British were considering a partition of the country as a solution to a Mid-East peace, the effect of which could seriously curtail or eliminate completely the immigration of refugees into that area.[6] And the accepted view in Europe was that German refugees were supposed to emigrate at an even greater speed, making room in these Western European countries for more transits.[7] With these conditions in mind, coupled with the concern pervading the White House from the Jewish-American sector, Roosevelt sought to alleviate the problems of Europe's refugees—in private.

Roosevelt was very concerned, as were America's Jews, with the ominous portent of future British policy in the Middle East and the effect that the policy would have vis-à-vis Jewish refugees. Roosevelt also saw that British policy toward Palestine—the possible partition of the country—was going to be more and more difficult to influence, particularly with the success rate previously obtained. Consequently, he decided to attempt to unite Jewish-American leadership behind his plan to assist refugees, and that meant that Rabbi Wise had to come to the White House.[8]

At their meeting in January of 1938, Roosevelt opened the conversation by alluding to the fact that there was "not room in Palestine for many more people—perhaps another hundred or hundred and fifty thousand." Even though it might be possible to get more Jews into Palestine, Roosevelt continued, Jewish-Americans ought to begin to think about finding some other large areas "as a second choice for the Jews." Wise was visibly upset. He believed that the British ambassador had filled Roosevelt's head with those figures, or possibly some non-Zionist or anti-Zionist like his close associate, Sam Rosenman. Wise corrected Roosevelt, explaining that conservative estimates for available space in Palestine showed that a million and one-half to two million refugees could be accommodated over a period of twenty-five years, and "that isn't all. In the larger territory of Trans-Jordania, to which we should and may have access, we could in time get homes for two to three millions, making four to five million in all."[9]

Roosevelt interrupted. He wanted Wise to listen to his plan, which "isn't a thing that we can talk about [publicly], but I am just thinking aloud....I haven't talked to a soul as yet, but I want to unburden myself." Roosevelt told Wise that, if the world powers could hold off from war for two or three years, he would call a world conference on the re-allocation of territories, especially unoccupied areas, and in these areas there could certainly be found large land areas suitable for Jewish colonization.[10]

Wise immediately pointed out that Jews have contributed, besides their lives and labor, over one hundred million pounds into Palestine, and that, aside from Britain, France, and the United States, Palestine was the only place that Jews cared to settle. Actually, both were keenly aware that the Jewish community was split over the desire to rescue fellow Jews in Europe and bring them to the United States as well as divided over the issue of Palestine becoming a Jewish State. However, to continue to rescue Jews, to continue to keep Palestine open to some immigration, and to continue to rely on a firm Anglo-American friendship, Roosevelt wanted Wise—and his pro-Zionist organization—to accept the prevalent view of the anti-Zionist Jewish community in the United States.[11] Wise and Roosevelt also knew that many Zionists desired additional outlets for refugees; that Palestine could not take all refugees, Wise admitted as much months before his meeting with Roosevelt, confiding to a friend that he would be willing to bargain with the British if they would provide territory for Jews in Uganda and Kenya.[12]

Roosevelt confessed that he did not want to offer a substitute for Palestine. However, if Jews in America were realistic, they would understand that Palestine was going to be exhausted as a refugee haven, and therefore the Jewish-American community "ought to have another card up your sleeve."[13] For all intents and purposes Wise agreed, even though he had grown to distrust the British, feeling that they would use Jews for their own self-interest and "kick us" if the situation demanded it.[14] He told Roosevelt to go ahead with his plans to acquire unoccupied territory for Jewish refugees, but qualified his approval by requesting Roosevelt's assurance that "in the meantime you help us to get all we can and all we are entitled to in Palestine." Roosevelt agreed.[15]

At his meeting with Roosevelt in January of 1938, Wise concurred with Roosevelt's desire to pursue in private havens for refugees other than Palestine, and from all indications, had it not been for the events following the Anschluss in Austria and the attempts in Congress to liberalize the immigration quotas, Roosevelt would have adopted this policy in conjunction with the British government. It should be noted that later in the year the British Cabinet did decide to produce a large-scale plan for the settlement of refugees, suggesting that British Guiana would be able to accommodate tens of thousands and that the rest of the British colonies and dominions would make similar commitments.[16] However, just as it appeared that Roosevelt had garnered the support from all factions of the Jewish-American community, thereby avoiding public agitation and accusations concerning the plight of the Jews, the sound of the German *Wehrmacht* entering Austria was heard around the world. Now, Roosevelt faced the politically sensitive question as to whether he would pursue and promote publicly what he planned and promised privately. Indeed, the political risk appeared great, but the concern engendered by being renounced by the Jewish-American community loomed ever greater.

On March 25, 1938, Roosevelt announced the call for the international committee to be formed, and, although he emphasized at his press conference that it also meant the rescue of a great number of Christians, there was no doubt in his mind or in the mind of the committee that was eventually formed that they were mainly concerned with the plight of the Jews. Myron Taylor, the

President's personal representative on the committee established at the Evian Conference, confided to Frances Perkins that he was primarily concerned with the treatment of Jews in Germany, how to get them out, and how to provide for their future.[17] In attempting to decide whether or not to take the lead and call this international conference, Roosevelt was primarily influenced by the activities of several Jewish-American congressmen in the House of Representatives and the upshot of those activities on public opinion, the leadership of the Jewish-American community, and the fate of the Jews in Europe.

At this time, America's immigration policy was closely intertwined with Roosevelt's rescue plans. Two bills were proposed in the House by Jewish Democratic congressmen from New York, Samuel Dickstein (chairman of the House Immigration Committee) and Emanuel Celler, hoping to open America's doors wide. Celler and Dickstein had been agitating in the House since 1937 to lift immigration quotas to assist refugees, and now their bills were to be introduced and hearings held.[18] In order for Roosevelt to call for an international committee to rescue Jews, he had to be certain that Congress would not discuss changes in the immigration quotas. From all indications, any liberalization of the immigration quotas, lifting restrictions and permitting the entrance of thousands of refugees, would not only be soundly defeated, but would also give a forum to those who would want the Roosevelt administration to be labeled as one run by Jews.

A *Fortune* magazine poll in July of 1938 substantiated the President's conviction that the American people were opposed to assisting refugees by changing the immigration laws. Approximately 67 percent of all respondents believed that the United States should try to keep them out. Only 18.2 percent agreed with Roosevelt that refugees should be permitted to enter the country, but not by raising the immigration quotas. Approximately 5 percent said that immigration quotas should be raised and refugees encouraged to live in the United States. And, interestingly enough, the following year almost 26 percent of Jewish-Americans surveyed stated that they were opposed to the opening of America's doors to a larger number of European refugees than were presently permitted entrance under the immigration quotas.[19]

Roosevelt and certain Jews, particularly Rabbi Wise, also feared that Congress would probably invoke stricter immigration laws and quotas, thereby further hindering any possibility of rescuing at least some Jews. Wise was amazed and horrified at Celler's resolution, which sought to increase the quota substantially. Wise likened Celler to an "agent provacateur," even though he knew that Celler was far from being an unscrupulous man. He believed that, if Celler's bill reached debate on the floor, the whole country would "go down on the President's proposal with a thud."[20] Roosevelt was in a precarious position. If he proposed an international refugee rescue committee and wished to appear to be sincere, he would have to likewise support legislation to allow a change in the quota system. But, according to knowledgeable leaders in the administration and on Capitol Hill, both actions would meet with defeat. Vice President John Nance Garner, counting votes in Congress, said at one of Roosevelt's Cabinet meetings that, "if any question were raised in Congress about immigration, a total exclusion act would probably be passed."[21] Moreover, the administration would be playing into the hands of Nazi propagandists, restrictionists, and anti-Semites in the United States. And this Roosevelt did not wish to do. Roosevelt knew, therefore, that if Congress severely limited or completely restricted immigration, his call to the nations of the world to open their doors to Jewish refugees would be looked upon as nothing more than pious rhetoric.

The hearings never did take place and the bills were withdrawn. Some pressure was exerted by a New York conference representing Protestant, Catholic, Jewish, and non-sectarian refugee Aid agencies who agreed that the Dickstein and Celler bills would be harmful, and Roosevelt's plans for the Evian Conference would be hindered by the publicity.[22] But, in actuality, it was the administration working through the intervention of Assistant Secretary of State George Messersmith, that alleviated this problem. Messersmith revealed that he "discreetly brought to the attention of Mr. Dickstein and others the desirability of hearings not being held on such bills for the present," stressing the fact that such hearings could hurt Roosevelt's efforts and interfere with the work of the proposed international refugee committee.[23] They agreed and consequently, rather than the door to America being shut to Jewish refugees, Roosevelt had kept it open, with of course the cooperation of several very prominent, Jewish-American congressmen.

The policy of calling for the Evian Conference was, for all intents and purposes, a compromise. By publicly divulging his desire to find havens for Jewish refugees, rather than pursuing this privately over a period of several years, Roosevelt satisfied the demands of both Zionist and anti-Zionist Jewish-Americans. By following the quota system and by not condoning the proposed increase in immigration quotas or special legislation to assist Jews specifically, he placated America's restrictionists, avoided the likelihood of widespread anti-Semitism that these proposals would exacerbate, and more important, he kept the American doors open to Jewish refugees. Moffat recorded that the genesis for the President's proposed policy occurred at a meeting between Roosevelt, Welles, and Morgenthau. And it was no coincidence that the meeting on this foreign policy venture took place in the office of Undersecretary of State Sumner Welles, for it was Welles, in collaboration with Morgenthau, who proposed this compromise plan to the President, with the influence and interest of Jewish-Americans in mind.[24]

Although evidence is not available to show absolutely that Wise influenced Roosevelt to announce publicly what he privately promised Wise at their meeting in January of 1938, one source close to the President does adhere to the fact that "Roosevelt did set up the Evian conference with Wise and Jewish-Americans in mind,"[25] and did so primarily as a "result of pressure upon him from Rabbi Wise, for whom he had a great deal of affection."[26] No doubt Wise was on Roosevelt's door step immediately after Anschluss. Actually, according to a prominent student of this period, Roosevelt was placed under enormous pressure not only by Wise, but also from all of his Jewish intimates—Morgenthau, Rosenman, Brandeis, Frankfurter, Bernard Baruch, and David Niles.[27]

The role of Morgenthau as a barometer of Jewish-American concerns and demands cannot be underestimated. Although Benjamin V. Cohen, personal advisor to the President, was said to have more influence with Roosevelt on Jewish matters than any other man,[28] with the exception of Felix Frankfurter, Cohen mentioned that he would primarily relay information from various Jewish groups, from Frankfurter, Brandeis, Wise, and others to Rosenman and Morgenthau, and they would pass it on to Roosevelt.[29] Roosevelt and Morgenthau were close friends and neighbors, living in the same county in New York State, and frequently lunched together at the White House. Morgenthau was not afraid to speak his mind to the President. And Jewish groups across the country, from B'nai B'rith to the American Jewish Congress, also spoke their mind and had their views duly noted.[30] In a letter to Frankfurter, Wise confided that he had learned from a friend, who had spoken to Roosevelt just after Anschluss, that Roosevelt's answer to Jewish-American pressure was to "keep your shirt on. We are going to do something big."[31]

As reported by the State Department, the pressure was exceedingly strong, with no let up in sight. For Moffat, the pressure groups were "obviously composed mainly of liberals and Jews."[32] Besides the protestations by Dorothy Thompson, the noted newspaper columnist who demanded an American effort to rescue Jews, a State Department memorandum coincided with Moffat's view that the principal sources of pressure were certain congressmen, like Celler and Dickstein, who represented large metropolitan constituencies. Consequently, to counteract this pressure, Hull, Welles, Messersmith, and Moffat gathered after Anschluss and decided to recommend to Roosevelt that, rather than resisting the pressure, the administration should "get out in front and attempt to guide the pressure, primarily with a view toward forestalling attempts to have the immigration laws liberalized." And, as soon as possible Welles suggested, a worldwide intergovernmental conference should be held.[33] After this meeting Welles met with Morgenthau, and together they approached Roosevelt.

Before leaving for Warm Springs on March 24, Roosevelt met with Welles and Morgenthau and at this meeting approved their recommendation to call for an international committee to rescue Jews from Austria and Germany.[34]

Whether this memorandum from Welles and Morgenthau was the same or similar to the State Department memorandum of late 1938 reviewing the year's refugee program and revealing the administration's motives for calling the Evian Conference, one cannot be certain. However, the memorandum clearly alludes to the fact that significant Jewish-American pressure motivated Roosevelt to initiate publicly the effort to deal with the Jewish refugee situation. So, while Roosevelt announced his plan for the Evian Conference, the American Jewish Committee, the B'nai B'rith, the Zionist Organization of America, and the American Jewish Congress met together to gather nation-wide support for Roosevelt to which, Wise said, he was "abundantly entitled."[35]

Even though the announced policy on March 25, 1938, was only to apply initially to refugees in Germany and Austria, Roosevelt included the other areas of Europe as well. He thoroughly upset the State Department. At his press conference at Warm Springs, Roosevelt claimed that Russia, Spain, Italy, Poland, Lithuania, Rumania, and Hungary could also find refuge for their Jews through the auspices of the international committee.[36] Roosevelt knew he was taking a political risk with this foreign policy initiative, but he hoped "that the narrow isolationists will not use this move of ours for purely partisan objectives—but no one can tell in these days." In writing to Irving Lehman, brother of the New York governor, Roosevelt revealed the political realities with which he had to deal in order to advance the cause of almost every Jewish-American. He explained that America's action "in regard to political refugees will have far reaching consequences even though, unfortunately, we cannot take care of more than a small proportion of them."[37] And to the Jewish-American governor of New York and his close friend, Herbert Lehman, Roosevelt similarly wrote that he hoped that the United States could help many refugees, "and I only wish we could do more."[38] Lehman knew that Roosevelt faced the impossibility of Congress ever changing the immigration laws and also knew that the American people, including a good percentage of Jewish-Americans, would not condone such a policy.[39] However, aside from the political realities of the immigration situation, the reaction from the American Jewish community was overwhelmingly joyful.

The American Jewish Congress, the B'nai B'rith, the Zionist Organization of America, the Jewish Labor Committee, and other national organizations concerned with the plight of Jewish refugees, now united in their efforts, informed Roosevelt that his action in extending an invitation to nine nations to assist in the emigration of Austro-German political fugitives was greatly appreciated.[40] Frankfurter similarly wrote the President to say "how wonderful I think your stand in regard to refugees. I dare say it will be enormously difficult to do, but it's so important to express the right feelings, and for us, as a nation, to take this position at this time, makes me proud."[41] Even Rabbi Wise and other prominent Jewish leaders were on their way to Washington to find out from the administration what they were "expected to do" to help.[42] Bernard Baruch, Roosevelt's economic advisor and member of the President's Advisory Committee for Political Refugees, was already at work, enthusiastically pursuing the possibility of "raising $500,000,000 in seed money" to help settle Jewish and other political refugees in Africa.[43]

Consequently, with Jewish-Americans pleased with the establishment in April of 1938 of the President's Advisory Committee for Political Refugees and with the convening of the Evian Conference in July, Jews turned their attention toward the obvious outcome of this cooperative international effort—the opening of numerous worldwide areas of refuge for their oppressed brethren in Europe. It would not take long to observe the results, whether one focused on Evian or on Palestine.

7

Palestine in 1938

The end of the Evian Conference brought bitter disappointment and a sense of hopelessness to Jews everywhere since it failed miserably in accomplishing its prime mission—to find areas of refuge throughout the world.[1] Only a few countries offered some land for just a minute number of the anxious, harassed victims of Nazi tyranny.

However, an International Committee of Refugees (ICR) was formed, with the guarantee of American participation and with the task of negotiating with Nazi Germany to facilitate the emigration of refugees. In addition, Jewish-Americans could still take comfort in the fact that refugees from Europe at least had Palestine to lure them and provide refuge. Cautious optimism reigned, but not for long. In the fall of 1938, the Palestine question appeared twice on Roosevelt's desk; once prompted by a proposed change in British policy in October, the other promoted by the shattering of broken glass—*Kristallnacht*—the night of broken glass that pervaded Germany in early November. On both occasions the Jewish-American community summoned its enormous strength and influence to persuade Roosevelt to act on their behalf. Once again, Roosevelt complied, but this time his efforts did not result in total success.

News was received in Washington early in October of 1938 that the British were considering a change in the Palestinian Mandate in order to make peace with the Arabs. The change specified that the British were "going to agree to the Arab demand to shut down on Jewish immigration."[2] Rabbi Wise quickly telegraphed Roosevelt that he had just received a cable from Weizmann in London that "the liquidation of the declared policy of the British government, in favor of a Jewish National Home in Palestine, is imminently threatened. Before Downing Street makes so grave and irrevocable a commitment, I beseech you to put in your word."[3] Weizmann's telegram urged Wise to mobilize as soon as possible the leaders of the Jewish-American community and make known their voice to the Roosevelt administration and the press. Moreover, the "Skipper"—as Roosevelt was frequently referred to by the Jewish "hierarchy"—should be told to intervene with the British ambassador in

Washington and to instruct him to relay the concern of America's Jews. Finally, the administration and American Jewry, Weizmann stated, should issue a statement declaring that Jews would not be pressured into giving up Palestine.[4]

After conveying Weizmann's remarks, Wise went on to remind Roosevelt of his past support in response to a Jewish-American plea to influence policy regarding Palestine, and "how effective was your word of two years ago when temporary stoppage of immigration was threatened! You alone averted it through a personal appeal to Neville Chamberlain."[5] Wise wanted Roosevelt to try again and, in order to avoid a fait accompli by the British, wished to meet with Roosevelt at Hyde Park to discuss strategy. Ben Cohen would join him, Wise said, as Cohen had just returned from London and had firsthand knowledge from several British officials and Zionist leaders. It would take one week for Roosevelt to reply and to act.[6]

Wise, Weizmann, and the leaders of the American Jewish community had cause to worry about the fate of immigration into Palestine. In October of 1938, the London press revealed that the British government was deliberating and implying that it would soon render a decision on the Woodhead Commission's report, which envisioned a partition of Palestine into a Jewish and Arab State, and the cessation of Jewish immigration. Several actions indicated that such a policy was contemplated or was even in the process of being implemented before a public announcement would be rendered. For example, the American Consul General in Jerusalem reported that the British Foreign Office, through its Commissioner for Migration in Palestine, had not issued any immigration schedules for the semester beginning on October 1 and that he gathered the distinct impression from conversations with British officials that the whole Palestine situation was being kept quiet until the publication of the commission's report and the final enunciation of British policy.[7]

Actually, Malcolm MacDonald, the British Colonial Secretary—when queried by Joseph Kennedy, America's ambassador to England, on the Palestine situation on two occasions in October—revealed that the Woodhead Commission's report would not be available to the government until the end of October and that the government could not reach a conclusion until after November 1. MacDonald told Kennedy not to worry about the decision of the British government; he would keep Kennedy informed and advise him from time to time.[8] However, when the British position on the Woodhead report was made public in November, Weizmann's suspicions proved correct. Upon speaking to MacDonald at that time, Kennedy learned that the British had intended to restrict immigration into Palestine, but they were influenced "by pressure from the United States and changed their ideas."[9] That pressure mounted almost immediately after Wise received Weizmann's telegram.

When news broke in the United States of the possibility of the British terminating immigration into Palestine, 6,000 telegrams arrived at the State Department within twenty-four hours, each demanding that the administration stop the British. Over one hundred members of the House and Senate registered similar views, and friends of Roosevelt and Hull swamped them with letters of protest, urging intervention.[10] A typical letter arrived from the future Speaker of the House of Representatives, John W. McCormack. Noting that Palestine was the only possible haven for the oppressed Jews of Europe, McCormack wanted Roosevelt to intervene with the British in order to safeguard Jewish national nights in Palestine and to adhere to the Balfour Declaration and the Mandate.[11] Congressman Robert L. Ramsey also told Roosevelt to use his powers of persuasion to have Great Britain either publicly renounce or modify the Balfour Declaration.[12] More significantly, Governor Herbert Lehman of New York wrote his friend, "Franklin," that it would be "a tragic anti-climax to what you tried to achieve through the Evian conference if, at this moment, Great Britain should stop Jewish immigration into Palestine and repudiate its obligations." Although it was not necessary, he reminded Roosevelt of the anxiety prevalent among all American-Jews and how grateful they would be if Roosevelt would strike the chord of action.[13]

By mid-October, the Jewish blitz on the Roosevelt administration produced the second largest number of telegrams ever handled on one subject by Western Union—34,000 cables reached the White House and the State Department on the Palestine question. The total number of telegrams delivered to government officials, Congress included, numbered about 65,000.[14] Jewish-American leadership also got into the act and submitted to Hull a memorandum, representative of every faction of organized Jewry in the United States. They too demanded the intercession of the American government to bring about a reversal of the proposed British policy to stop immigration into Palestine.[15]

Roosevelt reassured all who expressed concern in this most serious foreign policy matter. He publicly reiterated his desire to help establish a Jewish National Home in Palestine, and how he expected the British to respect America's interest in the welfare of Jewish refugees in Europe and Palestine. Moreover, in writing to Governor Lehman, he confided that the United States had "left no stone unturned—and will leave no stone unturned—to persuade the British Government to adopt a liberal policy with regard to the Refugees."[16] Unfortunately, the United States did not have any legal way to void British policy and therefore had to rely on presidential diplomatic pressure and the hope that such influence, strenuously demanded by Jewish-Americans, would change Britain's foreign policy. As Moffat succinctly put it, the problem was to find a formula that showed ample sympathy with the wishes of the Jewish-American community and yet stayed within the rights granted the United States by the Balfour agreement. Essentially, the United States could make its views known to the British, but had no final decision-making power.[17] Nevertheless, the legal position notwithstanding, Jewish-American leadership, in addition to overall group pressure, had gone to work on the President, and now Roosevelt was going to go to work for them, in private of course.

On October 12, Roosevelt answered Wise's cable. He told Wise that he hoped to find "an opportunity to be helpful as he endeavored to be a couple of years ago in a situation somewhat similar to that alluded to in your telegram," and thanked Wise for his "telegram of October sixth advising him of recent developments on the Palestine situation." Roosevelt also informed Wise that he had "talked with Mr. Felix Frankfurter about the Palestine situation over the weekend" and, in addition, had consulted with Louis D. Brandeis.[18] In his talk with Frankfurter, Roosevelt was extremely concerned with the importance of keeping Palestine whole and of keeping it Jewish. To Frankfurter, Roosevelt was "tremendously interested—and wholly surprised—on learning of the great increase in Arab population since the War; and on learning of the plentitude of land for Arabs in Arab countries, about which he made specific inquiries."[19] Roosevelt was ready to move.

Roosevelt suggested that Frankfurter dictate a draft of a note which Roosevelt, in turn, would send to Chamberlain in London. The note was dictated to presidential advisor, Ben Cohen. In it, Roosevelt urged the British to make no decision "which would close the gates of Palestine to the Jews." Owing to the failure of the Evian Conference, Roosevelt pointed out to Chamberlain the increased pressure on European Jewry and the significance of Palestine as the one last viable refuge for them.[20]

Besides contacting Chamberlain, the administration moved on two other fronts. Tracing a similar pattern followed by the administration in intervening with the British government in 1936 over this issue, Hull dispatched a message to Ambassador Kennedy. He instructed Kennedy to see Lord Halifax, British Foreign Secretary, as soon as possible, and inform him of the thousands of letters and telegrams received at the White House and the State Department protesting Britain's Palestine policy.[21]

Kennedy immediately met with Sir Alexander M.G. Cadogan, Permanent Under Secretary for Foreign Affairs, and verbally transmitted Hull's telegram. Halifax was out of London but would be informed upon his return. Malcolm MacDonald, the Colonial Secretary, was similarly approached, and Kennedy reported that the British would inform him of any proposed alterations in the Mandate.[22] Hull responded that any information from the British Cabinet regarding Palestine would be most helpful, particularly in view of the great concern in the United States.[23]

Finally, before Roosevelt played his second card—summoning Ronald Lindsay, the British ambassador, to the White House—the pressure on the British Cabinet was beginnng to show some results. In mid-October, Wise received a phone call from Weizmann. Weizmann reported that extreme action by the Cabinet "has probably been averted due to American pressure. That means that there will probably be no Arab State organized at present. I do not believe immigration will be completely halted, but it may be reduced to figures even lower than the present ones."[24] Moreover, Weizmann wanted the Jewish-American community and the American government to continue the pressure and go on with undiminished enthusiasm. One week later, MacDonald confirmed to Kennedy that even he would definitely recommend that immigration to Palestine for the Jews not be stopped or curtailed, and that he believed Jews everywhere would look favorably upon the British recommendations. MacDonald realized, Kennedy relayed to Hull, the enormous interest concerning Palestine in the United States and confessed that conditions would probably improve shortly.[25] Although the tension was easing, Roosevelt nevertheless decided to call Lindsay to the White House.

Roosevelt met with Lindsay on October 25. According to Adolf Berle, his Assistant Secretary of State, Roosevelt "was full of Palestine," and Lindsay quickly ascertained Roosevelt's interest in securing Palestine for Jewish refugees. Actually, Lindsay was taken aback by Roosevelt's commitment and plan. Roosevelt wanted the British—with the cooperation of the United States—to call a meeting of the Arab princes. The Arabs would be told that, since the Trans-Jordan desert could be irrigated, the American and British governments would provide about $200,000,000 to buy farms and dig wells for every Arab who left Palestine.[26] If that did not entice the Palestinian Arabs to move, then, according to Lindsay, Roosevelt said they should be "forced to do so if necessary, freeing their Palestine lands for Jews. Jews would be prohibited from emigrating to Jordan, and Arabs forbidden from emigrating to Palestine."[27] Lindsay promised to transmit Roosevelt's plan and his enthusiasm to Chamberlain as soon as possible.

From all indications, Roosevelt learned of the possibility of enacting the Iraq plan—irrigating the Trans-Jordan desert—from the State Department where for several years Edward A. Norman, working in collaboration with various leaders of the Jewish-American community, had presented to the Division of Near Eastern Affairs and to Undersecretary of State Sumner Welles, documents relating to the possible cooperation by the leaders of Iraq. Norman, characterized by a State Department official as an anti-Zionist, a gentleman of independent means, and highly reputable, spent a good deal of his time investigating the possibility of moving Palestinian Arabs to parts of Iraq where settlements could be established if massive irrigation projects were undertaken simultaneously.[28] As a member of the Democratic Party organization in New York City, Norman not only had close ties to the Arab leadership in the Middle East, but also received assurance from Weizmann and the senior officers of the Jewish Agency for Palestine early in 1938 that he had their blessing to pursue the Iraq plan in a quiet way so as to avoid repercussions from the Arab states.[29]

To Norman, the Iraqi leaders had to be kept unawares that the plan was devised in Jewish circles. Instead, he was attempting to plant in their minds the idea that Iraq's problem of under-population could be solved by a program of immigration of Arabs from Palestine, and, if they came forward with the Iraq plan, Roosevelt would be in a position to praise it and more importantly open up Palestine to Jewish immigration and control.[30] Later in 1939, Norman was told that Roosevelt had somehow learned of the possibilities of the Iraq plan and had proposed it to the British. Norman was delighted, thought it was splendid, but, as Roosevelt would soon discover, the British would reject it.[31] However, London would not go so far as to completely reject the efforts of Roosevelt and America's Jewish community to influence its Palestine policy.

In early November, Britain rejected the Woodhead Report which recommended partition of Palestine into Arab and Jewish states and announced that immigration would continue at the rate of 12,000 refugees per year.[32] However, London declared that preparations would continue for a conference between the Jewish Agency, Palestinian Arabs, and other Arab states to discuss their views on possible solutions to the Palestine question. The conference would be held in February and March of 1939, and immigration to Palestine would be given additional consideration.[33] What would happen then was open to speculation, but at least for the time being the threatened halt on Jewish immigration into Palestine was averted.

It was when the British government published its decision on the Woodhead Report that Kennedy learned from MacDonald that the Cabinet had planned to curtail immigration to Palestine, but was influenced by the pressure from the United States to change its view. As a prominent authority on this period concluded, British policy toward Jewish refugees and Palestine was altered, not only because of public opinion in Britain, but also due to the serious public outburst in the United States, where the refugee question threatened to upset Anglo-American relations. The center for pressure on Britain's Palestine policy was shifting from London to Washington.[34]

Publicly, no other group in the United States was more aware of the effort and commitment by Washington on this matter than the leadership of American Jewry. After the British announcement on the Palestine issue, Rabbi Wise transmitted Chaim Weizmann's feelings of joy over what the United States had contributed. Weizmann "spoke again with endless gratitude of what America had done," Wise informed Brandeis, "and urged the strongest possible American delegation [to the proposed British Conference on Palestine in February of 1939]. He spoke of Felix [Frankfurter], Ben [Cohen]. ... "[35] Even Malcolm MacDonald wanted Weizmann to give out a favorable statement on British policy, revealing that it was pressure from the United States that changed their ideas on restricting immigration.[36] Yet, it was Felix Frankfurter who best understood the role of Roosevelt in persuading the British government to look favorably upon Palestine as a homeland for Jewish refugees and not to block immigration. In writing to Roosevelt, Frankfurter thanked him for his "courageous resourcefulness" in making the Chamberlain government adhere to their obligation of keeping Palestine open to the victims of Nazi barbarism. "You have driven home your whole effort with Downing Street beautifully," Frankfurter concluded. "Thank God, say I, with millions upon millions of Americans, for the way in which you keep the flame of civilization aloft and burning brightly."[37] Roosevelt's efforts, however, to rescue Jews and keep Palestine open for the future possibility of establishing a Jewish homeland would come under even greater pressure by Jewish-Americans, Zionists and non-Zionists alike, with the arrival of *Kristallnacht* on November 10, 1938.

On the night of November 9-10, German troops and civilians went on a rampage. The objective: the destruction of Jewish shops, synagogues, hospitals, homes, children's schools, and homes for the aged. Nazi gun-butts, axes, and clubs made contact with glass and skulls, encouraging looting and burning throughout the Jewish neighborhoods by the terrorists. Forcing Jews into the night at this time of broken glass, referred to as *Kristallnacht* in Germany, between twenty-to-sixty thousand of them were rounded up and transported to concentration camps. And all of this occurred amid the daily expulsion of Jews by the Polish and German governments.[38]

During the weeks before *Kristallnacht,* and now as the news broke in the United States on November 10, Jewish-Americans flooded the White House and the State Department with tens of thousands of telegrams and letters urging that various actions be taken. To Moffat at the State Department, the pressure on the administration from Jews throughout the country was growing to such a peak that he felt a serious reaction would begin by the American people against their wishes. Although he sympathized with the horrible persecution of the Jews, as did Roosevelt and Hull, Moffat confessed that "no one likes to be subjected to pressure of the sort they are exerting."[39]

Even at the German Embassy in Washington, Hans Dieckhoff, German ambassador to the United States, informed the Fatherland that Jewish newspapers were writing more excitedly than ever before. Roosevelt, he said, was under enormous pressure from Jewish circles—owing to the German outburst and treatment of Jews—to exact some reprisals against Germany. Assistant Secretary of State George Messersmith, back at the State Department, corroborated Dieckhoff's estimate of the situation and strongly recommended to Roosevelt that, if some action was not forthcoming soon, the administration would run the risk of losing its position of leading public opinion.[40]

Before meeting with the anxious leadership of American Jewry, Roosevelt decided immediately after *Kristallnacht* to initiate several actions on his own which coincided with Jewish-American demands. The first involved the recall of Hugh Wilson, United States ambassador to Germany, for consultation. Much to the delight of Jewish-Americans, the German ambassador to the United States was likewise recalled.[41] Hoping to give Germany food for thought, Roosevelt knew that the recall of Wilson would not stop the atrocities against Jews and Catholics, but he believed it could "stem the orgy," and possibly result in the desire by the German government to cooperate with the nations of the world to assist the refugees.[42] Several weeks later, Germany made a change.

On December 15, 1938, Germany submitted to British officials and George Rublee, head of the International Committee on Refugees established at the Evian Conference and a Roosevelt appointee, a plan for the evacuation of refugees.[43] Whether the recalling of Wilson helped to alter the thinking of the Germans on a Jewish refugee plan cannot be known, but they were definitely concerned, as German records show, about the fact that Roosevelt was "anxious to place the onus [of the rupture of relations] on us."[44] The German government believed that, as far as assisting Jewish refugees was concerned, Roosevelt would support and initiate any measures demanded by American Jewry, and therefore Jewish-Americans would obtain their objectives.[45]

Those Jewish-American leaders whom Roosevelt relied upon to inform him of the attitudes within the Jewish community—Felix Frankfurter, Louis D. Brandeis, Ben Cohen, Sam Rosenman, Rabbi Wise—also influenced Roosevelt to implement policy demands espoused by Jewish-Americans after *Kristallnacht.* After several meetings with Frankfurter and Brandeis, it seemed as though Roosevelt could not do enough for Jewish-Americans, whether it be on the Palestine or the refugee situation. In fact, Cohen confided to Frankfurter that Roosevelt—who went south on a holiday in late November— would return to Washington "on short notice" to take further action if Brandeis deemed it necessary.[46] From the private utterances of several Jewish leaders, Roosevelt was deeply moved by the events surrounding *Kristallnacht;* privately, very bitter and outspoken about the horrors inflicted on European Jewry.[47] So, what did Roosevelt accomplish for his Jewish friends?

In a gesture to capitalize on the outburst of public support for Jewish refugees after *Kristallnacht* and not get involved in another quota controversy, Roosevelt announced that he was permitting some twelve-to-fifteen thousand German refugees who were in the United States on visitor's visas to remain in the country indefinitely.[48] Their visas would be extended for six months and thereafter renewed for as long as necessary. Although allowing aliens to reside in the United States without passports was contrary to American law and Roosevelt knew it, he nevertheless made it clear that he would not permit them to return to German concentration camps and certain punishment. Legal technicalities, he told the press, would not change his mind.[49]

Regarding immigration quotas, Roosevelt knew that very little could be accomplished in Congress regarding a change. Consequently, he sought to follow the advice of the Jewish leadership who believed that an increase in the quotas would only produce more anti-Semitism, and therefore was not in the best interests of the Jewish community. To one knowledgeable student of this period, the Roosevelt administration did not attempt to change the quota system because of the "curiously negative attitude of the American Jewish community to the prospect of any large influx of refugees into the United States, and the resultant refusal of the community's leaders to urge more than token changes in immigration law or procedures."[50] However, in response to Jewish pressure on the refugee situation in the aftermath of *Kristallnacht,* Roosevelt embarked on several approaches to finding havens for European Jews. Each effort was to end in failure; the first being another attempt to move the British government to support a plan recommended by their own Peel Commission in 1937 toward Palestine.

After the appeasement of Germany at Munich in October of 1938, and after *Kristallnacht,* the British government observed that American public opinion was becoming skeptical of Britain's policy of working for peace with Germany and was openly less sympathetic toward England. To Halifax, Anglo-American relations were at a critical stage. Jewish-Americans in particular were looking to Britain to alleviate the results of the German persecution of Jews, hoping for a change in their Palestine and refugee policies. Consequently, Halifax—believing that some promises of help had to be made to the Jews—suggested that Britain establish some area in the empire as a refuge for Jewish settlement. Britain's position in American public opinion, Halifax wrote, could be restored if the British took the initiative in the refugee situation.[51] So, after reviewing various areas, British Guiana emerged as the best choice.[52] Also, in order to avoid a deeper rift in Anglo-American relations, Lindsay in Washington was instructed to suggest to the State Department "that part of the unused British quota for immigration into the United States be made available instead for refugees from Germany."[53]

Like MacDonald—Britain's Colonial Secretary—the leadership of the Jewish-American community, particularly Brandeis and Frankfurter, knew that the offer of British Guiana would be more important politically to Britain than it would be for the settlement of Jewish refugees. British Guiana did not offer an area for a very large contingent of refugees, and it was not an acceptable substitute for Palestine. Consequently, after Lindsay delivered the British proposal to Welles at the State Department on November 17, Brandeis, Frankfurter, and other influential Jews met with Roosevelt on several occasions immediately thereafter to convince him to reject the British offer.[54] The meetings bore a fruitful response from the President.

Roosevelt met with Brandeis on two occasions, once on November 19. Brandeis believed that there was ample room in Palestine for 50,000 refugees per year and an equal number of settlers for every year in the near future. Roosevelt listened attentively to the position posed by Brandeis, and, according to Brandeis, "showed full appreciation of the absurdity of the British Guiana proposition and the value of Palestine." Brandeis actually congratulated Frankfurter and his associates who visited Roosevelt earlier for persuading Roosevelt to reject Guiana, noting that they had done "a good job with F.D."[55] Indeed they had, for Roosevelt confided to Morgenthau at that time that Guiana was unacceptable and it "would take the Jews from 25 to 50 years to overcome the fever and ... it's just no good."[56] Roosevelt was again ready to intervene on behalf of Palestine as a place of refuge.

After these meetings with the Jewish-American leadership, Roosevelt summoned Lindsay to the White House. Ben Cohen recorded the interview. Roosevelt told the British ambassador that he wanted to have a complete report on the refugee situation and that he wanted to express his views regarding Palestine. And in addition, Roosevelt wanted Lindsay to speedily communicate the content of their talk to London.[57]

Roosevelt suggested that the British convene a conference with the Arab leaders from Palestine and the adjacent Arab countries, explaining that ample land existed under their control to accommodate all of their people. Palestine and Trans-Jordan, Roosevelt continued, comprised probably no more than 5 percent of their territories, and therefore Jews going to Palestine would not interfere with their people; there was "plenty of land for all." Palestinian Arabs would be given even better land in the surrounding Arab countries, and the self-defeating conflict between the Arabs and Jews in Palestine would be alleviated.[58]

When Lindsay portrayed the hostility of the Arab and Moslem world toward Palestine, Roosevelt dismissed this opposition and "thought it due largely to British indecision and conflicting policy." Similarly, when Lindsay proposed British Guiana as an alternative to Palestine, Roosevelt echoed the attitudes of America's Jewish leadership that he "did not think this amounted to anything, and it would take 25 years to do anything there."[59] Roosevelt concluded the meeting by divulging his financial plan for Palestine. In one of his first references to public financing of refugee settlement, Roosevelt proposed that, if 100,000 families could be settled for $3,000 per family, the $300,000,000 could be raised in the following manner: 100 million from the United States government, 100 million from the French and British governments, and 100 million from private subscriptions, primarily Jewish.[60] As he headed for his southern holiday retreat, Roosevelt and the Jewish-American community awaited the outcome of their efforts to pamper the British lion.

Roosevelt's initiative regarding Palestine, as transmitted to the British government by Lindsay, met with only negative responses. In December of 1938, London informed the State Department that neither Britain "nor anyone else could promote a settlement primarily by economic sops or financial help however generous; although after a political settlement and when feeling has cooled down economic help may be able to play its part."[61] Future proposals by Roosevelt for Jewish refugees, promoted by the Jewish-American community, would meet a similar fate. As Morgenthau later confirmed in his diary, Roosevelt was really genuinely concerned in the rescue effort, but the "great trouble is there is nobody who is following him on the program."[62]

8

The British White Paper of 1939

Morgenthau could not have been more accurate in his observation that no one was following Roosevelt's lead in the rescue program. The earlier agreement and success that Roosevelt had garnered with the British government regarding Palestine and the refugee situation completely dissipated in the spring of 1939. It was in May of 1939 that the British issued their White Paper on Palestine, ending for years the Jewish-American attempt to influence British foreign policy in that area of the world. Specifically, the White Paper closed down Jewish immigration into Palestine—allowing only 75,000 Jews to enter over the next five years—and reversed the British position to convert Palestine into a Jewish State. London no longer desired to antagonize sixty million Arabs. But, from November to May—before the issuance of the White Paper—the intervention of the Roosevelt administration to alter British policy toward Palestine continued unabated. Like the British, Roosevelt did not wish to antagonize his allies either.

Although the British government rejected the Woodhead Report in November of 1938, which recommended the partition of Palestine into Arab and Jewish states, London did not cancel its conference to be held in February and March of 1939. Representatives of world Jewry, the Palestinian Arabs, and adjacent Arab countries, were invited to London to express their positions on how to solve the Palestine problem, and, as Malcolm MacDonald, the Colonial Secretary noted, the British government hoped that the Arab and Jewish delegations would arrive at an agreement on Palestine without a British-imposed settlement.[1] However, that was not to be the case.

The London Conference convened on February 7, 1939. At the opening session, the Arab delegation presented its proposals. While demanding complete independence in Palestine, the Arabs sought to have the British abandon their desire to establish a Jewish National Home in Palestine. With the abrogation of the Mandate, Palestine would become a sovereign Arab State, and as such the sale of land to Jews and the immigration of Jews to Palestine would cease.[2]

The Jewish delegation was represented by Chaim Weizmann, head of the World Zionist Organization. As part of the Jewish contingent in London were Rabbi Wise, Louis Lipsky, and Robert Szold, all of the American Jewish Congress. They countered the Arab argument by noting that the Mandate was the only common meeting ground for a settlement between the Arabs and Jews. Large-scale Jewish immigration was essential to any final agreement as was the fact that the British were obliged to safeguard Jews in their present minority status, never abandoning the right of Jews to return in greater numbers to their future homeland.[3] As the conference progressed, however, neither side agreed on a solution. Consequently, the British began to interject their own position.

The prime goal of British diplomacy throughout the London Conference was to guarantee England's strategic position in the Middle East. No solution to the Palestine problem could engender the establishment of hostile Arab states on the Palestine border. Moreover, if Britain pushed the Arab leadership too hard—supporting Jewish arguments toward Palestine—the Arabs might decide to move into the German and Italian camp, taking their oil reserves as well as their animosity with them.[4] London was in a dangerous and difficult position, and by early March it was obvious to the Jewish delegation at the conference that the plan espoused by the British was essentially the Arab plan.[5]

British strategy was to hold in reserve the provisions regarding immigration and land purchases by the Jews, thereby gaining the confidence of the Arabs and forcing the Jews to make the greatest concessions. This the British did until late February.[6] The British Foreign Office persistently hounded the Colonial Office not to open Palestine to unrestricted immigration, urging instead the establishment of refugee settlements in other areas of the empire. However, the Jewish delegation finally sensed the urgency of the situation when Weizmann received—evidently due to a clerical error—on the weekend of February 24-26 the British proposal to withdraw from the Palestine Mandate, leaving an independent Palestinian state where the majority would be Arab, and where Jewish immigration would cease after a five year period of limited access. And on March 8, the British Cabinet voted to approve this proposal on immigration. One week later on March 15, the London Conference ended with these proposals a fait accompli and the hopes of the Jewish delegation shattered.[7] It was during these last weeks of the conference that vibrations from the British proposals quickly travelled across the Atlantic; the Jewish delegation hoping that their impact on the American Jewish community and the Roosevelt administration would in some way reverberate to reverse Britain's Palestine policy.

With the persecution of Jews in Germany as a backdrop, Zionists and non-Zionists in the United States during the early months of 1939 united in their efforts to secure a haven in Palestine for European Jewry. Specifically, they demanded that the American government press the British for a continuation of immigration into Palestine. According to the State Department, non-Zionists joined Zionists in protest, not because non-Zionists "were convinced that Palestine was a solution of the Jewish problem and not because they believed in a Jewish State, but simply because no other haven appeared as a possible refuge for the Jews being driven out of Europe."[8] The State Department was disturbed by the clamor erupting in the Jewish-American community and awaited a visit by Jewish representatives.

On February 25, 1939, *The New York Times* reported that American Jews would soon meet with Roosevelt and also attempt to sway American public opinion against the British. Rabbi Wise and Louis Lipsky—Jewish representative at the London Conference—had just had a meeting with Ambassador Kennedy in London, the *Times* revealed, and presumably the British proposals were discussed.[9] The Jewish delegates visited Kennedy on numerous occasions during the conference. Several days later, *New Palestine,* organ of the Zionist Organizations of America, in its issue of March 3, 1939, confirmed that Wise, Lipsky, and Szold would sail from England and would divulge the content of the proceedings of the London Conference at a public meeting arranged by the Zionist Organization of America in Carnegie Hall in New York on March 13.[10] In addition to this public meeting, *New Palestine* also announced that, following news of the British Government's proposals concerning Palestine, national officers of the Zionist Organization of America and the Mazrach Organization of America would meet to formulate a program of action and that Jewish-American districts throughout the United States would form emergency committees similiar to those established during the immigration crisis of October 1938.[11] Soon the State Department was cognizant of the impact of the Jewish effort.

In early March, a "marked increase in correspondence" concerning Palestine was reported at the State Department, requesting the intervention of the American government on behalf of Jewish demands in Palestine. The Department believed that the pressure on State and on the White House would equal if not surpass the pressure exerted by America's Jews in October of 1938, with the White House bearing the brunt of the attack.[12] Jewish pressure was well organized, so much so that even the Egyptian minister in Washington (admittedly not an objective source) told the State Department that he was annoyed at the large percentage of Jews in support of the Zionist cause, far outweighing the support from any other country known to him.[13]

Additional pressure from the Jewish community reached the White House from London. No doubt Weizmann and Wise kept Brandeis and Frankfurter aware of the proposals and progress of the London Conference—both met with Roosevelt on several occasions in the spring of 1939—but on March 10

Weizmann saw the necessity of flying to Paris to contact Roosevelt directly through William Bullitt, American ambassador in Paris, pleading the Jewish position. In a personal telegram to Roosevelt, Bullitt relayed Weizmann's view that "the zero hour for the Jews of Palestine had now arrived." Weizmann had made every argument he could in London, Bullitt wrote, but to no avail. Weizmann believed that "nothing could save the Jews of Palestine or keep open the door for Jewish refugees except a quiet word from you to the British authorities."[14]

Hoping that Roosevelt would intervene as he did in October of 1938, Weizmann pressed Roosevelt to contact Chamberlain and ask for a delay in the issuance of Britain's long-term solution toward Palestine. Chamberlain had recently spoken to Weizmann and had told him that the world situation might change in six months. Palestine policy, therefore, could be re-evaluated. To Weizmann, it would be a tragedy for Britain to enact a permanent, long-term solution to a probably temporary emergency in Palestine which might end within several weeks. If Roosevelt could not stop or delay the announcement of Britain's proposed policy, Weizmann confessed, London would never reconsider it.[15] So, the Roosevelt administration now faced a situation strikingly similar to the one in October of 1938.

Roosevelt did not wait until after seeing Weizmann's telegram or until the end of the London Conference to act. On behalf of the Jewish-American community, Roosevelt followed a pattern similar to that taken in October of 1938. Ambassador Kennedy, on a winter vacation in Florida, was told by Roosevelt in an early February telephone conversation to cut his vacation short and return to London at the outset of the London Conference.[16] Whether Roosevelt directed Kennedy, as he had in October of 1938, on the telephone to inform Halifax, Chamberlain, and MacDonald of the concern of Jewish-Americans and the President that Palestine not be closed to Jewish immigration, or that the idea of a Jewish homeland not be terminated, is not known. What is known is that Kennedy was instructed to tell Halifax that the American position regarding Palestine was the same as the State Department statement of October 14, 1938. Specifically, Jewish immigration into Palestine should continue and the effort to establish a Jewish National Home in Palestine not cease.[17]

Although the American government did not wish to intervene in the conference and hoped that the British, the Jews, and the Arabs would work out their own plan, the State Department did record that Kennedy informed the British government on February 27, 1939, during the course of the London Conference on Palestine, that drastic restriction of Jewish immigration into that country and the abolition of the British Mandate over the Holy Land would have "a disastrous effect on public opinion in the United States."[18] To the press Kennedy denied making such a statement, but to the State Department he confided that he was meeting with Rabbi Wise and wanted additional suggestions to give to Halifax.[19] Recollecting Kennedy's role in October of 1938 concerning British policy in Palestine, one must agree with Kennedy's biographer that it was no doubt correctly rumored "that Kennedy told Halifax that the British plans would not be favorably received by the American public."[20] The British, according to Kennedy, were stalling for time, and in the process, were "giving the Arabs the better of it."[21]

On March 3, Kennedy met with MacDonald after MacDonald and Chamberlain had concluded a meeting with Weizmann, Wise, and others on the Jewish position. Kennedy learned from MacDonald that the British sought delays in the conference in order to "save themselves" from a further crisis at home and abroad and would eventually make a decision which would provoke as little trouble for the British as possible.[22]

Undoubtedly, Roosevelt received the same impression when he spoke to Chamberlain on two different occasions during the conference. The exact dates of Roosevelt's conversations with Chamberlain are not known. However, on March 1, Chamberlain did announce to his Cabinet that Roosevelt had contacted him and that on or about March 8 Roosevelt had sent another message stating that he expected anti-British demonstrations to take place in the United States if London carried out its proposed policy toward Palestine.[23]

In those conversations, Roosevelt told Chamberlain that the United States would not publicly interfere with Britain's proposals, but privately Roosevelt wanted London to reconsider the Iraq Plan; that is, the possibility of developing and settling Arabs from Palestine in Trans-Jordan, thereby opening Palestine to greater Jewish immigration and settlement and keeping alive the concept of a Jewish homeland in Palestine. From the evidence it was apparent that, when news of the contents of the proposed White Paper reached the United States, the leadership of the American Jewish community, particularly Brandeis and Frankfurter, discussed with Roosevelt the possibility of urging the British to again consider the Iraq Plan. According to Rabbi Solomon Goldman, president of the Zionist Organization of America, Roosevelt wanted the British to remove two-to-three hundred thousand Arabs from Palestine into Iraq. The cost—$300 million—would be financed equally by the British and French, the Americans, and world Jewry. To Roosevelt, the Arabs who had entered Palestine since World War I were not the rightful owners of the country, and Chamberlain should not be disturbed by their claims on Palestine.[24] Roosevelt's intervention, however, only landed on deaf ears.

Just prior to the announcement of the White Paper on May 17, an aide-memoire from the British Embassy in Washington summarized its government's position for Roosevelt regarding the Iraq Plan. London understood that Roosevelt had "frequently shown an interest in the possibility of some development and settlement either of Arabs from Palestine or else of Jews in Trans-Jordan." London also shared Roosevelt's concern, but indicated that expert investigators noted that such a program would not succeed. The authorities in Trans-Jordan would not consent to any type of Jewish settlement, and the Arab population still feared domination by a minority of Jews.[25] Although he failed in his endeavor at this time, Roosevelt was determined to propose the plan again as soon as tensions had abated.[26] His attention now turned to the plea from Weizmann and America's Jewish community to press the British government for a delay in announcing their policy toward Palestine.

The London Conference ended on March 15, and the British planned to announce their Palestine policy several days later.[27] Kennedy immediately informed Washington of this development on March 18, and one day later— amid the height of Jewish-American pressure—Roosevelt directed Kennedy to urge the British to delay publication.[28] Kennedy met at once with MacDonald and Halifax, discussed the Palestine situation, and subsequently notified Washington that British policy toward Palestine would be "held up in accordance with your suggestion and you will be notified before they put anything into effect."[29] Although the British government was anxious to satisfy the Arab states, MacDonald, Chamberlain, and Halifax did "not wish to ignore altogether the Jews primarily because of the latter's influence in the United States."[30] As Chamberlain noted, the British did not want to completely antagonize Washington over Palestine because, if war eventually broke out in Europe, London wanted the support and aid of the American government. Consequently, it was urged at several meetings of the British Cabinet, particularly by MacDonald, to take "some action to ease matters for the Jews."[31]

Arab delegates at the London Conference were convinced that the British government did ease up on the Jews—particularly permitting some immigration into Palestine—and failed to fulfill Arab demands because of the pressure exerted by the American government and its officials. One delegate, Assam Bey, the Egyptian minister in Iraq, confided to a State Department official that MacDonald was continually explaining to the Arab delegation that "such and such a thing could not be done because of American opposition."[32] Aly Maher Pasha, Chief of the Royal Cabinet of Egypt and an Arab delegate at the London Conference, also stated that it was the attitude of the United States over the Palestine issue that blocked any agreement between the Arabs and the British government.[33] As evidence of the change in British policy the British government, in an aide-memoire to the Roosevelt administration prior to the announcement of the White Paper, stated that, regarding immigration into

Palestine, "His Majesty's Government had resisted very strong pressure from many quarters in favour of the immediate and complete stoppage of Jewish immigration."[34] With the delay in effect, the British government proceeded to offer yet another opportunity to mollify the Jewish community before announcing the White Paper.

Knowing that the inclusion in the White Paper of some immigration into Palestine would in itself not be enough to satisfy the Jewish community, the British government, particularly the Foreign Office, saw the British Guiana Refugee Commission's report as a blessing. By issuing the report in May, the British government could take the lead in proposing a significant, constructive solution to the refugee problem. In addition, the Cabinet knew that the Guiana report would "take some of the heat out of the extreme adverse reactions which were nervously anticipated, particularly from the American Jewish community, to the new Palestine policy which was about to be announced in the White Paper."[35] Aware of the Zionist/anti-Zionist split in the Jewish community, though temporarily united since *Kristallnacht,* the British sought to appeal to that non-Zionist element which did not wish to see Palestine as the only area of refuge. Likewise, the State Department confirmed this trend after publication of the British proposals to obtain refugee areas in Guiana, Tanganyika, and in other territories. The Department noted that non-Zionists were returning to their previously held position, opposing the eventual establishment of a Jewish state in Palestine.[36] Consequently, at a meeting in the British Foreign Office on May 4, the conclusion was reached that vigorous action by the government regarding British Guiana would be stressed in order "to offer some consolation to the Jews, who would be bitterly disappointed by the decision of HM Government about Palestine."[37]

On May 10 the British Guiana Refugee Commission's report was published in Britain and the United States, one week before the announcement of the White Paper. On the following day, Chamberlain issued a statement applauding the British Guiana report and offered to begin the leasing of lands in Guiana to refugees.[38] Roosevelt and America's Zionist leaders recognized that their efforts on behalf of Palestine were suffering a serious setback. "What can I say to Justice Brandeis?" Roosevelt asked the State Department, as the British were about to issue the White Paper. "I still believe," Roosevelt said, "that any announcement about Palestine at this time by the British Government is a mistake, and I think we should tell them that."[39] In a copy of his letter to Brandeis in response to the judge's concern about the Palestine White Paper, Roosevelt wrote of the numerous times he had intervened with the British to make them cognizant of America's desire to see established a National Home for Jews in Palestine. Everything that could appropriately be done regarding Palestine, Roosevelt continued, was kept continually before the British. While he wanted to reassure Brandeis that London was fully aware of American public opinion on this question, Roosevelt also knew that the issuance of the White Paper was all but a fait accompli by mid-May.[40]

Roosevelt resigned himself to the fact that all that could have been accomplished regarding Palestine had been attempted. Any further pressure on the British, Roosevelt thought, would be unwise at that point, for London was deeply concerned with formulating a response to Hitler's occupation of Bohemia, Mussolini's destruction of Albania, and the debates in the American congress to change the neutrality laws.[41] Actually, Roosevelt confided to Assistant Secretary of State Adolph Berle that he doubted the present crisis would last five years and that "we might cross the Palestine bridge when we come to it, instead of now."[42]

However, the announcement of the British White Paper on May 17, 1939 was greeted by a bitter protest against Britain by Palestinian Jews and American Zionists. At the State Department, Hull summoned his advisors to discuss the White paper and how best to react to the demands of America's Jewish community, who were planning a campaign to influence the American government, urging intervention with the British on their behalf.[43] Several days later, Berle recorded that "a flying squad from the Zionist group, headed by Rabbi Wise, visited all the Congressmen yesterday, urging them to telephone us to request the British to hold up their White Paper on Palestine. The telephone calls came in thick and fast, likewise a delegation of Zionists, headed by Rabbi Wise; and there was an attempt to bring along a delegation of some 200 Zionists, as well."[44]

Before Wise arrived at the State Department for his meeting with Hull, Sol Bloom, chairman of the House Foreign Affairs Committee, met with Wise and the delegation. Bloom stressed that nothing could be accomplished by high-pressure tactics; quiet, thoughtful discussion with the State Department would render a greater service to the plight of Jews everywhere.[45] Actually, as spokesman for the American Jewish community, particularly the Zionist faction in this matter, Wise limited his endeavors to a quick protest toward the top diplomatic officials in Washington, avoiding a large-scale, public anti-British demonstration. He emphasized that Jews had come to Washington from every section of the United States to protest against the British, and that their sorrow and indignation should be heeded and immediately transmitted to London.[46]

Roosevelt and the State Department were aware and concerned about the reaction from the American Jewish community, but with the British position now publicly stated under its proper auspices as executor of the Palestinian Mandate, the United States was in no position to demand the revocation of the White Paper or be a party to the formulation of British policy toward Palestine. Roosevelt could only do what, in reality, he did; that is, to protest, try to get it postponed or abandoned, and in light of the war situation do what he could, but not to the point of upsetting Great Britain and losing an ally. Roosevelt did not like the White Paper but he saw both sides to the legal question and accepted the State Department's view, which was that the United States had no legal position, and therefore could not demand that the White paper was not binding.[47]

While understanding the legal position which confronted the United States, Roosevelt did react to Jewish pressure. Protests were, in fact, flooding the State Department, and Roosevelt himself empathized with the Jewish dismay over the eventual cessation of Jewish immigration into Palestine and the seemingly dashed hopes for a future Jewish homeland.[48] In a memorandum to Hull, Roosevelt thought that the British were violating the Palestine Mandate, not only by limiting immigration, but also by not moving to convert Palestine into a Jewish National Home.[49] However, the reaction of the Roosevelt administration only went so far as to instruct Kennedy on May 23, 1939 to inform Halifax of the disappointment in the United States over the White Paper, "especially in Zionist circles."[50] All parties concerned would have to wait for a more opportune moment to press for a reopening of the Palestine question.

Extremely disappointed, the leadership of the Jewish-American community—specifically Rabbi Wise—agreed with Roosevelt that a mammoth anti-British demonstration should be avoided. Wise confided to Brandeis that any demonstration against Britain "would merely furnish material to the Isolationists; in other words, give comfort to the enemies of F.D.R." This is the last thing in the world that Wise wished to do, "the last thing in the world we have the right to do."[51]

With World War II only a few months away, the attitude of most Jews, in addition to public opinion in the United States and Great Britain, seemed to be best portrayed by a former president of Israel, David Ben-Gurion. Although England had violated the Mandate in 1939, he said, Jews faced a greater emergency—to assist Britain in winning the war. Then, when victory was assured, Ben-Gurion concluded, "justice will be done us."[52] Roosevelt could not have expressed the intent of American foreign policy toward Palestine with any greater clarity.

Conclusion

On the basis of the foregoing study, it is apparent that ethnic groups in the 1930s had neither disappeared nor been assimilated. As assertive and highly organized groups, they sought to influence the political process wherever their homeland or ideological proclivity was threatened. And to a large degree they succeeded.

During negotiations with the Soviet Union concerning recognition and the establishment of diplomatic relations in 1933, Roosevelt insisted upon the inclusion of a clause on religious freedom and toleration as demanded by American Catholics. Maxim Litvinov, the Russian negotiator, exclaimed vociferously to Hull and to William Bullitt, America's first ambassador to the Soviet Union, how obsessed Roosevelt was over the insertion of the religious plank. Secretary of the Treasury Henry Morgenthau, Jr., recorded in his diary that during the negotiations Hull told him that if diplomatic relations began without first coming to an agreement on the religious issue, the Roosevelt administration would be overthrown at the next election. Roosevelt was clearly aware of Catholic-American pressure and influence, and indeed threatened to terminate the negotiations with Litvinov if the demands emanating from the Catholic community were not met. He would not have accorded diplomatic recognition in 1933 if Russia did not agree, as it did, to allow religious freedom to American nationals within its borders.

As soon as the outpouring of Catholic pressure over the recognition of Russia abated, anticlericalism and anti-Catholic activity erupted south of the border. The Mexican government in the early 1930s began a program of restricting and in some cases banning religious activities of the Catholic Church, dictating how many priests and churches were to function and who was to control the educational system. Catholic-Americans regarded these restrictions as obvious persecution, particularly the desire of the Mexican government with the apparent endorsement of America's ambassador to secularize education, traditionally the bastion of the Roman Catholic Church. Pressure applied by church members, the Church hierarchy, newspapers and magazines, and congressional pronouncements and committees, moved

Roosevelt to take an active role in quietly persuading the Mexican authorities to relax and desist from their campaign against the Church. Publicly, Roosevelt adhered to the policy of non-intervention—his Good Neighbor Policy—but privately, behind the scenes, he pursued a different course, collaborating with Father John J. Burke of the National Catholic Welfare Conference; with his friend and ambassador to Mexico, Josephus Daniels; with Undersecretary of State Sumner Welles; and with the Mexican ambassador, Castillo Najera. The record shows Roosevelt to be an astute, politically minded individual, anxious to appease this type of ethnic pressure. By working closely with his ambassador and influential Roman Catholic officials, Roosevelt helped to bring about a substantial improvement in Mexican religious conditions. Moreover, because of his covert intervention, the forecasted Catholic opposition to his reelection in 1936 did not materialize.

During the election of 1936 and shortly thereafter, Roosevelt was to once again feel the pressure of America's prominent Catholic minority. The Spanish Civil War erupted in the midst of American isolation and neutrality toward the rise of Fascism in Europe. Although Roosevelt publicly supported American neutrality legislation, he firmly desired to aid the Loyalist, legitimate government in Spain against the rebel, Facist Franco faction, even though the legitimate government contained obvious communist elements. For the most part, Catholic-Americans supported the forces of Franco. As discussion mounted within the administration for some form of intervention in this conflict, particularly on the side of the Loyalist faction, those close to Roosevelt, specifically Secretary of Interior Harold Ickes and Postmaster General James A. Farley (and Roosevelt himself), reported that his decision not to act was primarily dictated by Catholic-Americans. To have openly assisted the Loyalists, Roosevelt and Democratic party strategists feared the ultimate danger—the alienation of Catholic voters who were vital to Roosevelt's domestic programs and the continued proper functioning of the Democratic political machine. Consequently, when it seemed that aid to the Spanish government might become a reality, with the apparent blessing of the Roosevelt administration, Roosevelt leaked a story to the press that was specifically calculated to arouse Catholic opposition and defeat such a policy. Roosevelt's strategy proved a success, and the Congress, in light of Catholic opposition, could never achieve a program of support for the Loyalist government in Spain.

Similarly, while the election of 1936 was in full swing, Italian-American concern mounted over the role Roosevelt would play in curtailing trade and assistance from America to Italy during the Italo-Ethiopian War. Italian-American organizations, in conjunction with Generoso Pope, the influential editor of *Il Progresso Italo-Americano* and confidant of Roosevelt, flooded Washington with over one million letters from November of 1935 to February of 1936, when the administration's moral embargo proposal was defeated. Italian diplomatic and consular staffs also participated in the campaign, but it was Pope who reported that Roosevelt and the Congress were so deeply influenced by Italian-American pressure that they decided to extend the proposal for the passage of the Neutrality Act for another year and still sell United States manufactured goods to Italy at normal levels. The Italian-American victory—depriving Roosevelt of discretionary power to curtail trade to Italy—helped to assure Mussolini his hegemony in Ethiopia.

Equally important in the decision-making process of the Roosevelt administration were Jewish-Americans, the extent of whose influence far exceeded their relative population size. Two major foreign policy considerations affected the President—the refugee question and the formation of the state of Palestine as a Jewish homeland. Under the influential leadership of Rabbi Stephen S. Wise, president of the American Jewish Congress, and other Jewish leaders and organizations, Roosevelt and the Department of State were quick to attempt, whenever feasible, to assist refugees in their escape from Nazi Germany and Europe. When the British government proposed to terminate Jewish immigration into Palestine prior to the election of 1936 and during the fall of 1938, Roosevelt privately intervened and succeeded in altering British policy. Immigration of Jews into Palestine from 1936 to the announcement of the British White Paper in 1939, can be credited to the pressure exerted by Roosevelt on London in behalf of America's Jews.

Although Roosevelt exhibited profound empathy with the plight of the international Jewish community, evidence points to the fact that he was aware of the significant amount of anti-Semitism prevalent in the United States. In order not to exacerbate this attitude, which undoubtedly would hinder the war effort, Roosevelt proceeded with utmost caution in complying with Jewish-American demands to revise the quota system. At the same time he demanded that American officials find suitable alternate sites around the world for Jewish settlement and, after the Anschluss in the spring of 1938, called for the establishment of an international committee to be formed for the relief of refugees. Out of this concern was born the Evian Conference in 1938.

The support from Jewish-Americans for the fortunes of the Democratic party and for the presidential ambitions and elections of Franklin D. Roosevelt is well documented, and their desires in international affairs were given the highest consideration, particularly their concern for the state of Palestine. Roosevelt himself claimed to be a Zionist and supported the establishment of a Jewish homeland in Palestine. Although understanding the control exercised by Britain over the Middle East area, Roosevelt continually sought to persuade London to adhere to the Balfour Declaration and the League Mandate to relocate Palestinian Arabs in adjacent Arab states and convert Palestine into a Jewish National Home. After *Kristallnacht* in November of 1938, and on the eve of the British White Paper in 1939, Roosevelt revealed to London his financial plan to assist in the resettlement of Palestinian Arabs. On Downing Street, Roosevelt's efforts fell on deaf ears. While holding to his policies as a Zionist, he was also a pragmatist, firmly believing that, if he could not arrange for a Jewish homeland in Palestine before or during the war, such a reality would occur immediately thereafter.

On several occasions during Roosevelt's first two terms, the pressure exerted by some ethnic groups did not produce significant alterations in basic administration policy or contradict Roosevelt's foreign policy goals. The Catholic demand for a religious plank in exchange for the recognition of the Soviet Union, and Jewish pressure to assist refugees and promote the establishment of a Jewish National Home in Palestine, closely adhered to American policy positions. Roosevelt did not quarrel with accepting these positions as his own. However, major changes in administration policy did occur, particularly regarding the Good Neighbor Policy toward Mexico and neutrality legislation during the Italo-Ethiopian War. Roosevelt's private intervention in Mexico in compliance with the desires of the Catholic-American community completely overturned his public Latin America stand. And the pressure emanating from the highly organized Italian-American sector for continued American trade to Italy during the Italo-Ethiopian War provides perhaps the best example of the ethnic factor in the formulation of American foreign policy during this period.

The potential for ethnicity affecting diplomacy is evident. That it is more evident than previously shown in the making and implementing of foreign policy decisions is of utmost significance. Such pressure, interest, and influence, must be taken into consideration by future presidents, for the fact is apparent that an ethnic group will crystallize and consolidate its cultural heritage, organize it, and actively flaunt it when the ancestral homeland is in jeopardy, or its values and beliefs challenged. Overall, it seems fair to conclude that in the case of Franklin D. Roosevelt, at least, ethnic pressure was more of a factor than has thus far been realized, if one is to understand how foreign policy was made in the 1930s. The degree to which one can generalize on the basis of this case and suggest a need for more attention to ethnic factors for *all* of recent diplomatic history is a question which other scholars will have to decide.

Notes

Chapter 1

1. Herbert Feis, *1933: Characters in Crisis* (Boston: Little, Brown and Company, 1966), p. 308.

2. Ibid., p. 309.

3. Robert Paul Browder, *The Origins of Soviet-American Diplomacy* (Princeton: Princeton University Press, 1953), p. 109.

4. Ibid., p. 103.

5. Ibid.

6. Edward M. Bennett, *Recognition of Russia: An American Foreign Policy Dilemma* (Waltham, Massachusetts: Blaisdell Publishing Company, 1970), p. 86.

7. Farm Credit Diary, p. 17, in the Henry M. Morgenthau, Jr. Diaries, Franklin D. Roosevelt Library, Hyde Park, New York (hereafter referred to as FDRL).

8. Feis, *1933*, p. 307.

9. John J. Burke to Wallace Murray, January 3, 1933, Files of the office of the General Secretary of the National Catholic Welfare Conference, United States Catholic Conference, Washington, D.C. (hereafter referred to as NCWC, USCC).

10. Ibid.

11. Ibid.

12. *The Brooklyn Tablet,* March 25, 1933, p. 1. It must be said, however, that after the final position expressed by the hierarchy of the Church in September of 1933, *The Brooklyn Tablet* then publicly supported the view of the hierarchy and reversed its own prior to the negotiations with Litvinov. The front page editorial to Roosevelt on October 28, 1933, urged the President to "insist upon guarantees with regard to religious freedom . . . at the discussions in Washington. Otherwise recognition should be barred."

13. Memorandum, Marvin H. McIntyre to Cordell Hull, March 31, 1933, Official File 220 (Russia: 1933-1940), FDRL.

14. Louis Johnson to Franklin D. Roosevelt (hereafter FDR), June 17, 1933, Official File 220A (Russia: 1933), FDRL. In October of 1933, after Roosevelt decided to adopt the policy of the Catholic community to demand conditions and concessions on religious freedom from the Soviet government prior to discussing recognition, Walsh agreed to curtail his public protests and remain silent as Roosevelt negotiated with the Soviets in November.

15. *The Washington Star,* April 29, 1933, in Edmund A. Walsh Papers, Box 1932-1936, Georgetown University, Washington, D.C.

16. Response from Patrick Cardinal Hayes, under cover letter, Paul Marella to J.M. Gannon, March 10, 1933. All responses are attached to this cover letter in the file folder, entitled "Russia: Recognition by the United States," in the Files of the Office of the General Secretary of the NCWC, USCC.

17. Edmund A. Walsh to Patrick Cardinal Hayes, March 7, 1933, Walsh Papers, Section II, Folder #8, Georgetown University, Washington, D.C.

18. Response from Cardinal Hayes under cover letter, Marella to Gannon, March 10, 1933, USCC.

19. *The Brooklyn Tablet,* May 20, 1933, p. 1.

20. Feis, *1933,* p. 310.

21. Ibid., pp. 311-12.

22. Ibid., p. 313.

23. Hayes to FDR, June 16, 1933 and October 6, 1933, President's Personal File 628, FDRL.

24. Interview by John J. Burke with Jefferson Caffrey, July 21, 1933, Burke's Interview Book, USCC.

25. Interview by John J. Burke with William Phillips, July 24, 1933 (recorded on July 27, 1933), Burke's Interview Book, USCC.

26. Ibid.

27. Ibid.

28. Ibid.

29. Burke to Phillips, September 30, 1933, 861.01/2046, Record Group 59, Department of State File, National Archives, Washington, D.C. Hereafter, since all documents in this work are from the same record group at the National Archives, only the number, document, and date will be cited.

30. Hull to FDR, September 21, 1933, *Foreign Relations of the United States, Soviet Union: 1933-1939,* pp. 12-13 (hereafter referred to as FRUS).

31. Burke to Phillips, September 30, 1933, 861.01/2046.

32. Ibid.

33. Memorandum, William Bullitt to Cordell Hull, October 4, 1933, FRUS, pp. 16-17.

34. Browder, *Origins of Soviet-American Diplomacy,* p. 115.

35. Memorandum, Bullitt to FDR (no date) 1933, Official File 799, FDRL. The major points stressed by Bullitt included the following:
    1. Freedom of conscience be guaranteed in Russia for all Russian citizens and foreigners.
    2. The free exercise, both public and private, of religion and worship be guaranteed....
    3. Liberation be given to those imprisoned on account of religion.
    4. ... there be a cessation of persecution and propaganda against God in Russia and elsewhere, and that freedom be given to ministers of religion to exercise their ministry in Russia.

36. Written by FDR on memorandum, Bullitt to FDR (no date) 1933, Official File 799, FDRL.

37. Eleanor Roosevelt, *This I Remember* (New York: Harper and Brothers, 1949), p. 134.

38. Memorandum, R. Walton Moore to FDR, October 28, 1933, R. Walton Moore Papers, Box 18, FDRL.

39. Donald G. Bishop, *The Roosevelt-Litvinov Agreements: The American View* (Syracuse: Syracuse University Press, 1965), p. 70.

40. Farm Credit Diary, p. 81, in the Henry M. Morgenthau, Jr., Diaries, FDRL.

41. The Reminiscences of Henry A. Wallace, Vol. 2, Oral History Project, Columbia University, p. 267.

42. Walter G. Hooke to Marvin H. McIntyre, October 15, 1933, Official File 220A (Russia: 1933-1940), FDRL.

43. Memorandum, Edmund A. Walsh to FDR, October 31, 1933, Box 2, Unindexed papers at end of Decimal File: 1930-1939, "Interoffice Memo not included in Central Files," 1933, Record Group 59, National Archives.

44. Ibid.

45. Reverend Louis J. Gallagher, S.J., *Edmund A. Walsh, S.J.; A Biography* (New York: Benziger Brothers, Inc., 1962), p. 93.

46. Bennett, *Recognition of Russia*, p. 94; and George Q. Flynn, *American Catholics and the Roosevelt Presidency: 1932-36* (Lexington: University of Kentucky Press, 1968), p. 140. George Flynn's work is the best study of the reaction of the Catholic community toward Roosevelt's foreign policy. However, the major deficiency is that Flynn does not consult or exhaust the various collections or archival material that provide insight on Roosevelt's motives for his decisions and give a clearer conception of the extent of the influence of the ethnic factor.

47. Walsh to McIntyre, October 21, 1933, Official File 220A (Russia: 1933-1940), FDRL.

48. Press Release by Father Walsh, October 21, 1933, Files of the Office of the General Secretary of the NCWC, USCC: See also Walsh papers, Section II, Folder #7, Georgetown University, Washington, D.C.

49. *The Brooklyn Tablet,* November 18, 1933, p. 1.

50. Press Release by Most Reverend Joseph Schrembs, October 23, 1933, Files of the Office of the General Secretary of the NCWC, USCC.

51. *The Brooklyn Tablet,* October 28, 1933, p. 1.

52. Ibid.

53. Michael J. Ready to Anthony J. O'Driscoll, October 13, 1939, Files of the Office of the General Secretary of the NCWC, USCC. Father Ready succeeded Father Burke as General Secretary of the NCWC in 1936.

54. Personal interview with Grace Tully, Washington, D.C., November 11, 1976. Miss Tully was Roosevelt's personal secretary throughout his presidency and was initially the secretary to Cardinal Hayes.

55. Maurice S. Sheehy to Marvin H. McIntyre, November 3, 1933, Official File 220A, FDRL.

56. Robert I. Gannon, *The Cardinal Spellman Story* (Garden City: Doubleday and Company, Inc., 1962), p. 425. Although used by Gannon, the Spellman Papers are still restricted and are not available for scholarly perusal.

57. William Phillips Journal, Vol. 3, November 3, 1933, Phillips Papers, Houghton Library, Harvard University, Cambridge, Massachusetts (hereafter referred to as Harvard).

58. Walsh to FDR, November 7, 1933, Official File 220, FDRL.

59. Radio Address by R. Walton Moore on Recognition of Soviet Union, November 22, 1933, Moore Papers, Box 24, FDRL. According to Moore, "There were no stenographers present and no reports made, and thus, so far as the conferences are concerned, there will be a bare outline and not a full picture exposed to the eye of the future historian." A full picture, however, can be obtained using the papers of those cited and mentioned above.

60. Farm Credit Diary, p. 98, Morgenthau Diaries, FDRL.

61. Ibid., p. 99.

62. Ibid.

63. Ibid.

64. William Phillips Journal, Vol. 3, November 9, 1933, Phillips Papers, Harvard.

65. Gannon, p. 144.

66. Browder, p. 133, footnote 21. Bullitt's comments were recorded in his article, "How We Won the War and Lost the Peace," Part I, *Life*, August 30, 1948. See also Bishop, *Roosevelt-Litvinov Agreements*, p. 20.

67. Feis, *1933*, p. 320.

68. *The Brooklyn Tablet*, November 18, 1933, p. 1.

69. Feis, *1933*, p. 321.

70. Rexford G. Tugwell, *The Democratic Roosevelt* (Garden City: Doubleday and Company, Inc., 1957), p. 346.

71. James A. Farley, *The Jim Farley Story: The Roosevelt Years* (New York: McGraw-Hill Book Company, 1948), p. 44.

72. Ibid.

73. Personal interview with James A. Farley, New York City, February 17, 1975. See also, *New York Herald Tribune*, November 14, 1933, in Edmund A. Walsh Papers, Box 1932-1936 (folder: 1933), Georgetown University.

74. The Reminiscences of Frances Perkins, Vol. 4, Part 4, Oral History Project, Columbia University, pp. 548-551.

75. William Phillips Journal, Vol. 3, November 13, 1933, Phillips Papers, Harvard. According to Cardinal Spellman's papers, Kelley apparently played a significant role, in conjunction with Walsh and others, in convincing Roosevelt to insist on a religious clause prior to recognition. Gannon, p. 98.

76. FDR to Maxim Litvinov, and Maxim Litvinov to FDR, November 16, 1933, President's Secretary's File 67, FDRL.

77.   *New York Herald Tribune,* November 14, 1933, in Edmund A. Walsh Papers, Box 1932-1936 (folder: 1933), Georgetown University.

78.   Letter, Maurice S. Sheehy to Marvin H. McIntyre, November 17, 1933, President's Personal File 4996, FDRL.

79.   Robert F. Keegan to FDR, November 18, 1933, President's Personal File 628, FDRL.

80.   FDR to Robert F. Keegan, November 22, 1933, President's Personal File 628, FDRL.

81.   Sheehy to McIntyre, November 17, 1933, President's Personal File 4996, FDRL.

82.   Raymond Clapper Diaries, Box 8 (folder: Diaries 1933 #9), November 29, 1933, Clapper Papers, Manuscript Division, Library of Congress, Washington, D.C. (hereafter referred to as LC).

83.   *The Baltimore Catholic Review,* November 23, 1933, in Edmund A. Walsh Papers, Box 1932-1936 (folder: 1933), Georgetown University.

84.   Press clipping in letter, William Richardson to FDR, November 19, 1933, 861.404/367.

85.   Thomas Roth Maddux, "American Relations with the Soviet Union, 1933-1941" (Ph.D. dissertation, University of Michigan, 1969), pp. 53-54. Dissertation contains a section on Catholic-Americans and recognition, and is available at Roosevelt Library on Microfilm 385.

86.   George F. Kennan, *Memoirs: 1925-1950* (Boston: Little, Brown and Company, 1967), p. 53.

87.   Bishop, *Roosevelt-Litvinov Agreements,* p. 245

88.   Michael J. Ready to Anthony J. O'Driscoll, October 13, 1939, Files of the Office of the General Secretary of the NCWC, USCC.

89.   J.F.T. O'Connor to Marvin H. McIntyre, December 19, 1933, Official File 220A, FDRL.

90.   *The Brooklyn Tablet,* November 25, 1933, p. 3.

91.   *The Washington Post,* January 14, 1934, in Edmund A. Walsh Papers, Box 1932-1936 (folder: 1934), Georgetown University.

92.   Speech by Father Walsh on National Broadcasting System, December 9, 1933, Walsh Papers, Section II (folder: #8), Georgetown University.

Chapter 2

1.   David E. Cronon, "American Catholics and Mexican Anticlericalism, 1933-1936," *The Mississippi Valley Historical Review* 45 (September, 1958): 202.

2.   Frank Brandenburg, *The Making of Modern Mexico* (Englewood Cliffs: Prentice-Hall, Inc., 1964), p. 186.

3.   Ibid., p. 187.

4.   Ibid., p. 170.

5.   Memorandum, William F. Montavon to John J. Burke, September 12, 1934, National Catholic Welfare Conference/United States Catholic Conference Records, John J. Burke Private File on Mexico, Box 3, Catholic University of America, Washington, D.C. (hereafter referred to as Burke File on Mexico, CUA).

6. Ibid.

7. Ibid.

8. Cronon, "American Catholics," p. 202.

9. Cronon, "American Catholics," p. 205.

10. Memorandum by John J. Burke, May 7, 1934, Burke File on Mexico, Box 4, CUA. It should be noted that, more than any other person in the Catholic Church in the United States, Burke's work and private papers clearly reveal the influence of Catholic-American opinion on Roosevelt and the actions that Roosevelt took in response to Catholic pressure over the Mexican question. Father Burke, therefore, was in the middle between the Bishops' Administrative Committee of the NCWC and the Roosevelt administration, and as such, relayed such statements made by the committee to the Roosevelt administration that the United States must restore religious liberty in Mexico.

11. State Department Press Release, October 17, 1934, FRUS 4 (1935): 782.

12. John B. Sheerin, *Never Look Back: The Career and Concerns of John J. Burke* (New York: Paulist Press, 1975), pp. 160-61.

13. Ibid., p. 161.

14. Ibid., p. 160.

15. Agnes G. Regan to FDR, October 23, 1934, Official File 76-B (Folder: Church Matters, Catholic), FDRL.

16. Cronon, "American Catholics," pp. 209-213.

17. Memorandum by John J. Burke, October 1934, Burke File on Mexico, Box 4, CUA.

18. Memorandum by Burke, May 14, 1934, Burke File on Mexico, Box 4, CUA.

19. Memorandum, Montavon to Burke, September 12, 1934, Burke File on Mexico, Box 3, CUA.

20. Memorandum by Burke of interview with FDR, October 22, 1934, Burke File on Mexico, Box 5 CUA.

21. Memorandum of Telephone Conversation between Josephus Daniels and William Phillips, October 17, 1934, Daniels Papers, Box 643, LC.

22. Memorandum by Burke of interview with FDR, October 22, 1934, Burke File on Mexico, Box 5, CUA.

23. Ibid.

24. William Phillips Journal, Vol. 5, October 27, 1934, Phillips Papers, Harvard.

25. Memorandum by Burke of interview with FDR, November 12, 1934, Burke File on Mexico, Box 5, CUA.

26. Cordell Hull to Josephus Daniels, January 28, 1935, Daniels Papers, Box 82, LC.

27. Michael F. Doyle to Josephus Daniels, January 24, 1935, Daniels Papers, Box 643, LC.

28. Memorandum, Edward L. Reed to R. Walton Moore, February 5, 1935, 812.404/1549.

29. Cronon, "American Catholics," p. 215.

30. Senate Resolution 70, 74th Congress, 1st Session, FRUS 4 (1935): 786-88.

31. Key Pittman to Cordell Hull, February 5, 1935, 812.414/1549.

32. Maury Maverick to Cordell Hull, February 16, 1935, 812.404/1557.

33. William Phillip's Journal, Vol. 7, June 28, 1935, Phillips Papers, Harvard.

34. Martin H. Carmody to Frank A. Picard, April 15, 1935, Official File 28, FDRL.

35. Telegram, Martin H. Carmody to FDR, January 13, 1935, Official File 146-A (folder: Mexico 1935), FDRL.

36. Ibid.

37. Report on the Mexican Situation from Burke to chairman of the Administrative Board of the NCWC, October 15, 1935, Burke File on Mexico, Box 4, CUA.

38. *America,* March 2, 1935, pp. 491-93.

39. *The Baltimore Catholic Review,* March 8, 1935, p. 1.

40. *The Baltimore Catholic Review,* March 29, 1935, p. 1. It should be noted that many copies of this newspaper, to the exclusion of other Catholic papers, can be found in Roosevelt's White House files.

41. *The Brooklyn Tablet,* April 6, 1935, p. 1.

42. Memorandum by Burke, March 8, 1935, Burke File on Mexico, Box 5 CUA.

43. Cordell Hull to William G. McAdoo, February 12, 1935, FRUS 4 (1935): 794.

44. William E. Borah to E.J. Kelly, February 28, 1935, Borah Papers, Box 422, LC.

45. Memorandum by Hull, March 5, 1955, FRUS 4 (1935): 794.

46. Memorandum by Burke, July 11, 1935, Burke File on Mexico, Box 5, CUA.

47. Ibid.

48. Memorandum by Hull, March 5, 1935, FRUS 4 (1935): 794-96.

49. Ibid.

50. Memorandum by Burke, March 8, 1935, Burke File on Mexico, Box 5, CUA.

51. Ibid.

52. Memorandum by Burke, March 20, 1935, Burke File on Mexico, Box 5, CUA.

53. Memorandum by Burke, August 10, 1935, Burke File on Mexico, Box 5, CUA.

54. Memorandum by Burke, April 23, 1935, Burke File on Mexico, Box 5, CUA.

55. Ibid.

56. Ibid.

57. John F. Noll to FDR, May 13, 1935, President's Personal File 2406, FDRL.

58. FDR to John F. Noll, May 23, 1935, President's Personal File 2406, FDRL.

59. Memorandum by Burke of interview with FDR, May 2, 1935, Burke File on Mexico, CUA.

60. Ibid.

61. Ibid.

62. Ibid.

63. Memorandum by Burke, May 15, 1935, Burke File on Mexico, Box 5, CUA.

64. Ibid.

65. Ibid.

66. Memorandum by Burke, May 22, 1935, Burke File on Mexico, Box 5, CUA.

67. Josephus Daniels to FDR, June 25, 1935, President's Personal File 86, Box 1, FDRL.

68. Memorandum, R. Walton Moore to Cordell Hull, June 24, 1935, Moore papers, Box 10, FDRL.

69. Memorandum by Burke, June 6, 1935, Burke File on Mexico, Box 5, CUA.

70. Memorandum by Burke, June 25, 1935, Burke File on Mexico, Box 5, CUA; and memorandum of conversation between Sumner Welles and Francisco C. Najera, June 25, 1935, Moore papers, Box 10, FDRL.

71. Daniels to Roosevelt, June 25, 1935, President's Personal File 86, Box 1, FDRL.

72. Ibid.

73. Ibid.

74. Memorandum by Burke, June 25, 1935, Burke File on Mexico, Box 5, CUA.

75. Memorandum on conversation between Welles and Najera, June 25, 1935, Moore Papers, Box 10, FDRL.

76. Ibid.

77. Daniels to Roosevelt, June 25, 1935, President's Personal File 86, Box 1, FDRL.

78. Memorandum of conversation between Welles and Najera, June 25, 1935.

79. Ibid.

80. Memorandum by Burke, June 25, 1935, Burke File on Mexico, Box 5, CUA.

81. Telegram, Daniels to Hull, July 3, 1935, 812.404/1740.

82. Daniels to Sam D. McReynolds, July 2, 1935, Daniels Papers, Box 644, LC.

83. Report by Burke to the Chairman, Administrative Committee of the NCWC, October 31, 1935, Burke File on Mexico, Box 4, CUA.

84. Sumner Welles to FDR, June 25, 1935, President's Secretary's File 61, FDRL.

85. Memorandum, FDR to Myron Taylor, September 1, 1941, Taylor Papers, Box 11, FDRL.

86. Memorandum by Burke, June 25, 1935, Burke File on Mexico, Box 5, CUA.

87. Hull to Daniels, June 28, 1935, Daniels papers, Box 82, LC.

88. Flynn, *American Catholics and the Roosevelt Presidency: 1932-36,* p. 162.

89. Martin H. Carmody to FDR, June 23, 1935; Official File 28, FDRL.

90. Memorandum by Burke, July 11, 1935, Burke File on Mexico, Box 5, CUA.

91. Martin H. Carmody to Amleto Cicognani, July 15, 1935, Burke File on Mexico, Box 4, CUA.

92. Memorandum by Burke, July 11, 1935, Burke File on Mexico, Box 5, CUA.

93. Luke E. Hart to William E. Borah, July 11, 1935, Borah papers, Box 421, LC.

94. Petition relating to the religious rights of American citizens in Mexico, July 16, 1935, Official File 146-A (folder: Mexico, 1935), FDRL.

95. William Phillips Journal, Vol. 7, June 28, 1935, Phillips papers, Harvard.

96. Ibid.

97. Stephen Early to Charles S. MacFarland, July 24, 1935, Official File 164-a (folder: Mexico, 1935), FDRL. See also FRUS 4 (1935): 806.

98. Daniels to Welles, November 6, 1937, Daniels Papers, Box 106, LC.

99. Daniels to FDR, July 23, 1935. President's Personal File 61, FDRL.

100. Welles to FDR, July 12, 1935, President's Secretary's File 87, FDRL.

101. Memorandum by Burke, July 12, 1935, Burke File on Mexico, Box 5, CUA.

102. Memorandum by Burke, January 6, 1936, Burke File on Mexico, Box 5, CUA.

103. Memorandum by Burke, July 30, 1935, Burke File on Mexico, Box 5, CUA.

104. Daniels to Roosevelt, August 2, 1935, President's Secretary's File 61, FDRL.

105. Memorandum by Frank Tannenbaum in Letter, Daniels to FDR, August 26, 1935, President's Secretary's File 61, FDRL. See also Tannenbaum to Burke, September 1, 1935, Burke File on Mexico, Box 4, CUA.

106. P.H. Callahan to William F. Sands, September 27, 1935, 812.404/1792.

107. *The Commonweal,* November 22, 1935, p. 85.

108. Carmody to FDR, October 25, 1935, Official File 28, FDRL.

109. Frank A. Hall to Luke E. Hart, October 18, 1935, Burke File on Mexico, Box 3, CUA.

110. Memorandum by Burke, January 14, 1936, Burke File on Mexico, Box 5, CUA.

111. FDR to Carmody, November 13, 1935, Official File 28, FDRL.

112. Flynn, *American Catholics and the Roosevelt Presidency: 1932-36,* pp. 168-69.

113. *The Baltimore Catholic Review,* November 29, 1935, p. 1. This paper on pages 1 and 2 reported numerous editorials from the Catholic press throughout the United States.

114. Flynn, *American Catholics and Roosevelt,* p. 169.

115. Welles to Daniels, December 4, 1935, Daniels Papers, Box 106, LC.

116. Memorandum by Burke, December 12, 1935, Burke File on Mexico, Box 5, CUA.

117. Memorandum by Burke, December 14, 1935, Burke File on Mexico, Box 5, CUA.

118. Memorandum of conversation between Welles and Najera, December 12, 1935, 812.404/1829 A.

119. Memorandum by Burke, December 14, 1935, Burke File on Mexico, Box 5, CUA.

120. Memorandum of conversation between Welles and Najera, December 12, 1935, 812.404/1829 A.

121. Memorandum by Burke, December 14, 1935, Burke File on Mexico, Box 5, CUA.

122. Memorandum of conversation between Welles and Najera, December 12, 1935, 812.404/1829 A.

123. Michael F. Doyle to Marvin H. McIntyre, November 27, 1935, Official File 146-A (folder: Mexico, 1935), FDRL.

124. Memorandum, FDR to McIntryre, December 4, 1935, Official File 146-a (folder: Mexico, 1935), FDRL.

125. Doyle to Daniels, February 1, 1936, Daniels Papers, Box 226, LC.

126. Daniels to FDR, April 22, 1936, President's Secretary's File 61, FDRL. See also Daniel Papers, Box 96, LC.

127. Welles to Roosevelt, June 17, 1936, President's Secretary's File 61, FDRL.

128. Welles to FDR, June 17, 1936, President's Secretary's File 61, FDRL.

129. Memorandum by Burke, June 4, 1936, Burke File on Mexico, Box 5, CUA.

130. Memorandum by Burke, June 10, 1936, Burke File on Mexico, Box 5, CUA.

131. Sheerin, p. 171. See also Memorandum by Michael J. Ready (Father Burke's successor), March 5, 1937, Burke File on Mexico, Box 5, CUA.

132. Welles to Daniels, April 30, 1936, Daniels Papers, Box 106, LC.

133. NCWC Press Release, April 4, 1936, Burke File on Mexico, Box 1, CUA.

134. *The Brooklyn Tablet,* March 21, March 28, and May 23, 1936, p. 1.

135. Welles to Daniels, April 30, 1936, Daniels Papers, Box 106, LC.

136. Memorandum by Burke, May 4, 1936, Burke File on Mexico, Box 5, CUA.

137. Memorandum, S.N. Reed to Welles, May 13, 1936, 812.404/1890.

138. Memorandum by Michael J. Ready of Notes on conversation between Daniels and Hull, December 22, 1936, Burke File on Mexico, Box 3, CUA.

139. Josephus Daniels Diary, August 8, 1936, Daniels Papers, Box 8, LC.

140. Memorandum by Frank Tannenbaum for Daniels, August 21, 1936, Burke File on Mexico, Box 4, CUA. See also President's Secretary's File 61, FDRL.

141. Report of conversation between Daniels and Lazaro Cardenas, October 9, 1936, 812.404/2017.

142. Daniels to FDR, December 12, 1936, President's Secretary's File 61, FDRL.

143. Hull to Daniels, September 9, 1936, Daniels Papers, Box 82, LC.

144. Hull to Daniels, September 18, 1936, Daniels Papers, Box 82, LC.

145. Michael F. Doyle to Daniels, October 24, 1936, Daniels Papers, Box 229, LC.

146. *The Washington Post,* October 11, 1936, p. 1.

147.   Cronon, "American Catholics," p. 220.

148.   Ibid.

Chapter 3

1.   F. Jay Taylor, *The United States and the Spanish Civil War* (New York: Octagon Books, 1936), pp. 163-64. This work by Taylor, coupled with the studies of Richard Traina, *American Diplomacy and the Spanish Civil War* (Bloomington: Indiana University Press, 1968) and George Flynn, *Roosevelt and Romanism: Catholics and American Diplomacy, 1937-1945* (Westport, Connecticut: Greenwood Press, 1976) are the most authoritative sources on this topic. However, neither of these authors reach the conclusion set forth in this work.

2.   Taylor, *United States and Spanish Civil War*, p. 164.

3.   Traina, *American Diplomacy*, pp. 9-10.

4.   Robert A. Divine, *The Illusion of Neutrality* (Chicago: University of Chicago Press, 1962), p. 193.

5.   Ibid., pp. 64, 76.

6.   Ibid., p. 223.

7.   James H. Ryan to FDR, September 25, 1936, President's Personal File 3960, FDRL. See also Maurice S. Sheehy to Stephen Early, September 29, 1936, in same collection.

8.   Memorandum, Stephen Early to FDR, September 30, 1936, President's Personal File 3960, FDRL.

9.   Flynn, *American Catholics and the Roosevelt Presidency, 1932-36*, pp. 210-11.

10.   Edward J. Kelly to FDR, September 16, 1936, President's Personal File 321, FDRL.

11.   Memorandum, Stephen Early to FDR, September 30, 1936, President's Personal File 3960, FDRL.

12.   Memorandum, FDR to Marvin H. McIntyre, October 7, 1936, President's Personal File 3960, FDRL.

13.   William E. Leuchtenburg, *Franklin D. Roosevelt and the New Deal: 1932-1940* (New York: Harper and Row, Publishers, 1936), p. 184.

14.   Flynn, *American Catholics and The Roosevelt Presidency*, pp. 232-33.

15.   Sumner Welles, *The Time for Decision* (New York: Harper and Brothers Publishers, 1944), p. 60.

16.   The Reminiscenses of Norman Thomas, Oral History Project, Columbia University, pp. 138-39.

17.   Ibid., pp. 130, 134.

18.   Elliot Roosevelt and James Brough, *A Rendezvous with Destiny: The Roosevelts of the White House* (New York: G.P. Putnam's Sons, 1975), p. 191.

19.   *The New York Times*, May 17, 1938, p. 5.

20. Traina, *American Diplomacy*, p. 184.

21. Taylor, *United States and Spanish Civil War*, p. 158.

22. Traina, *American Diplomacy*, p. 195.

23. Memorandum, Sumner Welles to Marvin H. McIntyre, June 18, 1937, Official File 422 C, FDRL.

24. Taylor, *United States and Spanish Civil War*, pp. 158-59.

25. Memorandum, Welles to McIntyre, June 18, 1937, Official File 422 C, FDRL.

26. *The New York Times*, January 31, 1938, p. 1. See also Taylor, p. 156.

27. Traina, *American Diplomacy*, p. 127.

28. Taylor, *United States and Spanish Civil War*, p. 157.

29. Eleanor Roosevelt, *This I Remember* (New York: Harper and Brothers, 1949), pp. 161-62.

30. FDR to Louis Fischer, February 28, 1938, Fischer Papers, Box 70-4, LC.

31. Hadley Cantril, ed., *Public Opinion, 1935-1946* (Princeton: Princeton University Press, 1951), p. 808.

32. Ibid., p. 808.

33. Taylor, *United States and Spanish Civil War*, p. 174.

34. Traina, *American Diplomacy*, p. 140.

35. Breckinridge Long Diary, March 27, 1938, Long Papers, Box 5, LC.

36. Jay Pierrepont Moffat Diary, Vol. 40, March 24, 1938, Moffat Papers, Harvard.

37. Long Diary, March 27, 1938.

38. Moffat Diary, March 24, 1938.

39. Ibid.

40. Long Diary, March 27, 1938.

41. Ibid.

42. Ibid., March 31, 1938.

43. Ibid.

44. Ibid., April 1, 1938.

45. Ibid., April 10, 1938.

46. Ibid., April 1, 1938.

47. Moffat Diary, March 14, 1938.

48. Harold L. Ickes, *The Secret Diary of Harold L. Ickes,* 3 vols. (New York: Simon and Schuster, 1954), 2: 349-350.

49. Ibid., 2: 389.

50. Moffat Diary, April 4, 1938.

51. Traina, *American Diplomacy*, p. 130.

52. Moffat Diary, March 24, 1938.

53. James Roosevelt to Paul H. Todd, May 5, 1938, 852.24/624.

54. Traina, *American Diplomacy,* pp. 130-31.

55. Ibid., p. 130.

56. Moffat Diary, May 4, 1938.

57. Confidential Report attached to letter, Paul H. Todd to James Roosevelt, April 25, 1938, Official File 1561, FDRL.

58. Traina, *American Diplomacy,* p. 131.

59. Long Diary, May 8, 1938.

60. Personal interview with James A. Farley by George Q. Flynn, cited in his work *Roosevelt and Romanism: Catholics and American Diplomacy, 1937-1945,* p. XIV.

61. R. Walton Moore to Cordell Hull, May 5, 1938, 852.24/621.

62. James MacGregor Burns, *Roosevelt: The Lion and the Fox* (New York: Harcourt, Brace and World, Inc., 1956), p. 356. See also Taylor, *United States and Spanish Civil War,* p. 173.

63. Taylor, *United States and Spanish Civil War,* p. 185.

64. Claude Bowers, *My Life: The Memoirs of Claude Bowers* (New York: Simon and Schuster, 1962), p. 292.

65. Taylor, *United States and Spanish Civil War,* pp. 185, 195.

66. Donald F. Crosby, "Boston Catholics and the Spanish Civil War: 1936-39," *New England Quarterly* 44 (March 1971): 82-84.

67. Ibid., pp. 84-85.

68. Confidential Report attached to letter, Paul H. Todd to James Roosevelt, April 25, 1938, Official File 1561, FDRL.

69. James Roosevelt to the author, October 20, 1976. James A. Farley, chairman of the Democratic National Committee, similarly referred to Mundelein "as the leader of the American Catholics." Memorandum, Conversation between Arthur Krock and James A. Farley, March 7, 1940, Krock Papers, Box 25, The Seeley G. Mudd Library, Princeton University, Princeton, New Jersey.

70. Joseph P. Lash, *Eleanor and Franklin* (New York: W.W. Norton and Company, 1971), p. 569.

71. Flynn, *Roosevelt and Romanism,* p. 43.

72. Moffat Diary, May 2 and 3, 1938.

73. Ibid., May 3, 1938.

74. Ibid., May 4 and 5, 1938.

75. Ibid., May 3, 1938.

76. Ibid.

77. F.I. Israel, *Nevada's Key Pittman* (Lincoln: University of Nebraska Press, 1963), p. 157.

78. Moffat, Diary, January 23, 1939.

79. Ibid., May 5, 1938.

80. Ibid., May 9, 1938.

81. Traina, *American Diplomacy,* p. 132.

82. Moffat Diary, May 3, 1938.

83. Ibid., May 4, 1938.

84. Traina, *American Diplomacy,* pp. 131-32.

85. Moffat Diary, May 4, 1938.

86. Divine, *Illusion of Neutrality,* pp. 224-25.

87. Moffat Diary, May 4, 1938. Moffat's diary and the study of Traina refute the allegation of Divine and Taylor that Hull and his advisers agreed to lift the embargo for both sides in Spain.

88. Ibid.

89. Ibid., May 5, 1938.

90. Hugh Thomas, *The Spanish Civil War* (New York: Harper and Row 1977), pp. 824-825. See note 1 on page 825 and interview with Krock by Thomas on January 9, 1963. Without access to Sumner Welles's papers, one cannot be sure who leaked the story, but no matter who did plant the story, one can be assured that Roosevelt was contacted by wireless—as he had been on previous occasions—for his approval and consent. It should be noted, however, that in the Krock papers at Princeton University, Krock does reveal that he planted or "leaked" stories before this point in time for Cordell Hull. In 1948, he wrote to Hull, stating that he "wondered why you made no mention [in Hull's *Memoirs*] of *The New York Times* editorial in 1937 which I wrote at your instigation...." Krock to Hull, May 21, 1948, Krock Papers, Box 29, Princeton University.

91. Ibid., p. 824.

92. Ickes Diary, 2: 389. See also Robert Bendiner, *The Riddle of the State Department* (New York: Farrar and Rinehart, Inc., 1942), p. 61.

93. Traina, *American Diplomacy,* p. 135.

94. The Reminiscences of Arthur Krock, Oral History Project, Columbia University, p. 30.

95. *The New York Times,* May 5, 1938, p. 1.

96. Moffat Diary, May 10, 1938.

97. Guy E. Shipler to John W. McCormack, May 9, 1938, Montavon Papers, Box 2, CUA.

98. *The Brooklyn Tablet,* May 8, 1938, p. 1.

99. Ibid., May 14, 1938, p. 1.

100. A deletion from Ickes Diary, Vol. 2, May 7, 1938, in Ickes Papers, Microfilm, Reel 2, p. 2755, LC. Freda Kirchwey, the editor of *The Nation,* also wrote in a letter to Louis Fischer in Spain that one "can only say now that the Administration shows less and less willingness to face the implications of the Spanish embargo and the neutrality policy in general.... The President and Hull doubtles [sic] would like to lift the embargo, but the opinion inside the

State Department, doubtless reflecting Catholic-fascist opinion outside, is too much for them." Freda Kirchwey to Louis Fischer, April 22, 1938, Fischer Papers, Box 2, Princeton University.

101. *The Brooklyn Tablet,* May 21, 1938, p. 1.

102. The Reminiscences of Henry Wallace, Oral History Project, Columbia University, pp. 1686-87.

103. Personal interview by the author with James A. Farley, New York City, February 17, 1975.

104. Julio Alvarez del Vago, *Give Me Combat: The Memoirs of Julio Alvarez del Vago* (Boston: Little, Brown and Company, 1973), p. 184.

105. Memorandum of Conversation between Claude Bowers and Alvarez del Vago, May 9, 1938, 852.00/7931.

106. Max Lerner, "Behind Hull's Embargo," *The Nation* 146 (May 28, 1938): 609.

107. Traina, *American Diplomacy,* p. 184.

108. Personal interview by the author with John W. McCormack, Boston, Massachusetts, December 15, 1976.

109. Traina, *American Diplomacy,* p. 138.

110. Moffat Diary, May 9, 1938.

111. Ibid.

112. Ickes Diary, 2: 389-90.

113. A deletion from Ickes Diary, Vol. 2, May 12, 1938, in Ickes Papers, Microfilm, Reel 2, p. 2761, LC.

114. Personal interview by the author with Thomas G. Corcoran, Washington, D.C., November 19, 1976.

115. Moffat Diary, May 9, 1938.

116. *The New York Times,* May 16, 1938, p. 6. See also Hans Dieckhoff to Foreign Minister, May 16, 1938, in U.S., Department of State, *Documents on German Foreign Policy, 1918-1945,* 13 vols. (Washington, D.C.: U.S. Government Printing Office, 1949-1962), 3: 656-57.

117. Thomas, *Spanish Civil War,* p. 826. See note 1.

118. Moffat Diary, May 9 and 10, 1938.

119. Franklin D. Roosevelt, *Complete Presidential Press Conferences of Franklin D. Roosevelt,* 25 vols. (New York: Da Capo Press, 1972), 11: 407, 410.

120. Long Diary, May 11, 1938.

121. Traina, *American Diplomacy,* p. 139.

122. Moffat Diary, May 13, 1938.

123. Ibid.

124. Long Diary, May 17, 1938.

125. Divine, *Illusion of Neutrality,* p. 201.

126. Ibid., p. 236.

127. Ibid.

128. David J. Valaik, "Catholics, Neutrality, and the Spanish Embargo, 1937-1939," *The Journal of American History* 54 (June 1967): 78-79.

129. Michael F. Doyle to Marvin H. McIntyre, January 15, 1939, Official File 422 C, FDRL.

130. Valaik, pp. 81-82.

131. Moffat Diary, January 24, 1939.

132. Valaik, p. 80. Valaik, Traina, and Flynn give the best account of the organized Catholic-American pressure during this period.

133. Ibid., p. 81.

134. Moffat Diary, January 23, 1939.

135. Louis Fischer to Otto Simon, January 19, 1939, Fischer Papers, Box 2, Princeton University.

136. Israel, *Nevada's Key Pittman,* p. 157. See also Moffat Diary, January 19, 1939.

137. Divine, *Illusion of Neutrality,* p. 238.

138. Harold L. Ickes to Claude Bowers, January 11, 1939, Ickes Papers, Box 361, LC.

139. Claude Bowers to Josephus Daniels, May 2, 1939, Daniels Papers, Box 662, LC.

140. Moffat Diary, January 20, 1939.

141. Ickes Diary, 2: 586. See also *The Christian Science Monitor,* January 26, 1939, p. 1.

142. The Reminiscences of Henry Wallace, Oral History Project, Columbia University, p. 2280.

Chapter 4

1. Manfred Jonas, *Isolationism in America: 1935-1941* (Ithaca, New York: Cornell University Press, 1966), p. 172.

2. Ibid., pp. 172-73.

3. Cordell Hull, *The Memoirs of Cordell Hull,* 2 vols. (New York: The Macmillan Company, 1948), 1:192-93.

4. Brice Harris, Jr., *The United States and the Italo-Ethiopian Crisis* (Stanford: Stanford University Press, 1964), p. 80. This work is the best study of the American posture in the war and of the role of Italian-Americans in the formulation of American policy. Harris concluded that Italian-Americans noticeably influenced the outcome of neutrality legislation in 1936, but rather than citing numerous archival materials for his conclusions, Harris relied heavily on John Norman's article, "Influence of Pro-Fascist Propaganda on American Neutrality: 1935-36," in *Essays in History and International Relations* (Worcester: The Clark University Press, 1949), pp. 193-214, edited by Dwight E. Lee and George E. McReynolds. However, Norman did not reveal the actual extent of Italian-American pressure, as is documented in this work. For a recent study that is devoted, at least in part, to this topic but which unfortunately offers no new evidence substantially different from Harris and Norman, see Robert Dallek, *Franklin D. Roosevelt and American Foreign Policy, 1932-1945* (New York: Oxford University Press, 1979).

5.   Hull, *Memoirs,* 1: 417.

6.   Robert W. Bingham Diary, March 12, 1935, Bingham Papers, LC.

7.   Hull, L: 417.

8.   Ickes Diary, 1: 445-46.

9.   Hull, *Memoirs,* 1: 414.

10. Alexander DeConde, *Half-Bitter, Half-Sweet: An Excursion into Italian-American History* (New York: Charles Scribner's Sons, 1971), pp. 212-13.

11. Memorandum, "Italian Racial Stock in the United States," October 8, 1935, Official File 233-A, Box 2, FDRL.

12. John P. Diggins, *Mussolini and Fascism: The View from America* (Princeton: Princeton University Press, 1972), p. 304. Diggins does not portray in detail the impact and influence of the Italian-American community on the Roosevelt administration and its neutrality policy during the Italo-Ethiopian War. Even though numerous archival material was not consulted, he does conclude that "in Congressional circles it was obvious that Italian-American pressure helped defeat revision" of the Neutrality Act of 1935. See also Dallek, *Roosevelt and American Foreign Policy,* p. 119, for a similar portrayal.

13. Ibid., p. 307.

14. Telegram, Alexander Kirk to Cordell Hull, June 19, 1935, 765.84/386.

15. John P. Diggins, "Mussolini and America: Hero-Worship, Charisma, and the 'Vulgar Talent'," *The Historian* 28 (August 1966): 561.

16. Telegram, Kirk to Hull, June 19, 1935, 765.84/386.

17. John De Pastino to Augustine Lonergan to Cordell Hull, August 17, 1935, 765.84/877.

18. Telegram, Italo-American Employers and Workers Association to Senator Royal S. Copeland, September 28, 1935, 765.84/1744.

19. Diggins, *Mussolini and Fascism,* p. 302.

20. Harris, *U.S. and Italo-Ethiopian Crisis,* p. 79.

21. DeConde, *Italian-American History,* p. 217. See also John V. Cox, "The Italo-Ethiopian Crisis of 1935-1936 in the United States Foreign Relations" (Master's thesis, Naval War College, 1969), p. 102.

22. Telegram, Mattucci (no first name) to Hull, October 18, 1935, 765.84/1939.

23. *The New York Times,* October 31, 1935, p. 1.

24. FRUS 1 (1935): 812-13.

25. Memorandum, FDR to Henry Morgenthau, Jr., November 6, 1935, Official File 233-A, Box 2, FDRL. See also Official File 447, FDRL.

26. FRUS 1 (1935): 819.

27. Harris, *U.S. and Italo-Ethiopian Crisis,* p. 123.

28. Ettore Patrizi to A.P. Giannini to the White House, November 25, 1935, Official File 233-A, Box 2, FDRL.

29.   "Italians" to FDR, December 2, 1935, Official File 233-A, Box 2, FDRL.

30.   DeConde, *Italian-American History,* p. 219.

31.   Memorandum, FDR to Hull, November 23, 1935, Official File 233-A, Box 2, FDRL.

32.   Joseph Green to Jay Pierrepont Moffat, April 22, 1936, Moffat Papers, Volume 10, Harvard (hereafter referred to as Green to Moffat, April 22, 1936).

33.   R. Walton Moore to John Cudahy, November 7, 1935, Official File 20, Container 5, FDRL.

34.   Green to Moffat, April 22, 1936.

35.   U.S., Congress, Senate, Committee on Foreign Relations, *Neutrality, Hearings before Senate Committee on Foreign Relations.* S. 3474, 74th Cong., 2d sess., 1936; p. 209.

36.   *The New York Times,* November 27, 1935, p. 1.

37.   Long Diary, November 27, 1935.

38.   Ickes Diary, 1: 483.

39.   DeConde, *Italian-American History,* p. 220.

40.   Jonas, pp. 175-76. Jonas proposed that the "examination of isolationist policies and statements of the movement's leading spokesmen confirms that isolationism during the period just before the Second World War was not essentially an ethnic matter," and that in attempting to account for ethnic considerations in explaining isolationism "as applied to the entire isolationist tradition . . . is clearly inadequate." See pp. 19-21. While on the surface this explanation may seem reasonable, my examination of archival material and manuscripts indicates the opposite.

41.   Green to Moffat, January 9, 1936, Moffat Papers, Vol. 10, Harvard.

42.   Ibid.

43.   Norman, "Pro-fascist Propaganda," p. 201.

44.   Robert A. Divine, *The Illusion of Neutrality* (Chicago: University of Chicago Press, 1962), p. 132.

45.   Harold B. Hinton, "To Keep America Out of War," Current History (April 1936), p. 23.

46.   Diggins, *Mussolini and Fascism,* p. 304.

47.   Hinton, "To Keep America Out of War," p. 23.

48.   Norman, "Pro-Fascist Propaganda," pp. 205-210.

49.   *Il Progresso Italo-Americano,* January 28, 1936, p. 1.

50.   Divine, *Illusion of Neutrality,* p. 150.

51.   Philip Giordano (President, Italian-American Republican National League) to William Borah, January 16, 1936, Borah Papers, Box 439, LC.

52.   Dino Copello to Breckinridge Long, January 6, 1936, Long Papers, Box 115, LC.

53.   William Phillips Journal, Vol. 9, January 25, 1936, Phillips Papers, Harvard.

54.   Harris, *U.S. and Italo-Ethiopian Crisis,* p. 124.

55.   DeConde, *Italian-American History,* p. 220.

56. Norman, "Pro-Fascist Propaganda," p. 201.

57. U.S., Congress, House, Representative Marcantonio speaking about the Neutrality Bill of 1936, 74th Cong., 2d sess., February 17, 1936, *Congressional Record* 80: 2221.

58. Ibid., p. 2247. Speech by Representative Healey concerning the Neutrality Bill of 1936.

59. U.S., Congress, Senate, Committee on Foreign Relations, *Neutrality, Hearings before Senate Committee on Foreign Relations.* S. 3474, 74th Cong., 2d sess., 1936, p. 292.

60. Ibid., p. 192.

61. Ibid., p. 251.

62. Memorandum, Marvin H. McIntyre to FDR, January 23, 1939, Official File 1561, FDRL.

63. Memorandum by H.M. Kannee for the files, January 23, 1936, Official File 1561, FDRL.

64. Walton Moore to FDR, January 23, 1936, Official File 1561, Box 1, FDRL.

65. Harris, *U.S. and Italo-Ethiopian Crisis,* p. 124.

66. Divine, *Illusion of Neutrality,* p. 151. Although the extent of the Black-American influence cannot be shown adequately, the administration, fearful of losing the Black vote in the election of 1936, evidently considered this element in its decisions to impose the moral embargo against Italy in October of 1935 and to refrain from recognizing Italy's incorporation of Ethiopia in the new Italian empire. See William Phillips Journal, Vol. 16, July 5, 1938, Phillips Papers, Harvard.

67. Diggins, *Mussolini and Fascism,* p. 282.

68. Telegram, Cordell Hull to Breckinridge Long, February 1, 1936, 765.84111/79. See also William Phillips Journal, Vol. 9, January 31, 1936, Phillips Papers, Harvard.

69. Long to Hull, February 7, 1936, 765.84111/86.

70. Ibid.

71. Green to Moffat, April 22, 1936.

72. Long to Hull, February 7, 1936, 765.84111/86.

73. Ibid.

74. Green to Moffat, April 22, 1936.

75. Green to Moffat, April 22, 1936.

76. Telegram, Hull to Long, February 1, 1936, 765.84111/79.

77. Green to Moffat, April 22, 1936.

78. Ibid.

79. Ibid.

80. Ibid.

81. Divine, *Illusion of Neutrality,* p. 155.

82. Memorandum, Joseph C. Green to Carleton Savage, July 27, 1944, Green Papers, Carton 9, Mudd Library, Princeton University. In 1944, the State Department began to compile a history of neutrality legislation from 1935 to 1941. The State Department asked Green to

submit his recollection. At that time, Green was the only one, among R. Walton Moore, Key Pittman, and Sam McReynolds, left alive who had as much detailed knowledge of neutrality policy. Consequently, when the State Department completed its neutrality history, *Neutrality Legislation: 1935-1941,* Green was asked to correct any discrepancies in the work, written by one Ronald Young. In commenting, Green sent this memorandum to the State Department.

83. Green to Moffat, April 22, 1936.

84. Ibid.

85. Hinton, "To Keep America Out of War," p. 25.

86. Green to Moffat, April 22, 1936.

87. Memorandum, Green to Savage, July 27, 1944, Green Papers, Carton 9, Princeton University.

88. Memorandum R. Walton Moore, (no month or day) 1936, Moore Papers, Box 14, FDRL.

89. Norman, "Pro-fascist Propaganda," p. 212.

Chapter 5

1. For recent studies that are devoted, at least in part, to the influence of the Jewish-American community during this period with specific reference to the role of Rabbi Stephen S. Wise, see Melvin Urofsky's work, *A Voice That Spoke For Justice: The Life and Times of Stephen S. Wise* (Albany, New York: State University of New York Press, 1981) and the book cited previously, *Franklin D. Roosevelt and American Foreign Policy, 1932-1945,* by Robert Dallek. Touted as a comprehensive analysis of Roosevelt's foreign policy, Dallek's book unfortunately devoted only several pages to Jewish-American interests and concludes that "the Jewish dilemma did not command a very high priority" in the mind of FDR. The books by Henry Feingold, *The Politics of Rescue: The Roosevelt Administration and the Holocaust, 1938-1945* (New Brunswick: Rutgers University Press, 1970), and David S. Wyman, *Paper Walls: America and the Refugee Crisis, 1938-1941* (Amherst: The University of Massachusetts Press, 1968), are also particularly good on the Palestine issue in the 1930s, illustrating the relationship between the Roosevelt administration and Jewish-Americans. However, since both books begin in 1938, neither discusses the Palestine question as it evolved and affected Roosevelt in 1936.

2. Arthur Morse, *While Six Million Died: A Chronicle of American Apathy* (New York: Random House, 1967), p. 157. Although Morse attempted to document the apathy and neglect of the Roosevelt administration toward rescue efforts, he failed to document the actions of the administration toward the private initiatives pursued and accomplished by the President and his administration.

3. Hull to FDR, July 27, 1936, 867N.00/334.

4. Telegram, Leland B. Morris to Cordell Hull, May 18, 1936, FRUS 3 (1936): 442.

5. Ibid.

6. Hull to FDR, July 27, 1936, 867N.00/334.

7. Ibid.

8. Telegram, Wilbur J. Carr to Leland B. Morris, May 23, 1936, FRUS 3 (1936): 443.

9. Stephen S. Wise to Chaim Weizman, March 6, 1936, Wise Papers, Box 122, American Jewish Historical Society on the Brandeis University campus in Waltham, Massachusetts. Hereafter, AJHS.

10. Wise to FED, May 18, 1936, Official File 700, Container 1, FDRL.

11. FDR to Wise, June 8, 1936, Official File 700, Container 1, FDRL.

12. Ibid.

13. Telegram, Will Rosenblatt to S.H. Rifkind, July 15, 1936, President's Secretary's File 46, FDRL.

14. Samuel I. Rosenman to FDR, July 16, 1936, President's Secretary's File 46, FDRL.

15. Wise to Weizman, May 29, 1936, Wise Papers, Box 122, AJHS.

16. Telegram, Cordell Hull to Robert Bingham, July 27, 1936, FRUS 3 (1936): 444.

17. Ibid.

18. Telegram, Bingham to Hull, July 28, 1936, FRUS 3 (1936): 445.

19. Telegram, George Wadsworth to Cordell Hull, August 22, 1936, FRUS 3 (1936): 446-47.

20. Stephen S. Wise to David Niles, October 7, 1936, Wise Papers, Box 118, AJHS.

21. Ibid.

22. Memorandum by Wallace Murray, Chief of the Division of Near Eastern Affairs, September 22, 1936, FRUS 3 (1936): 451.

23. Memorandum, Wallace Murray to R. Walton Moore, September 10, 1936, 867N.00/383-1/2

24. Stephen S. Wise to Louis D. Brandeis, September 1, 1936, Wise Papers, Box 106, AJHS.

25. Telegram, Farley to FDR, August 31, 1936, Wise Papers, Box 68, AJHS.

26. Wise to Brandeis, September 1, 1936, Wise Papers, Box 106, AJHS.

27. Wise to Weizmann, October 26, 1936, Wise Papers, Box 122, AJHS.

28. Telephone conversation, Hull and Bingham, September 1, 1936, Hull Papers, Microfilm Reel 35, LC.

29. Ibid.

30. Ibid.

31. Ibid.

32. Ibid.

33. Ibid.

34. Wise to Brandeis, September 1, 1936, Wise Papers, Box 106, AJHS.

35. Memorandum of telephone conversation between Wise and Weizmann, September 1, 1936, Wise Papers, Box 122, AJHS.

36. Memorandum, Henry A. McBride to Hull, September 4, 1936, Hull Papers, Microfilm Reel 35, LC. See also Memorandum by Wallace Murray, September 22, 1936, FRUS 3 (1936): 450-51.

37. Wise to Hull, September 9, 1936, Wise Papers, Box 66, AJHS.

38. Brandeis to Wise, September 4, 1936, Wise Papers, Box 106, AJHS.

39. Memorandum of conversation with FDR by Wise, October 5, 1936, Wise Papers, Box 68, AJHS. See also Wise to Brandeis, May 21, 1937, Wise Papers, Box 106, AJHS; and Wise to McIntyre, November 13, 1936, 867N.01/725-1/2.

40. Ibid.

41. Ibid.

42. Hadley Cantril, ed., *Public Opinion: 1935-1946 (Princeton: Princeton University Press, 1951), p. 591.*

Chapter 6

1. Arthur D. Morse, *While Six Million Died: A Chronicle of American Apathy* (New York: Random House, 1968), pp. 199-201. See also Lucy S. Dawidowicz, *The War Against the Jews: 1933-1945* (New York: Holt, Rinehart, and Winston, 1975), pp. 374-75.

2. David S. Wyman, *Paper Walls: America and the Refugee Crisis, 1938-1941* (Amherst: The University of Massachusetts Press, 1968), p. 49.

3. Henry Feingold, *The Politics of Rescue: The Roosevelt Administration and the Holocaust, 1938-1945* (New Brunswick: Rutgers University Press, 1970), p. 25. Neither Wyman nor Feingold rely on the papers of Rabbi Wise, which provide new insights on the influence of the Jewish-American community on the Roosevelt administration during the period from 1936 to 1939.

4. Wyman, *America and the Refugee Crisis,* p. 33.

5. The Reminiscences of Frances Perkins, Book 7, Part 3, Oral History Project, Columbia University, p. 362.

6. Report of meeting between Wise and Roosevelt, January 22, 1938, Wise Papers, Box 181, AJHS.

7. Wyman, *America and the Refugee Crisis,* p. 33.

8. Report of meeting between Wise and Roosevelt, January 22, 1938, Wise Papers, Box 181, AJHS.

9. Ibid.

10. Ibid.

11. Ibid.

12. Will Rosenblatt to Stephen S. Wise, May 9, 1938, Wise Papers, Box 65, AJHS. Rosenblatt incorporated in this letter to Wise a 1937 letter from Wise, in which Wise divulged the attitude mentioned above.

13. Report of meeting between Wise and Roosevelt, January 22, 1938, Wise Papers, Box 181, AJHS.

14. Wise to Rosenblatt, May 9, 1938, Wise Papers, Box 65, AJHS.

15. Report of meeting between Wise and Roosevelt, January 22, 1938, Wise Papers, Box 181, AJHS.

16. John Harvey, ed., *The Diplomatic Diaries of Oliver Harvey, 1937-1940* (New York: St. Martin's Press, 1970), p. 220.

17. The Reminiscences of Frances Perkins, Book 7, Part 3, Oral History Project, Columbia University, p. 363.

18. Wyman, *America and the Refugee Crisis*, p. 67. Also personal interview with Emanuel Celler, New York City, July 20, 1976.

19. Hadley Cantril, ed., *Public Opinion: 1935-1946* (Princeton: Princeton University Press, 1951), p. 1150.

20. Stephen S. Wise, to Felix Frankfurter, March 30, 1938, Wise Papers, Box 109, AJHS.

21. Harold L. Ickes Diary, July 3, 1939, Ickes Papers, Microfilm reel 2, p. 2827, LC.

22. Wyman, *America and the Refugee Crisis*, pp. 67-68.

23. Memorandum, George Messersmith to Cordell Hull, March 31, 1938, 840.48 Refugees/84-1/2.

24. Moffat Diary, March 21, 1938.

25. Personal interview with Dr. Isador Lubin, New York City, July 21, 1976.

26. Feingold, *Roosevelt Administration and the Holocaust*, p. 23. Also from personal interview with Dr. Isodor Lubin, July 21, 1976.

27. Saul S. Friedman, *No Haven for the Oppressed* (Detroit: Wayne State University Press, 1973), p. 45.

28. Max Freedman, ed., *Frankfurter and Roosevelt: Their Correspondence, 1928-1945* (Boston: Little, Brown and Company, 1967), p. 451.

29. Personal interview with Benjamin V. Cohen, Washington, D.C., December 1, 1976.

30. Friedman, *No Haven for the Oppressed*, p. 45.

31. Letter, Wise to Frankfurter, March 30, 1938, Wise Papers, Box 109, AJHS.

32. Moffat Diary, March 19 and 20, 1938.

33. Memorandum, n.d. (late 1938), written by T.C. Achilles concerning refugee program under cover memorandum by N.N. Butler to Duggan and Drew (no first names), November 15, 1938, 840.48 Refugees/900-1/2.

34. Welles to FDR, April 6, 1938, 840.48 Refugees/117/2/7.

35. Wise to Frankfurter, March 30, 1938, Wise Papers, Box 109, AJHS.

36. Moffat Diary, March 25, 1938.

37. FDR to Irving Lehman, March 30, 1938, Official File 3186, Box 1, FDRL.

38. FDR to Herbert Lehman, April 4, 1938, Official File 3186, Box 1, FDRL.

39. The Reminiscences of Herbert Lehman, Oral History Project, Columbia University, p. 168.

40. Maldwin Fertig to FDR, March 25, 1938, President's Personal File 5029, FDRL.

41. Freedman, *Frankfurter and Roosevelt*, p. 450.

42. Wise to Frankfurter, March 30, 1938, Wise Papers, Box 109, AJHS.

43. Elliot Roosevelt and James Brough, *A Rendezvous with Destiny: The Roosevelts of the White House* (New York: G.P. Putnam's Sons, 1975), p. 225.

Chapter 7

1. David S. Wyman, *Paper Walls: America and the Refugee Crisis: 1938-1941* (Amherst: The University of Massachusetts Press, 1968), p. 51.

2. Moffat Diary, October 12, 1938.

3. Telegram, Wise to FDR, October 6, 1938, Wise Papers, Box 181, AJHS.

4. Telegram, Chaim Weizmann to Nahum Goldman, Stephen S. Wise, Louis Lipsky, October 6, 1938, Wise Papers, Box 122, AJHS.

5. Telegram, Wise to Roosevelt, October 6, 1938, Wise Papers, Box 181, AJHS.

6. Ibid.

7. Telegram, George Wadsworth to Cordell Hull, October 18, 1938, FRUS 2 (1938): 961.

8. Telegram, Joseph P. Kennedy to Cordell Hull, October 11, 1938, FRUS 2 (1938): 951-52.

9. Telegram, Kennedy to Hull, November 7, 1938, FRUS 2 (1938): 981.

10. Moffat Diary, October 12, 1938.

11. Telegram, John W. McCormack to FDR, October 11, 1938, Official File 700, Container 2, FDRL.

12. Robert L. Ramsey to FDR, October 12, 1938, President's Secretary's File 64, FDRL.

13. Herbert Lehman to FDR, October 10, 1938, President's Personal File 93, FDRL.

14. Memorandum by Paul H. Alling, Acting Chief of Division of Near Eastern Affairs, October 15, 1938, FRUS 2 (1938): 960.

15. Memorandum submitted to the Secretary of State by American Jewish Delegation, October 14, 1938, FRUS 2 (1938): 956-59. Several of the prominent members of the delegation included: Carl Austrian, New York, representing the American Jewish Committee; Dr. Stephen S. Wise, New York, President of the American Jewish Congress; George Backer, Vice-President of the American Joint Distribution Committee; Henry Monsky, Omaha, Nebraska, President of B'nai B'rith; Joseph Schlossberg, New York, representing the American Jewish Labor Committee; Dr. Solomon Goldman, Chicago, President of the Zionist Organization of America.

16. FDR to Herbert Lehman, October 13, 1938, President's Personal File 93, FDRL.

17. Moffat Diary, October 12, 1938.

18. Telegram, Marvin H. McIntyre to Stephen S. Wise, October 12, 1938, Wise Papers, Box 181, AJHS.

19. Felix Frankfurter to Stephen S. Wise, October 18, 1938, Wise Papers, Box 106, AJHS.

20. Max Freedman, ed., *Frankfurter and Roosevelt: Their Correspondence, 1928-1945* (Boston: Little, Brown and Company, 1967), p. 463.

21. Telegram, Hull to Kennedy, October 12, 1938, FRUS 2 (1938): 952-53.

22. Telegram, Hull to Kennedy, October 13, 1938, FRUS 2 (1938): 953.

23. Telegram, Hull to Kennedy, October 20, 1938, FRUS 2 (1938): 963.

24. Wise to Frankfurter, October 16, 1938, Wise Papers, Box 109, AJHS.

25. N.A. Rose, *The Gentile Zionists: A Study in Anglo-Zionist Diplomacy, 1929-1939* (London: Frank Cass and Company, Ltd., 1973), p. 169.

26. Adolf Berle, Jr., Diary, November 1, 1938, Berle Papers, Box 210 FDRL.

27. David D. Koskoff, *Joseph P. Kennedy: A Life and Times* (Englewood Cliffs: Prentice-Hall, Inc., 1974), p. 532. See footnote 69, contents of which he acquired from the British Foreign Office Files. Letter is from Ronald Lindsay to Lancelot Oliphant, November 3, 1938, reporting visit of October 25, 1938 with Roosevelt, and minutes of the conversation.

28. Sumner Welles to Wallace Murray, December 15, 1938, 867N.01/1360.

29. Edward A. Norman to Sumner Welles, November 20, 1939, 867N.01/1670.

30. Memorandum, Murray to Welles, July 31, 1939, 867N.01/1649.

31. Norman to Welles, July 27, 1939, 867N.01/1649.

32. A.J. Sherman, *Island Refuge: Britain and Refugees from the Third Reich, 1933-1939* (Berkeley: University of California Press, 1973), p. 163.

33. Ibid., pp. 210-11.

34. Ibid., p. 173.

35. Wise to Brandeis, November 11, 1938, Wise Papers, Box 106, AJHS.

36. Telegram, Kennedy to Hull, November 7, 1938, FRUS 2 (1938): 981.

37. Freedman, *Frankfurter and Roosevelt*, p. 466.

38. Wyman, *America and the Refugee Crisis*, pp. 71-72.

39. Moffat Diary, October 29 and 30, 1938.

40. Memorandum, George Messersmith to Cordell Hull, November 14, 1938, FRUS 2 (1938): 397.

41. Ibid.

42. Memorandum, Sumner Welles to Ronald Lindsay, November 18, 1938, FRUS 2 (1938): 402.

43. Samuel Rosenman, ed., *Public Papers and Addresses of Franklin D. Roosevelt,* 13 vols. (New York: Russell and Russell, 1938-1950), 7: 174.

44. *Documents on German Foreign Policy, 1918-1945,* 4: 644.

45. Ibid., 4: 656.

46. Benjamin V. Cohen to Felix Frankfurter, November 21, 1938, Frankfurter Papers, Box 45, LC.

47. The Reminiscences of Samuel Rosenman, Oral History Project, Columbia University, pp. 163-64.

48. *The Christian Science Monitor,* November 18, 1938, p. 7.

49. Morse, *Chronicle of American Apathy,* pp. 234-35.

50.   Sherman, *Britain and Refugees,* p. 265. See also Feingold, *Roosevelt Administration and the Holocaust,* p. 42; Memorandum by Sumner Welles, November 17, 1938, FRUS 1 (1938): 830.

51.   Sherman, *Britain and Refugees,* p. 173.

52.   Ibid., p. 174.

53.   Ibid., p. 177.

54.   Memorandum by Welles, November 17, 1938, FRUS 1 (1938): 829-31.

55.   Brandeis to Frankfurter, November 23, 1938, Frankfurter Papers, Box 29, LC. See also Ickes Diary, 2: 509-10.

56.   Morgenthau Diary, November 16, 1938, FDRL.

57.   Benjamin V. Cohen to Felix Frankfurter, November 21, 1938, Frankfurter Papers, Box 45, LC.

58.   Ibid.

59.   Ibid.

60.   Ibid.

61.   Memorandum, British charge d'affairs to Hull, December 20, 1938, 840.48 Refugees/1169-1/2. See also Koskoff, *Joseph P. Kennedy,* p. 532, footnote 69.

62.   Henry Morgenthau, Jr., Presidential Diaries, Vol. 1, June 19, 1939, Morgenthau Papers, FDRL.

Chapter 8

1.   A.J. Sherman, *Island Refuge: Britain and Refugees from the Third Reich, 1933-1939* (Berkeley: University of California Press, 1973), p. 263.

2.   Telegram, Herschel V. Johnson to Cordell Hull, February 11, 1939, FRUS 4 (1939): 706.

3.   Ibid., p. 707.

4.   Memorandum, Wallace Murray to R. Walton Moore, May 19, 1939, 867.01/1560-1/2.

5.   Memorandum, Murray to Hull, March 2, 1939, 867N.01/1472-1/2.

6.   Ibid.

7.   N.A. Rose, *The Gentile Zionists: A Study in Anglo-Zionist Diplomacy, 1929-1939* (London: Frank Cass and Company, Ltd., 1973), p. 188.

8.   Memorandum, Murray to Moore, May 19, 1939, 867N.01/1560-1/2.

9.   *The New York Times,* February 25, 1939, p. 1.

10.   Memorandum, Murray to Hull, March 4, 1939, 867N.01/1560-1/2. See also FRUS 4 (1939): 724.

11.   Ibid.

12.   Ibid.

13.   Memorandum of Conversation by Wallace Murray, Chief of Division of Near Eastern Affairs, March 1, 1939, FRUS 4 (1939): 719.

14. Telegram, William Bullitt to Cordell Hull, March 10, 1939, FRUS 4 (1939): 731-32.

15. Ibid.

16. Koskoff, *Joseph P. Kennedy,* p. 184.

17. Telegram, Hull to Kennedy, March 2, 1939, FRUS 4 (1939): 722.

18. Memorandum, Murray to Hull, April 27, 1939, 867N.01/1534.

19. Telegram, Kennedy to Hull, February 27, 1939, FRUS 4 (1939): 718.

20. Koskoff, *Joseph P. Kennedy,* p. 188.

21. Telegram, Kennedy to Hull, February 28, 1939, FRUS 4 (1939): 718.

22. Telegram, Kennedy to Hull, March 3, 1939, FRUS 4 (1939): 723.

23. Rose, *Study in Anglo-Zionist Diplomacy,* p. 187. No texts of the conversation between Roosevelt and Chamberlain exist, as far as we know, but from various memoranda, diaries, and letters, the content of the conversations can be deduced.

24. Samuel Halperin and Irvin Oder, "The United States in Search of a Policy: Franklin D. Roosevelt and Palestine," *Review of Politics* 24 (July 1962): 320-21. Original letter from Solomon Goldman to Chaim Weizmann, June 20, 1939, is in the Central Zionist Archives, Jerusalem.

25. Aide-Memoire, British Embassy to the Department of State, May 15, 1939, President's Personal File 64, FDRL.

26. Halperin, "Franklin D. Roosevelt and Palestine," p. 321.

27. Telegram, Kennedy to Hull, March 18, 1939, FRUS 4 (1939): 737.

28. Telegram, Welles to Kennedy, March 19, 1939, FRUS 4 (1939): 737.

29. Telegram, Kennedy to Hull, March 20, 1939, FRUS 4 (1939): 737-38.

30. Telegram, Bert Fish to Cordell Hull, April 15, 1939. FRUS 4 (1939): 742.

31. Sherman, *Britain and Refugees,* p. 232.

32. Memorandum, Murray to Hull, July 18, 1939, 867N.01/1635.

33. Memorandum, Murray to Hull, May 12, 1939, 867N.01/1545.

34. Aide-Memoire, British Embassy to the Department of State, May 15, 1939, President's Personal File 64, FDRL. See also FRUS 4 (1939): 750.

35. Sherman, *Britain and Refugees,* p. 231.

36. Memorandum, Murray to Moore, May 19, 1939, 867N.01/1560-1/2.

37. Sherman, *Britain and Refugees,* p. 231.

38. Ibid., p. 233.

39. Memorandum, FDR to Hull, May 10, 1939, FRUS 4 (1939): 748.

40. FDR to Brandeis, May 9, 1939, 867N.01/1542A.

41. Ibid.

42. Berle Diary, May 26, 1939.

43.   Moffat Diary, May 18, 1939.

44.   Berle Diary, May 23, 1939.

45.   Memorandum of Conversation by Wallace Murray, May 22, 1939, FRUS 4 (1939): 760-61.

46.   Wise to Hull, May 22, 1939, FRUS 4 (1939): 761.

47.   Personal interview by author with Benjamin V. Cohen, Washington, D.C., December 1, 1976.

48.   Berle Diary, May 26, 1939.

49.   Memorandum, FDR to Hull, May 17, 1939, President's Personal File 64, FDRL.

50.   Hull, Memoirs 2: 1530-31.

51.   Wise to Brandeis, July 19, 1939, Wise Papers, Box 106, AJHS.

52.   David Ben-Gurion to Felix Frankfurter, July 17, 1946, Frankfurter Papers, Box 23, LC.

Bibliography

Archival Material

The Franklin D. Roosevelt Library, Hyde Park, New York.

A. Franklin D. Roosevelt Papers.
   1. Map Room File
   2. Official File
   3. President's Personal File
   4. President's Secretary's File
B. Louis Bean Papers.
C. Adolf Berle, Jr., Papers.
D. Oscar Cox Papers.
E. Louis Fischer Papers.
F. Harry Hopkins Papers.
G. R. Walton Moore Papers.
H. Henry Morgenthau, Jr., Diaries and Papers.
I. Eleanor Roosevelt Papers.
J. James Roosevelt Papers.
K. Samuel I. Rosenman Papers.
L. Myron Taylor Papers.
M. Rexford Tugwell Papers.

Manuscripts Division, Library of Congress, Washington, D.C.

A. Robert W. Bingham Diary and Papers.
B. William Borah Papers.
C. Emanuel Celler Papers.
D. Raymond Clapper Papers.
E. Thomas Connally Papers.
F. Josephus Daniels Diary and Papers.
G. Joseph Davies Papers.
H. Norman Davis Papers.
I. James A. Farley Papers.
J. Herbert Feis Papers.
K. Felix Frankfurter Papers.
L. Harold Ickes Diary and Papers.
M. Cordell Hull Papers.
N. Phillip Jessup Papers.

O.   William Leahy Papers.
P.   Breckinridge Long Diaries and Papers.
Q.   Key Pittman Papers.
R.   Laurence Steinhardt Papers.
S.   Myron Taylor Papers.

Diplomatic Branch, National Archives, Washington, D.C.

   The Department of State Records, Record Group 59, 1933-1939.

Federal Records Center, National Archives, Suitland, Maryland.

   Records of the Office of Strategic Services, Foreign Nationalities Branch.

American Jewish Historical Society, Brandeis University, Waltham, Massachusetts.

   Stephen S. Wise Papers.

Catholic University of America, Washington,D.C.

A.   National Catholic Welfare Conference Papers.
B.   John J. Burke Papers.
C.   William Montavon Papers.
D.   John A. Ryan Papers.

Oral History Project, Columbia University, New York, New York.

A.   Adolf Berle, Jr.
B.   Claude Bowers.
C.   Edward J. Flynn.
D.   Arthur Krock.
E.   Herbert H. Lehman.
F.   Frances Perkins.
G.   William Phillips.
H.   Eleanor Roosevelt.
I.   Samuel I. Rosenman.
J.   Norman Thomas.
K.   Henry A. Wallace.

School of International Affairs, Columbia University, New York, New York.

A.   Herbert H. Lehman Papers.
B.   James G. McDonald Papers.

Georgetown University, Washington, D.C.

A.   Robert F. Wagner, Sr., Papers.
B.   Edmund A. Walsh Papers.

Harvard University, Cambridge, Massachusetts.

A.   Joseph C. Grew Papers.
B.   Jay Pierrepont Moffat Papers.
C.   William Phillips Papers.

New York City Municipal Archives and Record Center, New York, New York.

    Fiorello LaGuardia Papers.

Princeton University, Princeton, New Jersey.

A.   Bernard M. Baruch Papers.
B.   Louis Fischer Papers.
C.   Joseph C. Green Papers.
D.   George F. Keenan Papers.
E.   Arthur Krock Papers.
F.   Norman Thomas Papers.

University of Virginia, Charlottesville, Virginia.

A.   Homer S. Cummings Papers.
B.   Louis A. Johnson Papers.
C.   Edward R. Stettinius Papers.
D.   Edwin M. Watson Papers.

Yale University, New Haven, Connecticut.

A.   Arthur Bliss Lane Papers.
B.   Henry L. Stimson Papers.

United States Catholic Conference, Washington, D.C.

    File of the Office of the General Secretary, National Catholic Welfare Conference.

Interviews

Louis H. Bean
Emanuel Celler
Benjamin V. Cohen
Thomas G. Corcoran
Charles E. Coughlin
James A. Farley
W. Averall Harrriman
Isador Lubin
Archibald MacLeish
John W. McCormack
John W. Pehle
James Roosevelt
Grace Tully

Published Primary Sources: Documents and Letters

Cantril, Hadley, ed. *Public Opinion: 1935-1946.* Princeton: Princeton University Press, 1951.
Freedman, Max, ed. *Roosevelt and Frankfurter: Their Correspondence, 1928-1945.* Boston: Little, Brown and Company, 1967.
Loewenheim, Francis L.; Langley, Harold D.; and Jonas, Manfred, eds. *Roosevelt and Churchill: Their Secret Wartime Correspondence.* New York: E.P. Dutton and Company, Inc., 1975.

Nixon, Edgar B., ed. *Franklin D. Roosevelt and Foreign Affairs.* 3 vols. Cambridge: The Belknap Press of Harvard University Press, 1969.

Polier, Justin Wise and Wise, James Waterman, eds., *The Personal Letters of Stephen Wise.* Boston: The Beacon Press, 1956.

Roosevelt, Elliot, ed. *The Roosevelt Letters: Being the Personal Correspondence of Franklin Delano Roosevelt.* 3 vols. London: George G. Harrap and Company, Ltd., 1952.

———, ed. *F.D.R.: His Personal Letters: 1928-1945.* 3 vols. New York: Duell, Sloan and Pearce, 1950.

Roosevelt, Franklin D. *Complete Press Conferences of Franklin D. Roosevelt.* 25 vols. New York: Da Capo Press, 1972.

Rosenman, Samuel I., ed. *The Public Papers and Addresses of Franklin D. Roosevelt.* 13 vols. New York: Russell and Russell, 1938-1950.

Taylor, Myron C., ed. *Wartime Correspondence between President Roosevelt and Pope Pius XII.* New York: The MacMillan Company, 1947.

U.S. Congress. House. 74th Cong., 2d sess., 1936. *Congressional Record,* vol. 80.

U.S. Congress. Senate. Committee on Foreign Relations. *Neutrality, Hearings before Senate Committee on Foreign Relations on S. 3474.* 74th Cong., 2d sess., 1936.

U.S. Department of State. *Documents on German Foreign Policy, 1918-1945.* 13 vols. Washington, D.C.: U.S. Government Printing Office, 1949-1962.

U.S. Department of State. *Foreign Relations of the United States.* Volumes 1933-1939. Washington, D.C.: U.S. Government Printing Office, 1951-1956.

Voss, Carl Hermann, ed. *Stephen S. Wise: Servant of the People: Selected Letters.* Philadelphia: The Jewish Publications Society of America, 1969.

Published Primary Sources: Memoirs and Diaries

Baruch, Bernard M. *Baruch: The Public Years.* 2 vols. New York: Holt, Rinehart and Winston, 1960.

Beneš, Eduard. *Memoirs of Dr. Eduard Beneš.* London: George Allen and Unwin, Ltd., 1954.

Berle, Beatrice Bishop, and Travis Beal Jacobs, eds. *Navigating the Rapids: 1918-1971: From the Papers of Adolf A. Berle.* New York: Harcourt Brace Jovanich, Inc., 1973.

Biddle, Francis. *In Brief Authority.* Garden City: Doubleday and Company, Inc., 1962.

Bloom, Sol. *The Autobiography of Sol Bloom.* New York: G.P. Putnam's Sons, 1948.

Blum, John Morton, ed. *From the Morgenthau Diaries: Years of Crisis, 1928-1939.* Boston: Houghton Mifflin Company, 1959.

———. *From the Morgenthau Diaries: Years of Urgency, 1938-1941.* Boston: Houghton Mifflin Company, 1965.

———. *The Price of Vision: The Diary of Henry A. Wallace, 1942-1946.* Boston: Houghton Mifflin Company, 1973.

Bohlen, Charles E. *Witness to History: 1929-1969.* New York: W.W. Norton and Company, 1973.

Bowers, Claude. *My Life: The Memoirs of Claude Bowers.* New York: Simon and Schuster, 1962.

———. *My Mission to Spain.* New York: Simon and Schuster, 1954.

Bullitt, Orville H., ed. *For the President, Personal and Secret: Correspondence Between Franklin D. Roosevelt and William C. Bullitt.* Boston: Houghton Mifflin Company, 1972.

Byrnes, James F. *Speaking Frankly.* New York: Harper and Brothers, 1947.

Campbell, Thomas M; and Herring, George C., eds. *The Diaries of Edward R. Stettinius, Jr., 1943-1946.* New York: New Viewpoints, 1975.

Celler, Emanuel. *You Never Leave Brooklyn: The Autobiography of Emanuel Celler.* New York: The John Day Company, 1953.

Childs, Marquis W. *I Write From Washington.* New York: Harper and Brothers, 1942.

Churchill, Winston S. *The Second World War*. Vol. 5: *Closing the Ring*. Boston: Houghton Mifflin Company, 1951.

———. *The Second World War*. Vol 6: *Triumph and Tragedy*. Boston: Houghton Mifflin Company, 1953.

Ciechanowski, Jan. *Defeat in Victory*. Garden City: Doubleday and Company, Inc., 1947.

Coughlin, Charles E. *A Series of Lectures on Social Justice*. New York: DeCapo Press, 1971.

Daniels, Josephus. *Shirt-Sleeve Diplomat*. Chapel Hill: The University of North Carolina Press, 1947.

Daniels, Jonathan. *White House Witness: 1942-1945*. Garden City: Doubleday and Company, 1975.

Dodd, William E. *Ambassador Dodd's Diary: 1933-1938*. New York: Harcourt, Brace and Company, 1941.

Farley, James A. *Behind the Ballots: The Personal History of a Politician*. New York: Harcourt, Brace and Company, 1938.

Farley, James A. *Jim Farley's Story: The Roosevelt Years*. New York: McGraw-Hill Book Company, 1948.

Feis, Herbert. *1933: Characters in Crisis*. Boston: Little, Brown and Company, 1966.

Goldmann, Nahum. *The Autobiography of Nahum Goldmann*. New York: Holt, Rhinehart and Winston, 1969.

Harriman, W. Averell, and Abel, Elie. *Special Envoy to Churchill and Stalin: 1941-1946*. New York: Random House, 1975.

Hassett, William D. *Off the Record with F.D.R.: 1942-1945*. New Brunswick: Rutgers University Press, 1958.

Hooker, Nancy Harvison, ed. *The Moffat Papers: Selections from the Diplomatic Journals of Jay Pierrepont Moffat: 1919-1943*. Cambridge: Harvard University Press, 1956.

Hull, Cordell. *The Memoirs of Cordell Hull*. 2 vols. New York: The Macmillan Company, 1948.

Ickes, Harold L. *The Secret Diary of Harold L. Ickes*. 3 vols. New York: Simon and Shuster, 1954.

Israel, Fred L., ed. *The War Diary of Breckinridge Long: Selections from the Years 1939-1944*. Lincoln: University of Nebraska Press, 1966.

Kennan, George F. *Memoirs: 1925-1950*. Boston: Little, Brown and Company, 1967.

Lane, Arthur Bliss. *I Saw Poland Betrayed: An American Ambassador Reports to the American People*. New York: The Bobbs-Merrill Company, 1948.

Lash, Joseph P. *Eleanor and Franklin: The Story of their Relationship, based on Eleanor Roosevelt's Private Papers*. New York: W.W. Norton and Company, 1971.

———. *Eleanor: The Years Alone*. New York: W.W. Norton and Company, 1972.

Lilienthal, David E. *The Journals of David E. Lilienthal: Venturesome Years: 1950-1955*. New York: Harper and Row, 1966.

Marcantonio, Vito. *I Vote My Conscience: Debates, Speeches, and Writings of Vito Marcantonio: 1935-1950*. New York: the Vito Marcantonio Memorial, 1956.

Moley, Raymond. *The First New Deal*. New York: Harcourt, Brace and World, Inc., 1966.

Perkins, Frances. *The Roosevelt I Knew*. New York: Viking Press, 1946.

Phillips, William. *Venture in Diplomacy*. Boston: The Beacon Press, 1952.

Roosevelt, Eleanor. *This I Remember*. New York: Harper and Brothers, 1949.

Roosevelt, Elliot, and Brough, James. *A Rendezvous with Destiny: The Roosevelts of the White House*. New York: G.P. Putnam's Sons, 1975.

Rosenman, Samuel I. *Working with Roosevelt*. New York: Harper and Brothers, Publishers, 1952.

Standley, William H., and Ageton, Arthur A. *Admiral Ambassador to Russia*. Chicago: Henry Regnery Company, 1955.

Stettinius, Jr., Edward R. *Roosevelt and the Russians: The Yalta Conference*. Garden City: Doubleday and Company, Inc., 1949.

Tully, Grace. *F.D.R. My Boss.* New York: Charles Scribner's Sons, 1949.

Vandenberg, Arthur H. Jr., ed. *The Private Papers of Senator Vandenberg.* Boston: Houghton Mifflin Company, 1952.

Weizmann, Chaim. *Trial and Error: The Autobiography of Chaim Weizmann.* New York: Harper and Brothers, 1949.

Welles, Sumner. *Seven Decisions that Shaped History.* New York: Harper and Brothers, 1950.

––––––. *The Time for Decision.* New York: Harper and Brothers, Publishers, 1944.

––––––. *We Need Not Fail.* Boston: Houghton Mifflin Company, 1948.

––––––. *Where Are We Heading?* New York: Harper and Brothers, 1946.

Wilson, Hugh R., Jr. *A Career Diplomat: The Third Chapter: The Third Reich.* New York: Vantage Press, 1960.

Wise, Stephen. *Challenging Years: The Autobiography of Stephen Wise.* New York: G.P. Putnam's Sons, 1949.

Published Primary Sources: Newspapers

Il Progresso Italo-Americano
The Baltimore Catholic Review
The Brooklyn Tablet
The Christian Science Monitor
The Indiana Catholic and Record
The Italian Weekly
The Jewish News
The New York Post
The New York Times
The Pilot
The Washington Post
The Washington Star

Dissertations

Bateman, Herman Edward. "The Election of 1944 and Foreign Policy." Ph.D. dissertation, Stanford University, 1952.

Cox, John V. "The Italo-Ethiopian Crisis of 1934-1936 in United States Foreign Relations." Master's Thesis, Naval War College, 1969.

Fitzgerald, Paul A. "American Neutrality and the Italo-Ethiopian Conflict." Ph.D. dissertation, Georgetown University, 1953

Friedman, Saul S. "Official United States Policy Toward Jewish Refugees." Ph.D. dissertation, The Ohio State University, 1969.

Gottlieb, Moshe. "The Anti-Nazi Boycott Movement in the American Jewish Community: 1935-1951." Ph.D. dissertation, Brandeis University, 1967.

Hasting, Martin Franklin. "United States-Vatican Relations: Policies and Problems." Ph.D. dissertation, University of California at Berkeley, 1952.

Karmarkovic, Alex. "The Myron Taylor Appointment: Background; Religious Reaction, Constitutionality." Ph.D. dissertation, University of Minnesota, 1967.

Maddus, Thomas Roth. "American Relations with the Soviet Union, 1933-1941." Ph.D. dissertation, University of Michigan, 1969.

Neal, Nevin Emil. "A Biography of Joseph T. Robinson." Ph.D. dissertation, University of Oklahoma, 1958.

Oder, Irwin. "The United States and the Palestine Mandate, 1920-1948: A Study of the Impact of Interest Groups on Foreign Policy." Ph.D. dissertation, Columbia University, 1956.

Pechota, Henry Lee. "Neutrality Legislation of the United States (1935, 1936, and 1937)." Ph.D. dissertation, University of Southern California, 1939.

Quigley, Robert Edward. "American Catholic Opinions of Mexican Anticlericalism: 1910-1936." Ph.D. dissertation, University of Pennsylvania, 1965.

Ragland, James Franklin. "Franklin D. Roosevelt and Public Opinion: 1933-1940." Ph.D. dissertation, Stanford University, 1954.

Smith, William Barry. "The Attitude of American Catholics Toward Italian-Fascism Between the Two World Wars." Ph.D. dissertation, Catholic University of America, 1969.

Valaik, John David. "American Catholics and the Spanish Civil War: 1931-1939." Ph.D. dissertation, The University of Rochester, 1964.

Whitehead, Donald F. "The Making of Foreign Policy During President Roosevelt's First Term: 1933-1937." Ph.D. dissertation, The University of Chicago, 1951.

Secondary Sources: Articles

Alvarez, David D. "The United States, the Vatican, and World War II." *Research Studies* 40 (December 1972): 239-50.

Bierbrier, Doreen. "The American Zionist Emergency Council." *American Jewish Historical Quarterly* 60 (September 1970): 82-105.

Braddick, Henderson B. "A New Look at American Policy during Italo-Ethiopian Crisis, 1935-1936" *Journal of Modern History* 34 (March 1962): 64-73.

Cannistraro, Philip V. "Fascism and Italian-Americans in Detroit, 1933-1935." *The International Migration Review* 9 (Spring 1975): 29-40.

Cole, Wayne S. "Senator Key Pittman and American Neutrality Policies: 1933-1940." *The Mississippi Valley Historical Review* 46 (March 1960): 644-62.

Cronon, E. David. "American Catholics and Mexican Anticlericalism, 1933-1936." *The Mississippi Valley Historical Review* 45 (September 1958): 201-230.

Crosby, Donald F. "Boston Catholics and the Spanish Civil War: 1936-1939." *New England Quarterly* 44 (March 1971): 82-100.

Diggins, John P. "Mussolini and America: Hero-Worship, Charisma, and the 'Vulgar Talent'." *The Historian* 28 (August 1966): 559-85.

_____. "The Italo-American Anti-Fascist Opposition." *The Journal of American History* 54 (December 1967): 579-98.

Gerson, Louis. "Immigrant Groups and American Foreign Policy," in *Issues and Conflicts: Studies in Twentieth Century American Diplomacy,* ed. George L. Anderson. Lawrence: University of Kansas Press, 1959, pp. 171-92.

Halperin, Samuel and Oder, Irvin. "The United States in Search of a Policy: Franklin D. Roosevelt and Palestine." *Review of Politics* 24 (July 1962): 320-41.

Hinton, Harold B. "To Keep America out of War." *Current History,* April, 1936, pp. 22-45.

Lerner, Max. "Behind Hull's Embargo." *The Nation,* May 28, 1938, pp. 607-610.

Lubell, Samuel. "Who Votes Isolationist and Why." *Harper's,* April, 1951, pp. 29-36.

Norman John. "Influence of Pro-Fascist Propaganda on American Neutrality: 1935-46," in *Essays in History and International Relations,* eds. Dwight E. Lee and George E. McReynolds. Worcester: The Clark University Press, 1949, pp. 193-214.

Patterson, James T. "Eating Humble Pie: A Note on Roosevelt, Congress, and Neutrality Revision in 1939." *The Historian* 31 (May 1969): 407-414.

Perkins, Dexter. "Foreign Policy in Presidential Campaigns." *Foreign Affairs* 35 (January 1957): 213-24.

Roucek, Joseph S. "American Foreign Policy and American Minorities." *The Indian Journal of Political Science* 17 (July-September 1956): 241-60.

Shafir, Shlomo. "American Diplomats in Berlin (1933-1939) and their Attitude to the Nazi Persecution of the Jews." *Yad Yashem Studies* 9 (1973): 71-104.

_____. "George S. Messersmith: An Anti-Nazi Diplomat's View of the German-Jewish Crisis." *Jewish Social Studies* 35 (January 1973): 32-41.

Shenton, James P. "The Coughlin Movement and the New Deal." *Political Science Quarterly* 73 (September 1958): 351-73.

Szajkowski, Zoza. "The Attitude of American Jews to Refugees from Germany in the 1930's." *American Jewish Historical Quarterly* 61 (December 1971): 101-143.

Thorning, Joseph F. "Mexico: An American Problem." *America,* March 2, 1935, pp. 491-93.

Valaik, J. David. "Catholics, Neutrality, and the Spanish Embargo, 1937-1939." *The Journal of American History* 54 (June 1967): 73-85.

Secondary Sources: Books

Bailey, Thomas A. *The Man in the Street: The Impact of American Public Opinion on Foreign Policy.* New York: The Macmillan Company, 1948.

Beard, Charles A. *President Roosevelt and the Coming of the War: 1941.* New Haven: Yale University Press, 1948.

Bemis, Samuel Flagg. *The Latin American Policy of the United States: An Historical Interpretation.* New York: W.W. Norton and Company, 1943.

Bendiner, Robert. *The Riddle of the State Department.* New York: Farrar and Rinehart, Inc., 1942.

Bennett, Edward M. *Recognition of Russia: An American Foreign Policy Dilemma.* Waltham, Massachusetts: Blaisdell Publishing Company, 1970.

Bishop, Donald G. *The Roosevelt-Litvinov Agreements: The American View.* Syracuse: Syracuse University Press, 1965.

Bishop, James. *FDR's Last Year: April 1944-April 1945.* New York: William Morrow and Company, 1974.

Blanshard, Paul. *The Irish and Catholic Power.* Boston: The Beacon Press, 1953.

Blum, John Morton. *Roosevelt and Morgenthau.* Boston: Houghton Mifflin Company, 1970.

_____. *V was for Victory: Politics and American Culture During World War II.* New York: Harcourt Brace Jovanich, 1976.

Borchard, Edwin, and Lage, William Potter. *Neutrality for the United States.* New Haven: Yale University Press, 1937.

Brandenburg, Frank. *The Making of Modern Mexico.* Englewood Cliffs, New Jersey: Prentice-Hall Inc., 1964.

Browder, Robert Paul. *The Origins of Soviet-American Diplomacy.* Princeton: Princeton University Press, 1973.

Burns, James MacGregor. *Roosevelt: The Lion and the Fox.* New York: Harcourt, Brace and World, Inc., 1956.

_____. *Roosevelt: The Soldier of Freedom.* New York: Harcourt, Brace and World Inc., 1970.

Cline, Howard F. *The United States and Mexico.* Cambridge: Harvard University Press, 1953.

Cohen, Naomi W. *American Jews and the Zionist Idea.* New York: KTAV Publishing House, Inc., 1975.

Cronon, E. David. *Josephus Daniels in Mexico.* Madison: The University of Wisconsin Press, 1960.

Dallek, Robert. *Franklin D. Roosevelt and American Foreign Policy, 1932-1945.* New York: Oxford University Press, 1979.

Dawidowicz, Lucy S. *The War Against the Jews: 1933-1945.* New York: Holt, Rhinehart, and Winston, 1975.

Dawson, Raymond H. *The Decision to Aid Russia, 1941: Foreign Policy and Domestic Politics.* Chapel Hill: The University of North Carolina Press, 1959.

DeConde, Alexander. *Half-Bitter, Half-Sweet: An Excursion into Italian-American History.* New York: Charles Scribner's Sons, 1971.

Diggins, John P. *Mussolini and Fascism: The View from America.* Princeton: Princeton University Press, 1972.

Divine, Robert A. *The Illusion of Neutrality.* Chicago: University of Chicago Press, 1962.

Farnsworth, Beatrice. *William C. Bullitt and the Soviet Union.* Bloomington: Indiana University Press, 1967.

Feingold, Henry L. *The Politics of Rescue: The Roosevelt Administration and the Holocaust: 1938-1945.* New Brunswick: Rutgers University Press, 1970.

Fleming, Denna Frank. *The United States and the World Court.* Garden City: Doubleday, Doran and Company, 1945.

Flynn, George Q. *American Catholics and the Roosevelt Presidency: 1932-1936.* Lexington: University of Kentucky Press, 1968.

_____. *Roosevelt and Romanism: Catholics and American Diplomacy, 1937-1945.* Westport, Connecticut: Greenwood Press, 1976.

Friedman, Saul S. *No Haven for the Oppressed: U.S. Policy toward Jewish Refugees, 1938-1945.* Detroit: Wayne State University Press, 1973.

Gallagher, Rev. Louis Jr., S.J. *Edmund A. Walsh, S.J.: A Biography.* New York: Benziger Brothers, Inc., 1962.

Gannon, Robert I. *The Cardinal Spellman Story.* Garden City: Doubleday and Company, Inc., 1962.

Gerson, Louis L. *The Hyphenate in Recent American Politics and Diplomacy.* Lawrence: The University of Kansas Press, 1964.

Glazer, Nathan, and Moynihan, Daniel P., eds. *Ethnicity: Theory and Experience.* Cambridge: Harvard University Press, 1975.

Gosnell, Harold F. *Champion Campaigner: Franklin D. Roosevelt.* New York: The Macmillan Company, 1952.

Gunther, John. *Roosevelt in Retrospect.* New York: Harper and Brothers, 1950.

Guttman, Allen, ed. *American Neutrality and the Spanish Civil War.* Boston: D.C. Heath and Company, Inc., 1963.

_____. *The Wound in the Heart: America and the Spanish Civil War.* New York: The Free Press of Glencoe, 1962.

Harris, Brice Jr. *The United States and the Italo-Ethiopian Crisis.* Stanford: Stanford University Press, 1964.

Harvey, John, ed. *The Diplomatic Diaries of Oliver Harvey, 1937-1940.* New York: St. Martin's Press, 1970.

Herring, George C., Jr. *Aid to Russia: 1941-1946.* New York: Columbia University Press, 1973.

Hinton, Harold B. *Cordell Hull: A Biography.* Garden City: Doubleday, Doran and Company, 1942.

Israel, F.I. *Nevada's Key Pittman.* Lincoln: University of Nebraska Press, 1963.

Jonas, Manfred. *Isolationism in America: 1935-1941.* Ithaca: Cornell University Press, 1966.

Kantowicz, Edward R. *Polish-American Politics in Chicago: 1888-1940.* Chicago: The University of Chicago Press, 1975.

Key, V.O., Jr. *Politics, Parties, and Pressure Groups.* New York: Thomas Y. Crowell Company, 1942.

Kogan, Norman. *Italy and the Allies.* Cambridge: Harvard University Press, 1956.

Koskoff, David E. *Joseph P. Kennedy: A Life and Times.* Englewood Cliffs, New Jersey: Prentice-Hall, Inc., 1974.

Langer, William L., and Gleason, S. Everett. *The Challenge to Isolation: 1937-40.* New York: Harper and Brothers, 1952.

———. *The Undeclared War: 1940-41.* New York: Harper and Brothers Publishers, 1953.

Lash, Joseph P. *Eleanor: The Years Alone.* New York: W.W. Norton and Co., Inc., 1972.

Leigh, Michael. *Mobilizing Consent: Public Opinion and American Foreign Policy, 1937-1947.* Westport, Connecticut: Greenwood Press, 1976.

Leuchtenburg, William E. *Franklin D. Roosevelt and the New Deal: 1932-1940.* New York: Harper and Row, Publishers, 1963.

Lubell, Samuel. *The Future of American Politics.* New York: Harper and Brothers, Publishers, 1951.

Marcus, Sheldon. *Father Coughlin.* Boston: Little, Brown and Company, 1973.

Markel, Lester, ed. *Public Opinion and Foreign Policy.* New York: Harper and Brothers, 1949.

McAvoy, Thomas T. *A History of the Catholic Church in the United States.* Notre Dame: University of Notre Dame Press, 1969.

McKenna, Marian. *Borah.* Ann Arbor: The University of Michigan Press, 1961.

Mooney, Booth. *Roosevelt and Rayburn.* Philadelphia: J.B. Lippincott Company, 1971.

Morrison, Joseph L. *Josephus Daniels: The Small-d Democrat.* Chapel Hill: The University of North Carolina Press, 1966.

Morse, Arthur D. *While Six Million Died: A Chronicle of American Apathy.* New York: Random House, 1968.

Nevins, Allan. *The New Deal and World Affairs: 1933-1945.* New Haven: Yale University Press, 1950.

Rollins, Alfred B. *Roosevelt and Howe.* New York: Alfred A. Knopf, 1962.

Roos, Hans. *A History of Modern Poland: From the Foundation of the State in the First World War to the Present Day.* London: Eyre and Spattiswoode, 1961.

Rose, N.A. *The Gentile Zionists: A Study in Anglo-Zionist Diplomacy, 1929-1939.* London: Frank Cass and Company, Ltd., 1973.

Rozek, Edward J. *Allied Wartime Diplomacy: A Pattern in Poland.* New York: John Wiley and Sons, Inc., 1958.

Salvemini, Gaetano. *Prelude to World War II.* Garden City: Doubleday and Company, Inc., 1954.

Schlesinger, Arthur M., Jr. *The Imperial Presidency.* Boston: Houghton Mifflin Company, 1973.

Shannon, William V. *The American Irish.* New York: The Macmillan Company, 1963.

Sheerin, John B. *Never Look Back: The Career and Concerns of John J. Burke.* New York: Paulist Press, 1975.

Sherman, Ari Jr. *Island Refuge: Britain and Refugees from the Third Reich: 1933-1939.* Berkeley. University of California Press, 1973.

Sherwood, Robert E. *Roosevelt and Hopkins: An Intimate History.* New York: Harper and Brothers, 1948.

Stewart, William Jr., ed. *The Era of Franklin D. Roosevelt.* Hyde Park: The Franklin D. Roosevelt Library, 1967.

Stiles, Lela. *The Man Behind Roosevelt: The Story of Louis McHenry Howe.* New York: The World Publishing Company, 1954.

Stolberg, Benjamin. *Tailor's Progress.* Garden City: Doubleday, Doran, and Company, Inc., 1944.

Thomas, Gordon, and Wills, Max Morgan. *Voyage of the Damned.* New York: Stein and Day, 1974.

Thomas, Hugh. *The Spanish Civil War.* New York: Harper and Row, 1977.

Thompson, Dorothy. *Refugees: Anarchy or Organization?* New York: Random House, 1938.

Tugwell, Rexford. *The Democratic Roosevelt.* Garden City: Doubleday and Company, Inc., 1957.

Tansill, Charles Callan. *Back Door to War: The Roosevelt Foreign Policy: 1933-1941.* Chicago: Henry Regency Company, 1952.

Taylor, F. Jay. *The United States and the Spanish Civil War*. New York: Octagon Books, 1956.

Traina, Richard P. *American Diplomacy and the Spanish Civil War*. Bloomington: Indiana University Press, 1968.

Tull, Charles J. *Father Coughlin and the New Deal*. Syracuse: Syracuse University Press, 1965.

Urofsky, Melvin. *A Voice That Spoke For Justice: The Life and Times of Stephen S. Wise*. Albany: State University of New York Press, 1981.

Wyman, David S. *Paper Walls: America and the Refugee Crisis: 1938-1941*. Amherst: The University of Massachusetts Press, 1968.

Index